# MaiNtENaNt[20]

A JOURNAL OF CONTEMPORARY DADA WRITING & ART

**PETER CARLAFTES & KAT GEORGES**
EDITORS

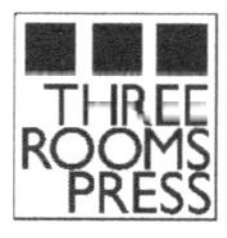


NEW YORK

WWW.THREEROOMSPRESS.COM
*EACH BOOK BORN IN GREENWICH VILLAGE*

**MAINTENANT: A JOURNAL OF CONTEMPORARY DADA WRITING & ART**
**ISSUE 20**

**Editors**
Peter Carlaftes & Kat Georges

**Design & Production**
KG Design International

**Inspiration**
Arthur Cravan

ON THE COVER:
"THE SHADOW OF THE STORM"
*Painting, oil on canvas, 60" X 96"*
NICKY NODJOUMI


Born in Kermanshah, Iran, Iranian-American artist Nicky Nodjoumi received his Bachelor's of Art from Tehran University of Fine Arts and his MFA from CUNY, before returning to Tehran to teach at his alma mater. During this period, he began designing political posters inspired by the revolutionary spirit sweeping the country, only to be forced into exile once again following the 1979 revolution. Nodjoumi's political engagement in his work continues today. His work is held in numerous prominent institutional collections worldwide, including The Metropolitan Museum of Art in New York, the British Museum in London, the Guggenheim Museum in Abu Dhabi, the DePaul Art Museum in Chicago, and the National Museum of Cuba. He lives and works in Brooklyn.

Special thanks to Danica Wei, all the contributors, and the readers, museums, galleries, performance venues, and booksellers who support *Maintenant*.

**Maintenant 20 is dedicated to**
**Cabaret Voltaire, birthplace of the Dada art movement**



ISBN: 978-1-953103-74-1 ISSN 2333-2034 TRP-127



MAINTENANT: A JOURNAL OF CONTEMPORARY DADA WRITING & ART
is published annually by Three Rooms Press, New York, NY
Current and back issues of MAINTENANT are available at www.threeroomspress.com/shop
For submission details, visit www.threeroomspress.com or email info@threeroomspress.com

**For inquiries about obtaining the MAINTENANT series for your educational or cultural institution archives or classroom, please email editor@threeroomspress.com**

Three Rooms Press hosts numerous US and international Dada salons and workshops, in conjunction with contributors to the MAINTENANT series. To download a free digital booklet with photos and information about nearly two decades of performances, please visit: https://threeroomspress.com/2025/01/3rp-dada-salons

**To schedule a workshop, presentation, or Dada salon, email editor@threeroomspress.com**

Distributed by Ingram / Publishers Group West (www.pgw.com)

## INTRODUCTION:
## IMPROPERGANDA

Politics has taken its turn to arrive at the worst and the creatures involved have become LOLiticians—laughable in their every move. The same unfathomable injustice persists as the poor become even more deprived and the press can't concede even one shred of Truth.

**A Theme for an Age of Disinformation:** MAINTENANT 20 tackles the global crisis of truth, exploring propaganda, media manipulation, and moral distortion through the Dadaist lens: subverting, questioning, and ridiculing modern "truth industries."

**The Media is Owned and So are We—Dada for the 21st Century:** MAINTENANT 20 renews the anti-art spirit of Dada, transforming protest and nonsense into tools of critical reflection, challenging readers to confront complicity, absurdity, and the erasure of fact.

**Moving Forward:** We are here to expose the formulated bias and unravel the way of the world by expanding the ideal of Freedom in every mind capable of thinking for all; this issue redefines propaganda as art's battlefield, reclaiming absurdity as the last honest response to a dishonest world.

MAINTENANT 20 dives into the intersection of politics, misinformation, and the post-truth era. A must-read for academics, artists, and anyone reckoning with modern media.

*—Peter Carlaftes and Kat Georges, editors*

## CONTENTS

# MaiNtENaNt[20]

**PAUL INDREK KOSTABI**

PIERMONT, NEW YORK

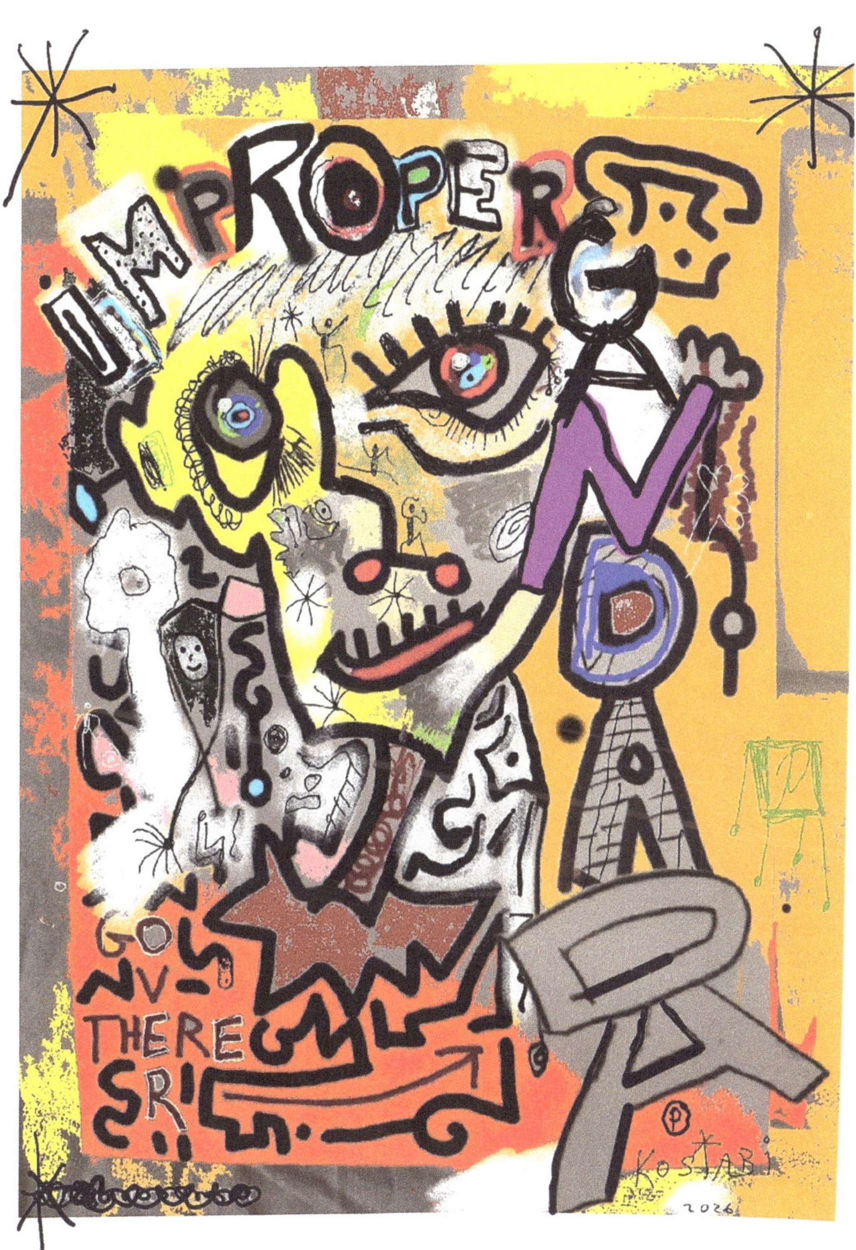


## IMPROPERGANDA(DA)

*Painting*

## JÓZSEF BÍRÓ

BUDAPEST, HUNGARY

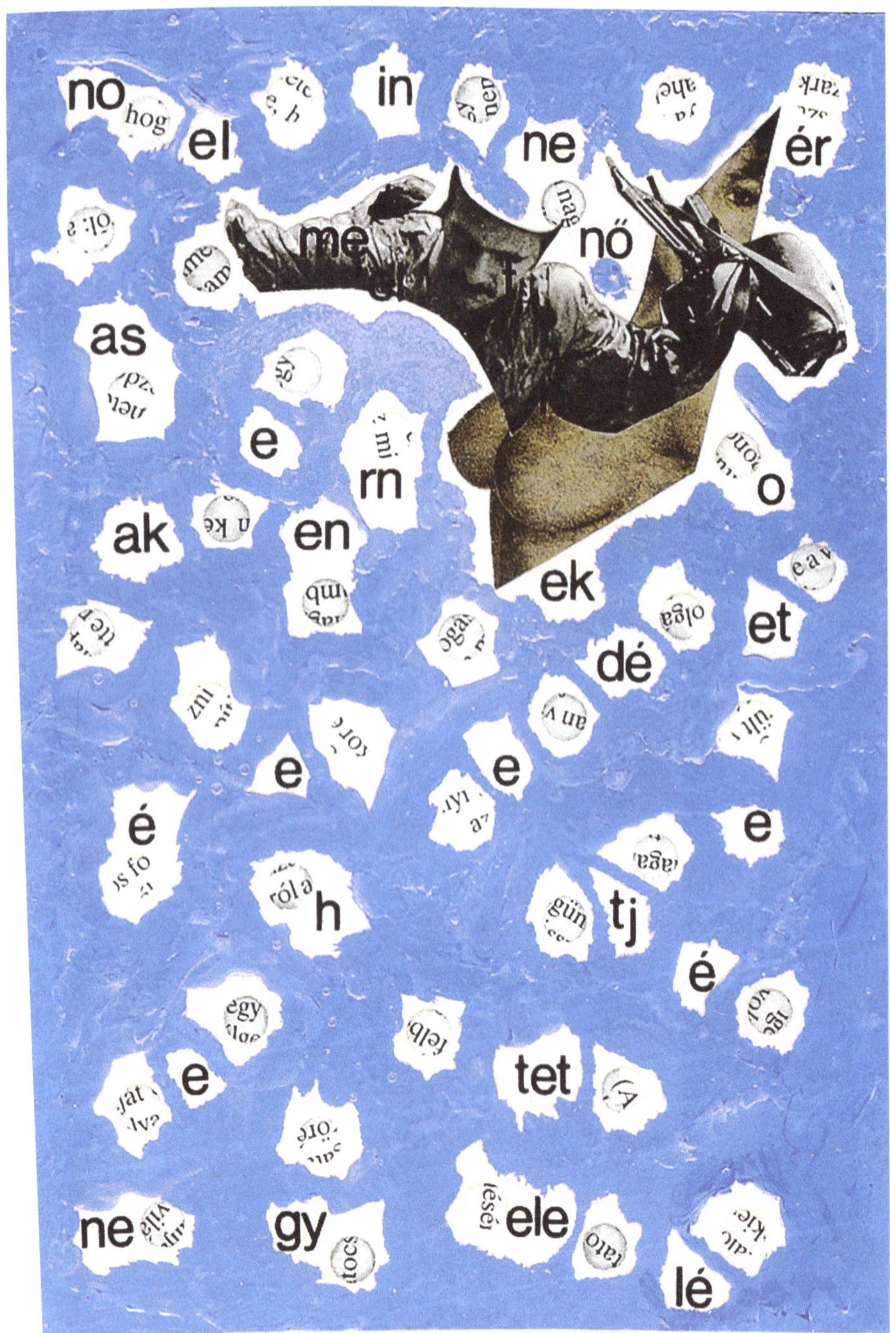

**AGAINST ALL WAR**

*Digital collage*

**MICHAEL GEORG BREGEL**

BERLIN, GERMANY

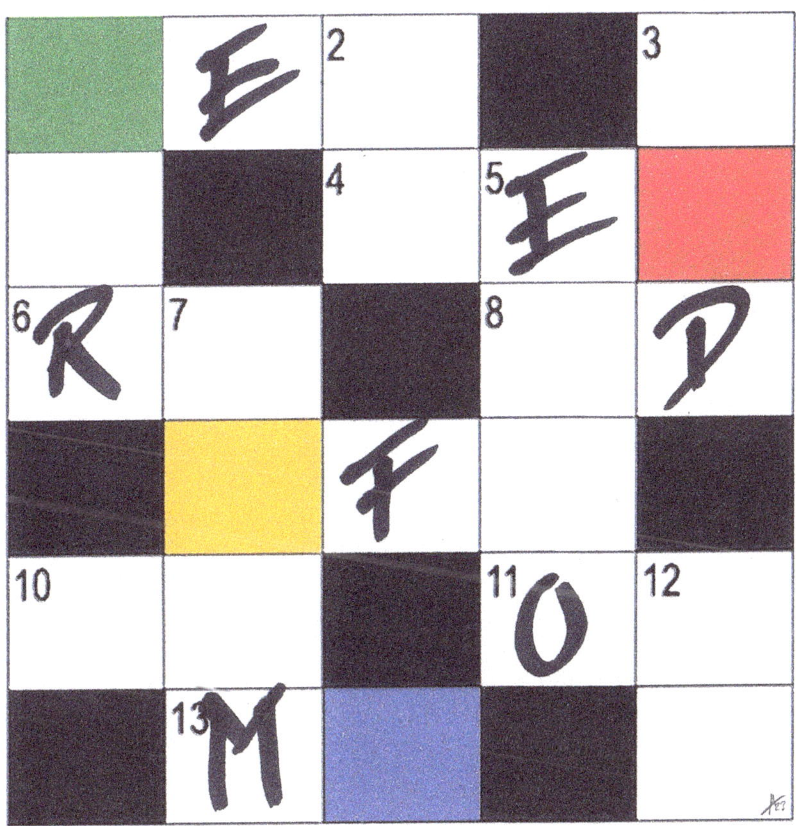


## PUZZLE FREEDOM

*Digital art*

**JOHN M. BENNETT**
COLUMBUS, OHIO

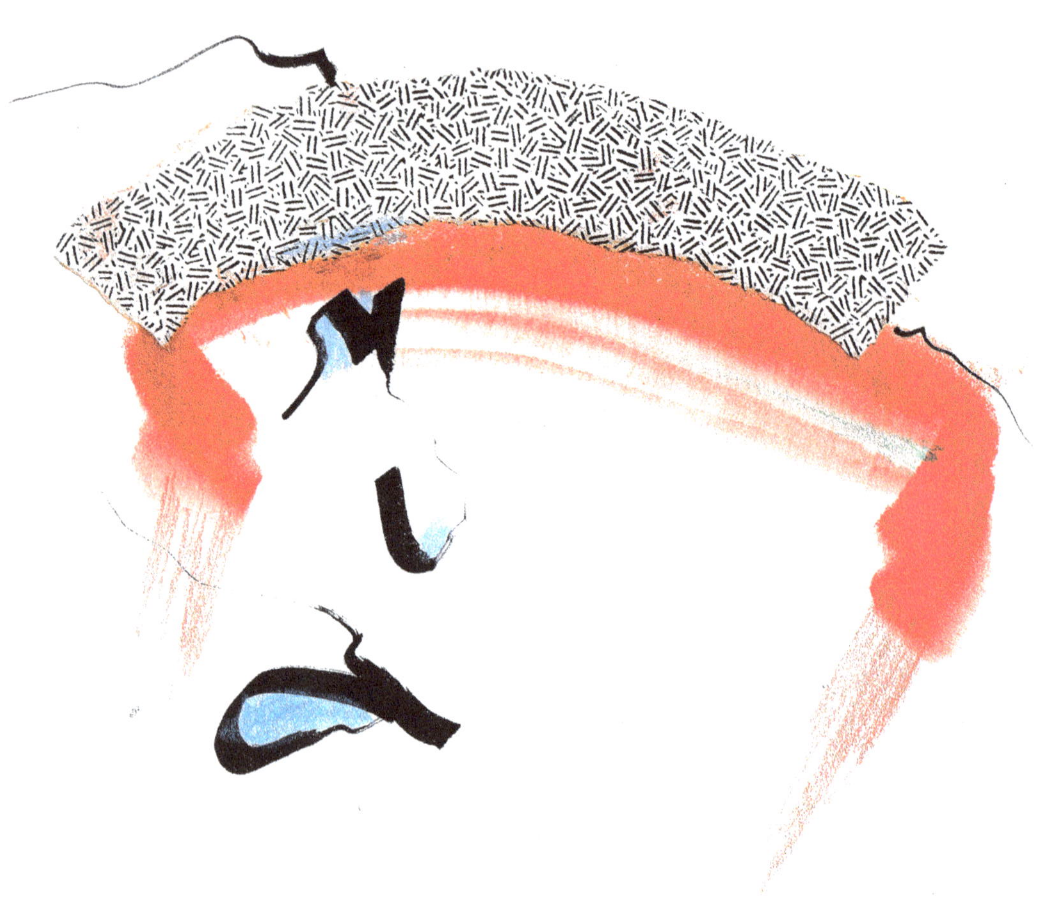

## MUD

*Visual poem, 6 in x 5 in*

**ANDREI CODRESCU**
BROOKLYN, NEW YORK

## I ALMOST JUMPED

*for Peter and Kat*

I want to take off my clothes and leap
into that lake where my new body waits for me
a deepfake as deep as the bottomless lake
of language that refuses to rhyme its
impropaganda with anything but Rwanda
but marketing in Rwanda works no different
than it does in the puddle of self that dreams
its every day "I am human" propaganda

## EDEL RODRIGUEZ

MT. TABOR, NEW JERSEY

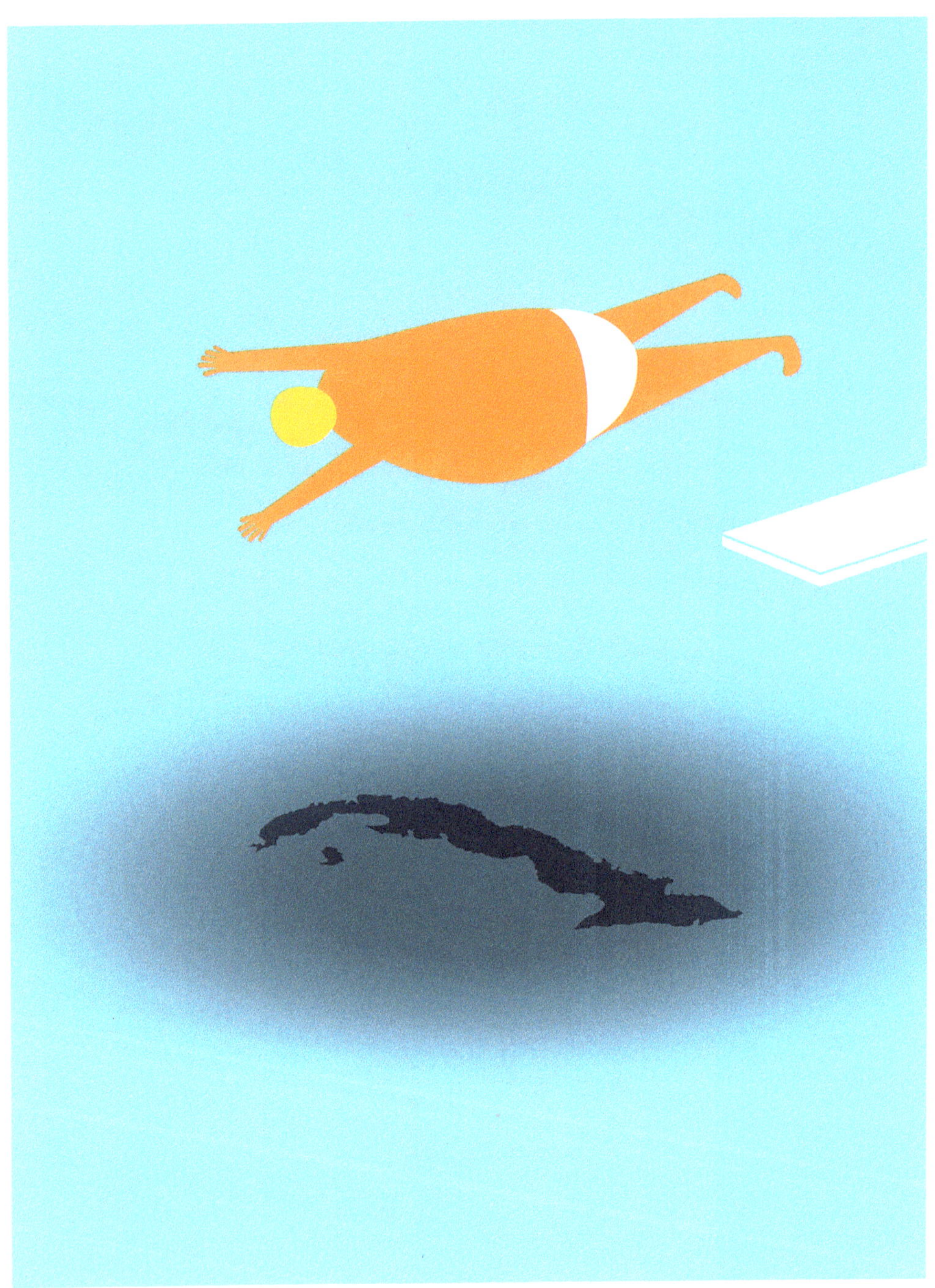

**BELLY FLOP**

*Digital art*

## ANNIE RACHELE LANZILLOTTO

YONKERS, NEW YORK

ROOM IS A BUNKER THE BALLROOM IS A BUNKER THE BALL ROOM IS A BUNKER THE
NKER THE BALLROOM IS A BUNKERTHE BALLROOM IS A BUNKER THE BALLROOM IS A
ROOM IS A BUNKER THE BALLROOM IS A BUNKER THE BALLROOM IS A BUNKER THE B
ER THE BALLROOM IS A BUNKER THE BALLROOM IS A BUNKER THE BALLROOM IS A B
OOM IS A BUNKERTHE BALLROOM IS A BUNKERTHE BALLROOM IS A BUNKERTHE BAL
ER THE BALLROOM IS A BUNKER THE BALLROOM IS A BUKN ER THE BALL ROOM IS ABUI
OM IS A BUNKER THE BALLROOM IS A BUNKER THE BALLROOM IS A BUNKER THE BAL
ER THE BALLROOM IS A BUNKER THE BALLROOM IS A BUNKER THE BALLROOM IS A BU
OM IS A BUNKER THE BALLROOM IS A BUNKER THE BALLROOM IS A BUNKERTHE BALL
THE BALLROOM IS A BUNKER THE BALLROOM IS A BUNKER THE BALLROOM IS A BUN
M IS A BUNKER THE BALLROOM IS A BUNKER THE BALLROOM IS A BUNKER THE BALLR
HE BALLROOM IS A BUNKER THE BALLROOM IS A BUNKER THE BALLROOM IS A BUNK
IS A BUNKER THE BALLROOM IS A BUNKER THE BALLROOM IS A BUNKER THE BALLRO
E BALLROOM IS A BUNKER **THE BALLROOM IS A BUNKER** THE BALLROOM IS
LROOM IS A BUNKER THE BALLROOM IS A BUNKERTHE BALLROOM IS A BUNKER THE
UNKER THE BALLROOM IS A BUNKER THE BALLROOM IS A BUNKER THE BALLROOM IS
LROOM IS A BUNKER *THE BALLROOM IS A BUNKER* THE BALLROOM IS A BUNKER THE
NKER THE BALLROOM IS A BUNKER THE BALLROOM IS A BUNKER THE BALLROOM IS
LROOM IS A BUNKER THE BALLROOM IS A BUNKER THE BALLROOM IS A BUNKER THE
NKER THE BALLROOM IS A BUNKER THE BALLROOM IS A BUNKER THE BALLROOM IS A
ROOM IS A BUNKER THE BALLROOM IS A BUNKER THE BALLROOM IS A BUNKER THE B
ER THE BALLROOM IS A BUNKER THE BALLROOM IS A BUNKER THE BALLROOM IS A
OOM IS A BUNKER THE BALLROOM IS A BUNKERTHE BALL ROOM IS A BUNKER THE B
ER THE BALLROOM IS A BUNKER THE BALLROOM IS A BUNKER THE BALLROOM IS A
OOM IS A BUNKER THE BALLROOM IS A BUNKER THE BALLROOM IS A BUNKER THE
NKER THE *BALLROOM IS A BUNKER* THE BALLROOM IS A BUNKER THE BALLROOM IS A
ROOM IS A BUNKER THE BALLROOM IS A BUNKER THE BALLROOM IS A BUNKER THE E
NKER THE BALLROOM **IS A BUNKER** THE BALL ROOM IS A BUNKER THE BALL ROOM I
LL ROOM IS A BUNKER THE BALL ROOM IS A BUNKER THE BALLROOM IS A BUNKER TH
UNKER THE BALLROOM IS A BUNKER THE BALL ROOM IS A BUNKER THE BALL ROOM
LLROOM IS A BUNKER THE BALL ROOM IS A BUNKER THE BALLROOM IS A BUNKERTI
BUNKER THE BALL ROOM IS A BUNKER THE BALL ROOM IS A BUNKERTHE BALL ROOM
BALLROOM IS A BUNKER THE BALLROOM IS A BUNKER THE BALLROOM IS A BUNKER T
A BUNKER THE BALL ROOM IS A BUNKER THE BALLROOM IS A BUNKERTHE BALL ROOM
BALLROOM IS A BUNKER THE BALLROOM IS A BUNKER THE BALLROOM IS A BUNKER
A BUNKER THE BALLROOM IS A BUNKER THE BALL ROOM IS A BUNKER THE BALL ROOM
BALL ROOM IS A BUNKER THE BALL ROOM IS A BUNKER THE BALL ROOM IS A BUNKE
S A BUNKER THE BALL ROOM IS A BUNKER THE BALL ROOM IS A BUNKER THE BALL R
HE BALLROOM IS A BUNKER THE BALLROOM IS A BUNKER THE BALLROOM IS A BU
M IS A BUNKERTHE BALLROOM IS A BUNKERTHE BALLROOM IS A BUNKERTHE BALLR
HE BALLROOM IS A BUNKERTHE BALLROOM IS A BUNKER THE BALLROOM IS A BUNK
S A BUNKER THE BALLROOM IS A BUNKER THE BALLROOM IS A BUNKERTHE BALLROC
E BALLROOM IS A BUNKERTHE BALLROOM IS A BUNKER THE BALLROOM IS A BUNKER
A BUNKER=ROOM IS A BUNKER THE BALLROOM IS A BUNKER THE BALLROOM IS A BUN
M IS A BUNKER THE BALLROOM IS A BUNKERTHE BALLROOM IS A BUNKERTHE BALLR
HE BALLROOM IS A BUNKERTHE BALLROOM IS A BUNKER THE BALLROOM IS A BUNKE
ROOM IS A BUNKER THE BALLROOM IS A BUNKER THE BALLROOM IS A BUNKER THE E
NKER THE BALLROOM IS A BUNKERTHE BALLROOM IS A BUNKERTHE BALLROOM IS
LROOM IS A BUNKERTHE BALLROOM IS A BUNKER THE BALLROOM IS A BUNKERTHE E
NKER THE BALLROOM IS A BUNKER THE BALLROOM IS A BUNKER THE BALLROOM
ALLROOM IS A BUNKERTHE BALLROOM IS A BUNKERTHE BALLROOM IS A BUNKERTH
UNKERTHE BALLROOM IS A BUNKER THE BALLROOM IS A BUNKER THE BALL ROOM IS
LROOM IS A BUNKER THE BALL ROOM IS A BUNKER THE BALL ROOM IS A BUNKER TH
UNKERTHE BALL ROOM IS A BUNKER THE BALLROOM IS A BUNKER THE BALL ROOM IS
LROOM IS A BUNKER THE BALL ROOM IS A BUNKER THE BALL ROOM IS A BUNKER THE
UNKER THE BALLROOM IS A BUNKER THE BALLROOM IS A BUNKER THE BALLROOM IS
LROOM IS A BUNKER THE BALLROOM IS A BUNKER THE BALLROOM IS A BUNKER THE
NKER THE BALLROOM IS A BUNKER THE BALLROOM IS A BUNKER THE BALLROOM IS
OOM IS A BUNKER THE BALLROOM IS A BUNKER THE BALLROOM IS A BUNKER THE E

### THE BALLROOM IS A BUNKER

*Text art*

**SANTIAGO AMAYA**
HACIENDA HEIGHTS, CALIFORNIA

## SPANGLISH GUNPOWDER

It's the denial of provocation
the nomadic nature of blame
that seems to frolic out of focus

Plausible deniability and systemic degradation
Twoisms that are one in the same
Riddled amongst the suburban locusts

The devolution of a think piece
featuring every single buzz word
from Fox News to Al Jazeera to your local communist

The general contractors of crisis acting
have modeled the propagandist machine
after the human centipede

To exude a unique thought against the
Frankensteins of our time is but a blasphemy to
the very manufacturers of our sepsis

The constant finger pointing has caused us all
to end up in the Chinese finger trap
of American freedom marked by an asterisk

The conditional love of a parent who only gets
you on holidays, relying on a transactional
adoration that deems you a functional member of society

It's been established that this is normal now
The dysfunctional essence of it being just a matter of fact

The famine that follows the drought
The corruption soaked vampires that preach religious morality
The freedom of speech that'll get you shot down from the guard tower

The beggar that holds the sign that attempts to garner your sympathy
As you scroll on a black screen and add righteous lacquer to your wishlist

It's all about choices
At least that's what the mirage has lead us to
As the last droplets of water evaporate into the conglomerate of flesh
that have become the billionaire class

They'll monetize the sun before they reconsider the damage they've done or
continue to do
They'll create a million conspiracy theories before they embrace the truth

Hiding our peoples bones in the marsh
and attributing the death to natural causes
Looking the other way like we just heard a tire screech and a metallic collision
praying it all sorts itself out as everyone else does the same

And who am I but a sinner with no faith
All I believe in is the end of the world,
deepfakes and that the murder of political candor will be a cold case

I turn my head to the bottle and suddenly the news announces a ceasefire
In the same breath I raise my glass to celebrate
the news announces the end of the ceasefire
So I raise my glass in defeat as I scroll onto the next 30 second news reel
and feel accomplished
that I've done my part in making the world a better place

**BOB HOLMAN**
NEW YORK, NEW YORK

## ALIENS IN THE WHITE HOUSE

They come from Outer Space
Can't look you in the face
Scenario's worst-case
*Got Aliens in the White House!*

They got delusional disorder
Huh? Stop aliens at the border?
Aliens infest the White House stink slime
Crack egg farts with they teeth! smells like it

Go head! pronounce yourself King
Cover yr flappy crap ass with bling
Cringe, Platypusnik, cringe as we sing
*We got Aliens in the White House!*

We're a nation of immigrantés
With a outerspace alien presidenté
Who survives by drinking blood inocenté
Alienate the Aliens! Aliens in the White House!

Pilgrim aliens rock Plymouth Rock
Double down, Citizens, Fight their doubletalk
His signature looks like it's a heart attack
He's on amphetamine ketamine BigMac crack!

Stop and romp! Clomp chomp, Chump
t-Rumpasaurus! Alien Dinosaurus! Fruckrump!
*We got Aliens in the White House!*
Aliens in the White House!

## JACK SEIEI

TOKYO, JAPAN

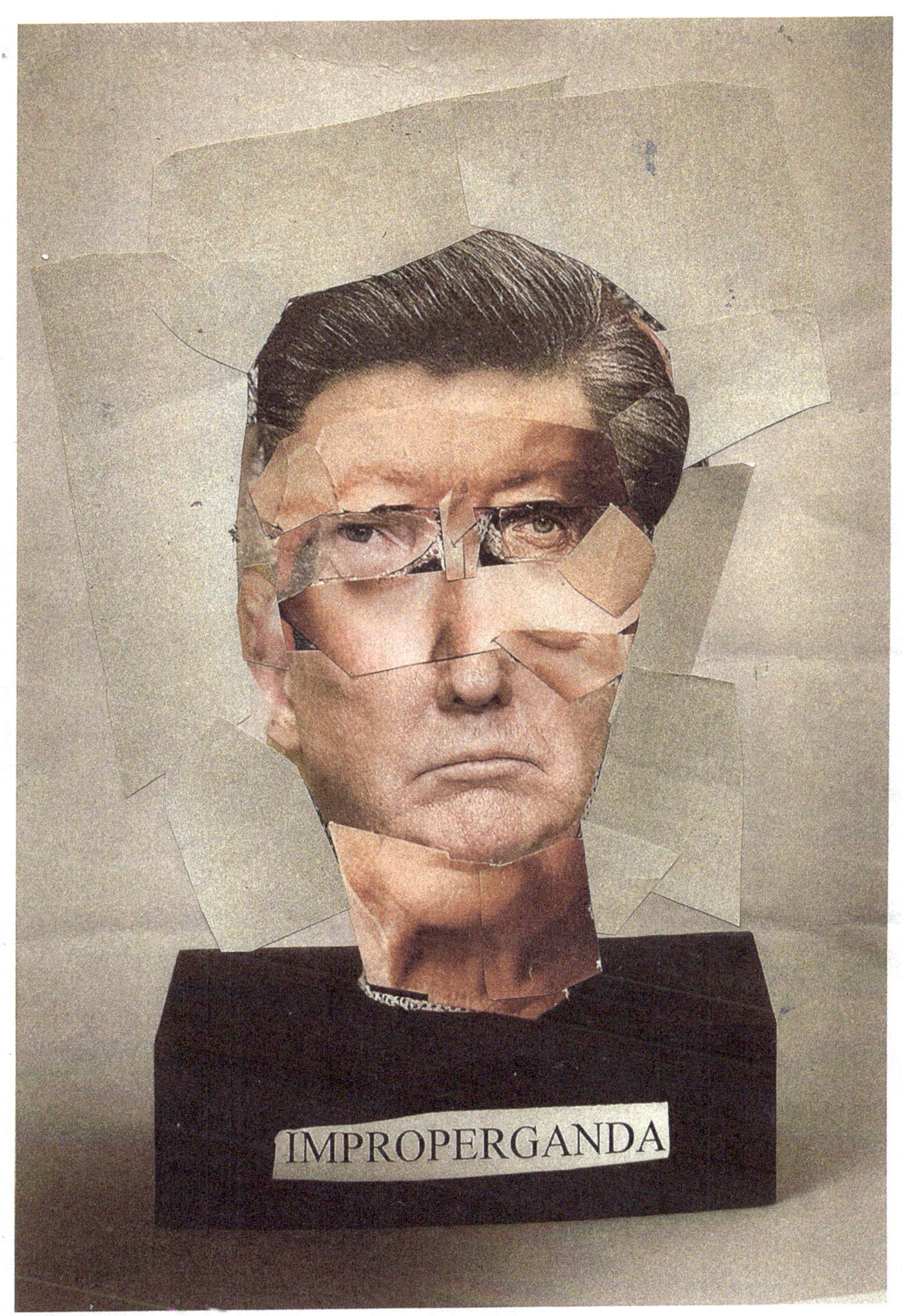


**IMPROPERGANDA**

*Collage, A4*

**PETER CARLAFTES**

NEW YORK, NEW YORK

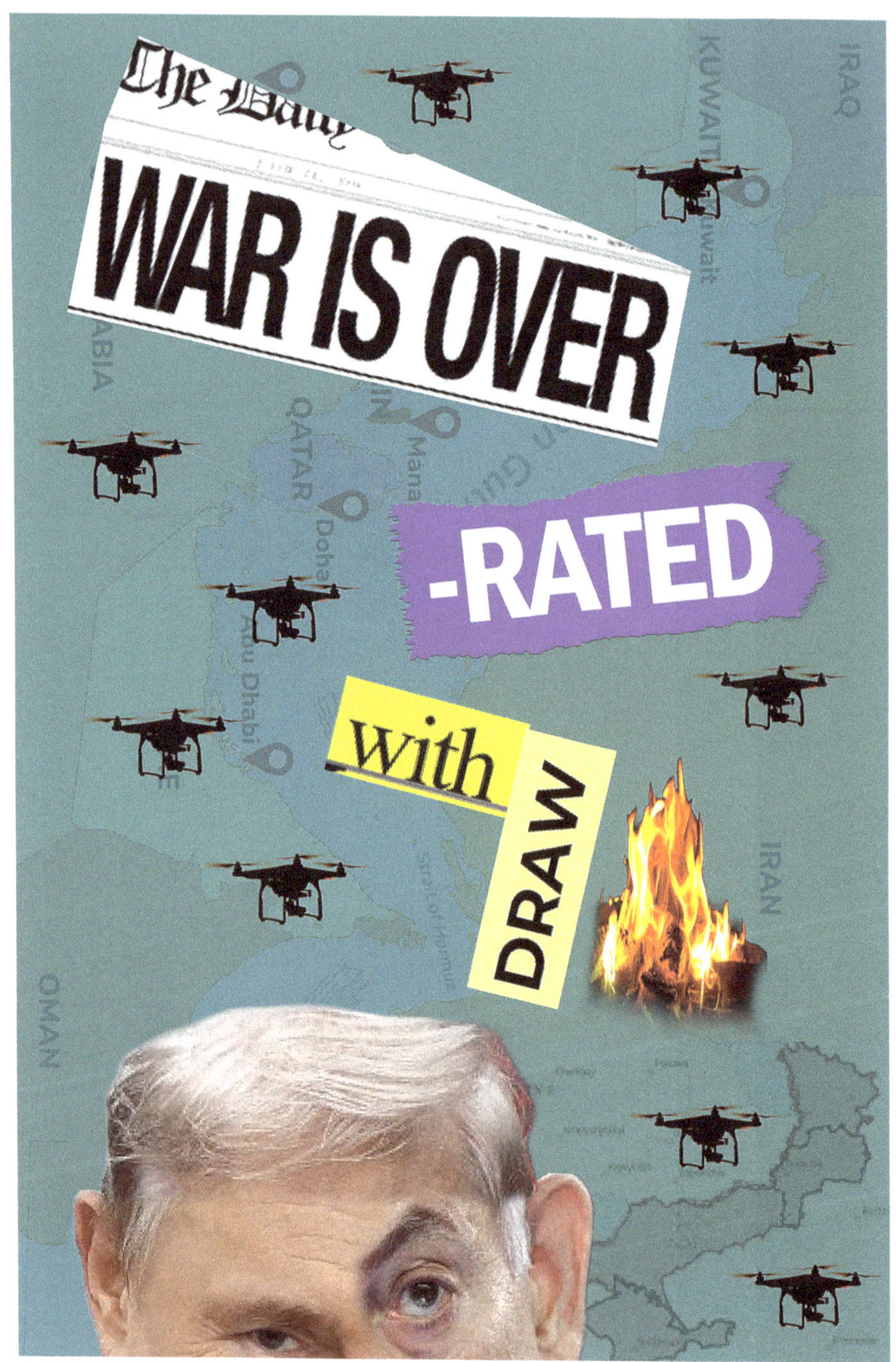


**OVER-RATED**

*Digital collage*

**KAT GEORGES**

NEW YORK, NEW YORK

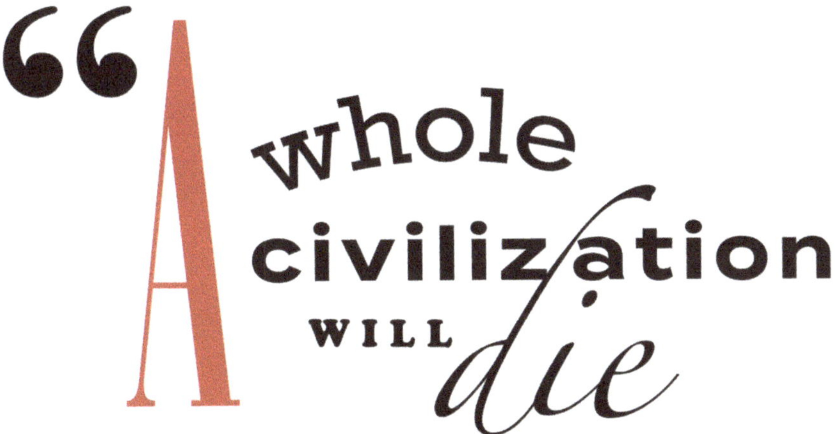


TONIGHT

never to be brought back again
never to be brought back again
never to be brought back again
never to be brought back again
never to be brought back again
never to be brought back again
never to be brought back again
never to be brought back again
never to be brought back again

I don't WANT that
TO happen BUT
it probably WILL"

D J T

**KEEP THE FAITH**

*Visual poetry*

**KAREN HILDEBRAND**

BROOKLYN, NEW YORK

# VALENTINE

*Address to the Munich Security Conference delivered by Marco Rubio on February 14, 2026, Valentine's Day.*

We gather here today as members of a historic alliance, an alliance that saved and changed the world. When this conference began in 1963, it was in a nation -- actually, it was on a continent -- that was divided against itself. The line **between** communism and freedom ran through the **heart** of Germ**an**y. The first barbe**d fence**s of the Berlin Wall had gone up just two years prior. And just months before that first conference, before our predecessors first met here, here in Munich, the Cuban Missile Crisis had brought the world to the brink of nuclear destruction. Even as World War II still burned fresh in the memory of Americans and Europeans alike, **we found** ourselves staring down the barrel of a new global catastrophe -- one with the potential for a new kind of destruction, more apocalyptic and final than anything before in the history of mankind. At the time of that first gathering, Soviet communism was on the march. Thousands of years of Western civilization hung in the balance. At that time, victory was far from certain. But we were driven by a common purpose. We were unified not just by what we were fighting against; we were unified by what we were fighting for. And together, Europe and America prevailed and a continent was rebuilt. Our people prospered. In time, the East and West blocs were reunited. A civilization was once again made whole. That infamous wall that had cleaved this nation into two came down, and with it an evil empire, and the East and West became one again. But the **euphoria** of this triumph led us to a dangerous delusion: that we had entered, quote, "the end of history;" that every nation would now be a liberal democracy; that the ties formed by trade and by commerce alone would now replace nationhood; that the rules-based global order -- an overused term -- would now replace the national interest; and that we would now live in a world without borders where everyone became a citizen of the world. This was a foolish idea that ignored both human nature and it ignored the lessons of over 5,000 years of recorded human history. And it has cost us dearly. In this delusion, we embraced a dogmatic vision of free and unfettered trade, even as some nations protected their economies and subsidized their companies to systematically undercut ours -- shuttering our plants, resulting in large parts of our societies being deindustrialized, shipping millions of working and middle-class jobs overseas, and handing control of our critical supply chains to both adversaries and rivals. We increasingly outsourced our sovereignty to international institutions while many nations invested in massive welfare states at the cost of maintaining the ability to defend themselves. This, even as other countries have invested in the most rapid military buildup in all of human history and have not hesitated to use hard power to pursue their own interests. To appease a climate cult, we have imposed energy policies on ourselves that are impoverishing our people, even as our competitors exploit oil and coal and natural gas and anything else -- not just to power their economies, but to use as leverage against our own. And in a pursuit of a world without borders, we opened our doors to an unprecedented wave of mass migration that threatens the cohesion of our societies, the continuity of our culture, and the future of our people. We made these mistakes together, and now, together, we owe it to our people to face those facts and to move forward, to rebuild. Under President Trump, the United States of America will once again take on the task of renewal and restoration, driven by a vision of a future as proud, as sovereign, and as vital as our civilization's past. And while we are prepared, if necessary, to do this alone, it is our preference and it is our hope to do this together with you, our friends here in Europe. For the United States and Europe, we belong together. America was founded 250 years ago, but the **roots** began here on this continent long before. The man who settled and built the nation of my birth arrived on our shores carrying the memories and the traditions and the Christian faith of their ancestors as a sacred inheritance, an unbreakable link between the old world and the new. We are part of one civilization -- Western civilization. We are bound to one another by the deepest bonds that nations could share, forged by centuries of shared history, Christian faith, culture, heritage, language, ancestry, and the sacrifices our forefathers made together for the common civilization to which we have fallen heir. And so this is why we Americans may sometimes come off as a little direct and urgent in our counsel. This is why President Trump demands seriousness and reciprocity from our friends here in Europe. The reason why, my friends, is because we care deeply. We care **deeply** about your future and ours. And if at times we disagree, our disagreements come from our profound sense of concern about a Europe with which we are connected -- not just economically, not just militarily. We are connected spiritually and we are connected culturally. We want Europe to be strong. We believe that Europe must survive, because the two great wars of the last century serve for us as history's constant reminder that ultimately, our destiny is and will always be inter**twined** with yours, because we know -- because we know that the fate of Europe will never be irrelevant to our own. National security, which this conference is largely about, is not merely series of technical questions -- how much we spend on defense or where, how we deploy it, these are important questions. They are. But they are not the fundamental one. The fundamental question we must answer at the outset is what exactly are we defending, because armies do not fight for abstractions. Armies fight for a people; armies fight for a nation. Armies fight for a way of life. And that is what we are defending: a great civilization that has every reason to be proud of its history, confident of its future, and aims to always be the master of its own economic and political destiny. It was here in Europe where the ideas that planted the **seeds of** liberty that changed the world were born. It was here in Europe where the world -- which gave the world the rule of law, the universities, and the scientific revolution. It was this continent that produced the **genius** of Mozart and Beethoven, of Dante and Shakespeare, of Michelangelo and Da Vinci, of the Beatles and the Rolling Stones. And this is the place **W**h**e**re the vaulted ceilings of the Sistine Chapel and the towering spires of the great cathedral in Cologne, they testify not just to the greatness of our past or to a faith in God that inspired these **marvel**s. They foreshadow the wonders that await us in our future. But only if we are unapologetic in our heritage and proud of this common inheritance can we together begin the work of envisioning and shaping our economic and our political future. Deindustrialization was not inevitable. It was a conscious policy choice, a decades-long economic undertaking that stripped our nations of their wealth, of their productive capacity, and of their independence. And the loss of our supply chain sovereignty was not a function of a prosperous and healthy system of global trade. It was foolish. It was a foolish but voluntary transformation of our economy that left us dependent on others for our needs and dangerously vulnerable to crisis. Mass migration is not, was not, isn't some fringe concern of little consequence. It was and continues to be a crisis which is transforming and destabilizing societies all across the West. Together we can reindustrialize our economies and rebuild our capacity to defend our people. But the work of this new alliance should not be focused just on military cooperation and reclaiming the industries of the past. It should also be focused on, together, advancing our mutual interests and new frontiers, unshackling our ingenuity, our creativity, and the dynamic spirit to build a new Western century. Commercial space travel and cutting-edge artificial intelligence; industrial automation and flex manufacturing; creating a Western supply chain for critical minerals not vulnerable to extortion from other powers; and a unified effort to compete for market share in the economies of the Global South. Together we can not only take back control of our own industries and supply chains -- we can prosper in the areas that will define the 21st century. But we must also gain control of our national borders. Controlling who and how many people enter our countries, this is not an expression of xenophobia. It is not hate. It is a fundamental act of national sovereignty. And the failure to do so is not just an abdication of one of our most basic duties owed to our people. It is an urgent threat to the fabric of our societies and the survival of our civilization itself. And finally, we can no longer place the so-called global order above the vital interests of our people and our nations. We do not need to abandon the system of international cooperation we authored, and we don't need to dismantle the global institutions of the old order that together we built. But these must be reformed. These must be rebuilt. For example, the United Nations still has tremendous potential to be a tool for good in the world. But we cannot ignore that today, on the most pressing matters before us, it has no answers and has played virtually no role. It could not solve the war in Gaza. Instead, it was American leadership that freed captives from barbarians and brought about a fragile truce. It had not solved the war in Ukraine. It took American leadership and partnership with many of the countries here today just to bring the two sides to the table in search of a still-elusive peace. It was powerless to constrain the nuclear program of radical Shia clerics in Tehran. That required 14 bombs dropped with precision from American B-2 bombers. And it was unable to address the threat to our security from a narcoterrorist dictator in Venezuela. Instead, it took American Special Forces to bring this fugitive to justice. In a perfect world, all of these problems and more would be solved by diplomats and strongly worded resolutions. But we do not live in a perfect world, and we cannot continue to allow those who blatantly and openly threaten our citizens and endanger our global stability to shield themselves behind abstractions of international law which they themselves routinely violate. This is the path that President Trump and the United States has embarked upon. It is **the path** we ask you here in Europe to join us on. It is a path **we** have **walk**ed **together** before and hope to walk together again. For five centuries, before the end of the Second World War, the West had been expanding -- its missionaries, its pilgrims, its soldiers, its explorers pouring out from its shores to cross oceans, settle new continents, build vast empires extending out across the globe. But in 1945, for the first time since the age of Columbus, it was contracting. Europe was in ruins. Half of it lived behind willing and able to defend it. And this is why we do not want allies to rationalize the broken status quo rather than reckon with what is necessary to fix it, for we in America have no interest in being polite and orderly caretakers of the West's managed decline. We do not seek to separate, but to revitalize an old friendship and renew the greatest civilization in human history. What we want is a reinvigorated alliance that recognizes that what has ailed our societies is not just a set of bad policies but a malaise of hopelessness and complacency. An alliance -- the alliance that we want is one that is not paralyzed into inaction by fear -- fear of climate change, fear of war, fear of technology. Instead, we want an alliance that boldly races into the future. And the only fear we have is the fear of the shame of not leaving our nations prouder, stronger, and wealthier for our children. An alliance ready to defend our people, to safeguard our interests, and to preserve the freedom of action that allows us to shape our own destiny -- not one that exists to operate a global welfare state and atone for the purported sins of past generations. An alliance that does not allow its power to be outsourced, constrained, or subordinated to systems beyond its control; one that does not depend on others for the critical necessities of its national life; and one that does not maintain the polite pretense that our way of life is just one among many and that asks for permission before it acts. And above all, an alliance based on the recognition that we, the West, have inherited together -- what we have inherited together is something that is unique and distinctive and irreplaceable, because this, after all, is the very foundation of the transatlantic bond. Acting together in this way, we will not just help recover a sane foreign policy. It will restore to us a clearer sense of ourselves. It will restore a place in the world, and in so doing, it will rebuke and deter the forces of civilizational erasure that today menace both America and Europe alike. So in a time of headlines heralding the end of the transatlantic era, let it be known and clear to all that this is neither our goal nor our wish -- because for us Americans, our home may be in the Western Hemisphere, but we will always be a child of Europe. Our story began with an Italian explorer whose adventure into the great unknown to discover a new world brought Christianity to the Americas -- and became the legend that defined the imagination of a our pioneer nation. Our first colonies were built by English settlers, to whom we owe not just the language we speak but the whole of our political and legal system. Our frontiers were shaped by Scots-Irish -- that proud, hearty clan from the **hill**s of Ulster that gave us Davy Crockett and Mark Twain and Teddy Roosevelt and Neil Armstrong. Our great midwestern **heartland** was built by German farmers and craftsmen who transformed empty **plain**s into a global agricultural powerhouse -- and by the way, dramatically upgraded the quality of American beer. Our expansion into the interior followed the **footsteps of** French fur traders and explorers whose names, by the way, still adorn the street signs and towns' names all across the Mississippi Valley. Our **horses**, our r**a**nches, our rodeos -- the entire **romance** of the cowboy archetype that became synonymous with the American West -- these were born in Spain. And our largest and most iconic city was named New Amsterdam before it was **named New York**. And do you know that in the year that my country was founded, Lorenzo and Catalina Geroldi lived in Casale Monferrato in the Kingdom of Piedmont-Sardinia. And Jose and Manuela Reina lived in Sevilla, Spain. I don't know what, if anything, they knew about the 13 colonies which had gained their independence from the British empire, but here's what **I** am certain of: They **could** have **never imagine**d that 250 years later, one of their direct descendants would be back here today on this continent as the chief diplomat of that infant nation. And yet here I am, reminded by my own story that both our histories and our fates will always be linked.

## WAYNE ATHERTON

DOVER, NEW HAMPSHIRE

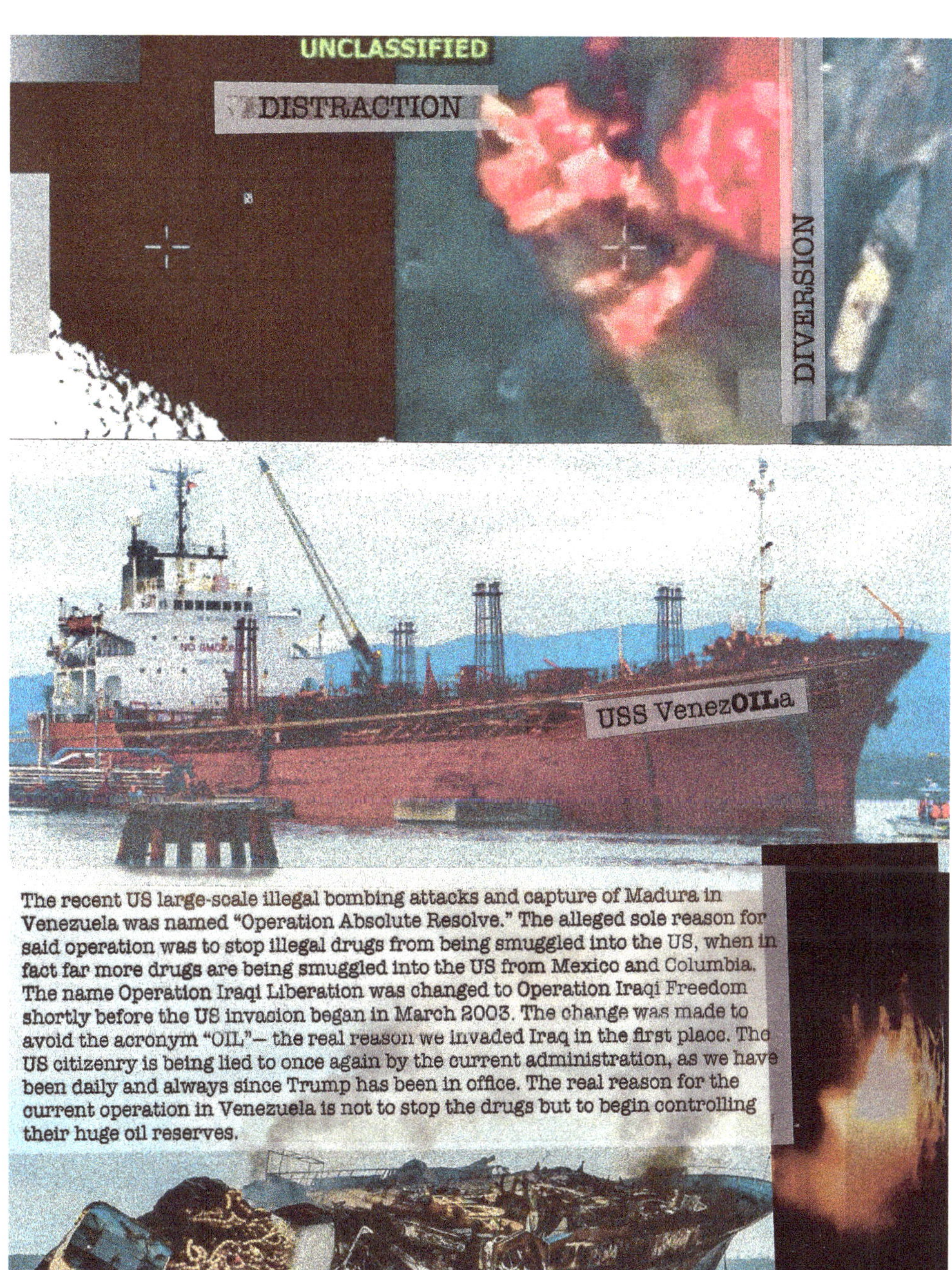


### UNCLASSIFIED DISTRACTION

*Mixed media collage on paper, 11 in x 8 in*

## BERTHOLDUS SIBUM

MEPPEL, THE NETHERLANDS

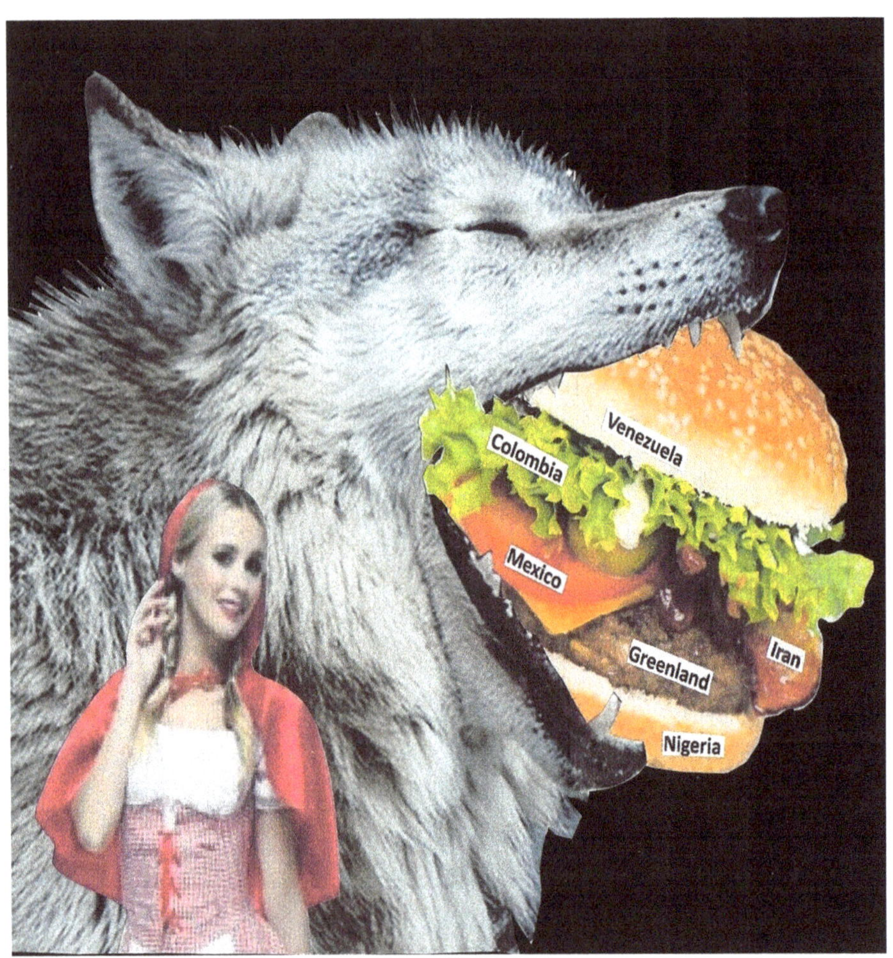


**YOU KNOW HOW THE FAIRY TALE ENDED**

*Digital art, 1400 px x1350 px*

**ROGER CONOVER**
FREEPORT, MAINE

## HOW TO CATCH A FAIRY

You can light a candle near the tub but you're not going to catch me that way.
That's like putting a bell on a cat's collar before it goes hunting
Or putting a fish on a hook to catch another one.
If you think this is too much advice don't read it.
I'm tired of words too.
I've never given the color brown much of a chance.
And if someone asks me to name an animal with paws, I think monkey.
Was it Schopenhauer who said
If you touch something too much it will die
But if you see things grownups don't you're alive?
Sometimes I place bones on the ground to read the weather.
If I could just get past the idea of skin
bones would tell me everything.
Why would you want to catch me anyway?
To pluck out my wings and drown me
The way you did that cricket in the toilet?

## SARA MAINO

ARCO, ITALY

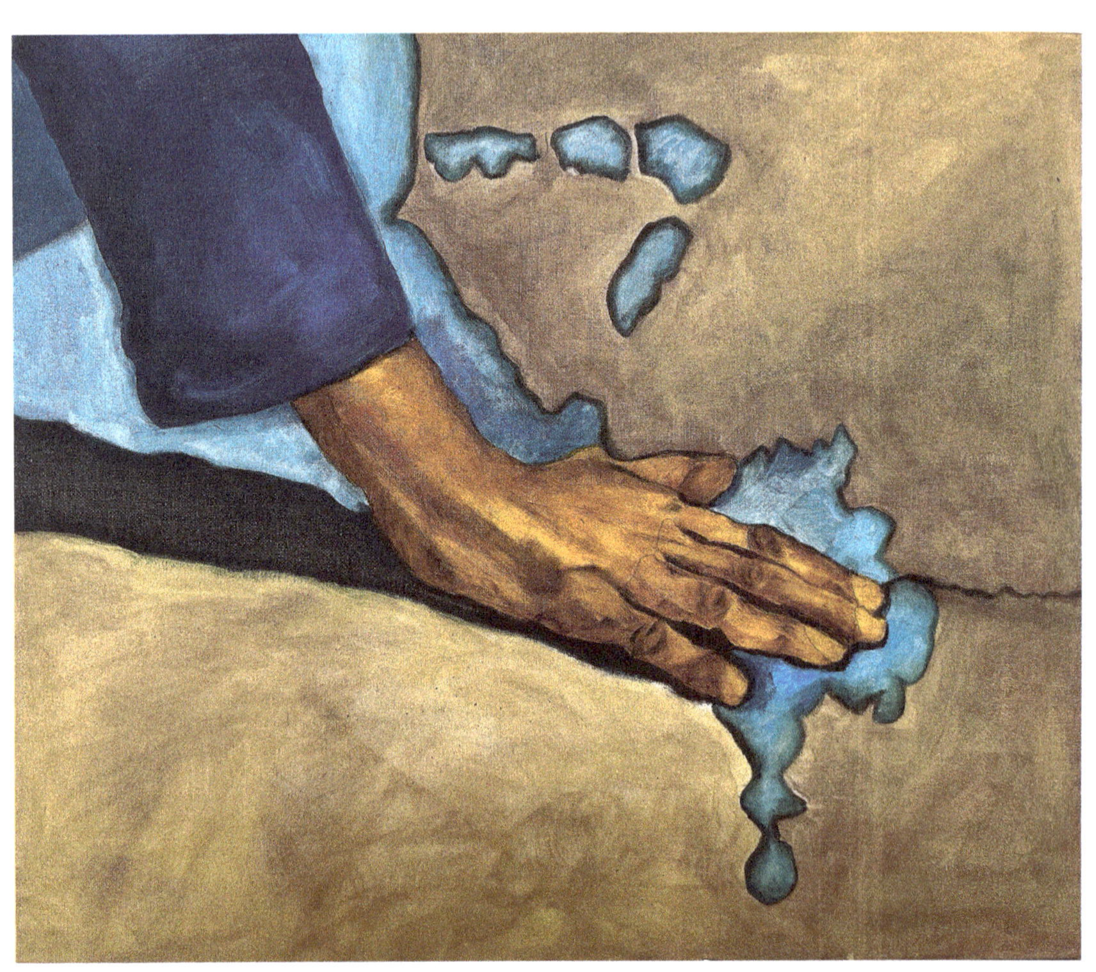

**MA(INO)FESTO**

*Oil on canvas, 58 cm x 48 cm*

**MARINA KAZAKOVA**
MOMIGNIES, BELGIUM

# PRAVDA

A childhood like any other:
I got five kopecks from my grandfather,
6 days a week,
To hurry down to the news booth
To buy a copy of "The Truth."
La Vérité, La Verità,
Al-Ḥaqq, Die Wahrheit, Zhēnlǐ Bào!
A childhood like any other:
I took 5 kopecks, brought him "Pravda," 6 days a week, without fail,
He'd smile relieved and freed, and say:
"The Truth" brings peace, the truth is art,
Unspoken deal was clear-cut -
Newspaper for the courtyard time,
The courtyard was my sacred dime,
There,
Through fights, in blood, in black-and-blue's
I sought and found sober truth.
Back then, we played the games in teams
— pre-Internet, pre-vandalism!
Always two camps:
"Cossacks and robbers," "hide and seek,"
sometimes a "dodgeball"!
The courtyard was its own world,
Far from the school, from written rules,
The courtyard was a court — a hall
Of justice, peace, of love, support!
Today that courtyard is a parking lot!
The age of "Truth" has left the Earth,
The age of "Trump" swept in, is on!
An adulthood like any other:
I got the memories of grandfather,
Only one fleeting truth that still remains —
The one that comes to me in dreams:
A secret, miracle inexplicAble,
That makes me smile without trouble,
Without trust in truth,
To stars
that look at me through fragile glass.

**NARGES BABAEI**

GRAZ, AUSTRIA

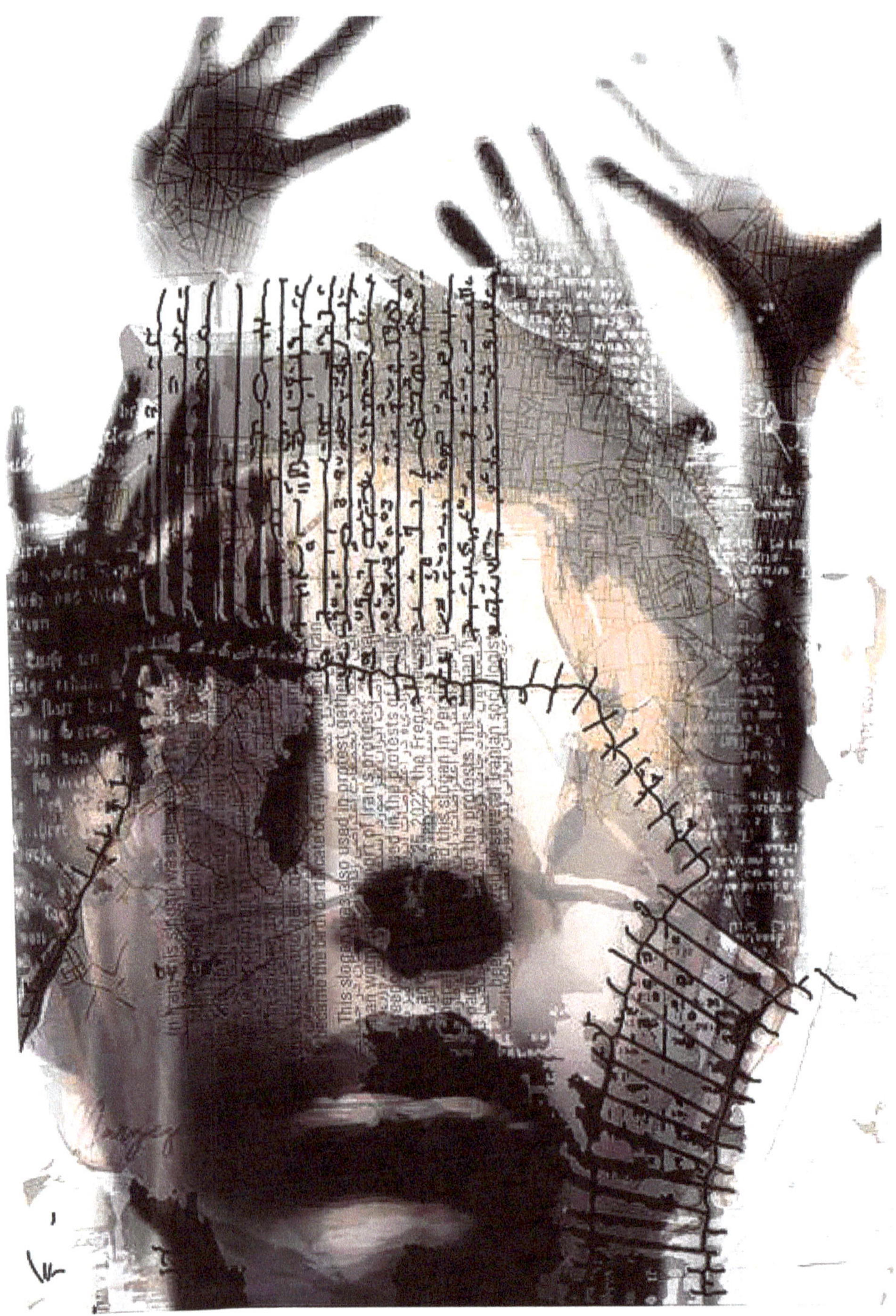

## INTERFERED IDENTITY

*Photomontage and collage, 1280 px x 1833 px*

**ANNA O'MEARA**
SEATTLE, WASHINGTON

## OLD COUNTRY

Gun sales and white lace.

The old country is here in the knickknacks and the wall calendars and the drinking and the laughing and the screaming and the leprechauns and the fairies and the football and the oatmeal and the disaffected tone and the apathy and the guilt and the woe and the not eating and the God.

The old country screams here.

Red wine on turquoise carpet. Andrew Wyeth's *Christina's World* on the wall.

I used to have dreams of my grandmother.

I used to wear my grandmother's moccasins after she died.

I was her favorite because I was graceful, thin, frail, depressed.

I did not see her vision.

I inherited my grandmother in my mother's animosity.

My grandmother seethes in my mother's resentment.

Resentment, a ghost from the old country,

The grudges we hold to the grave.

My grandpa's properties – were they charitable or decrepit?

What counts as a "slum lord"?

Here's one thing that makes me old country:

I know how to use words to hurt people.

## SAM DODSON

BRENTFORD, UNITED KINGDOM

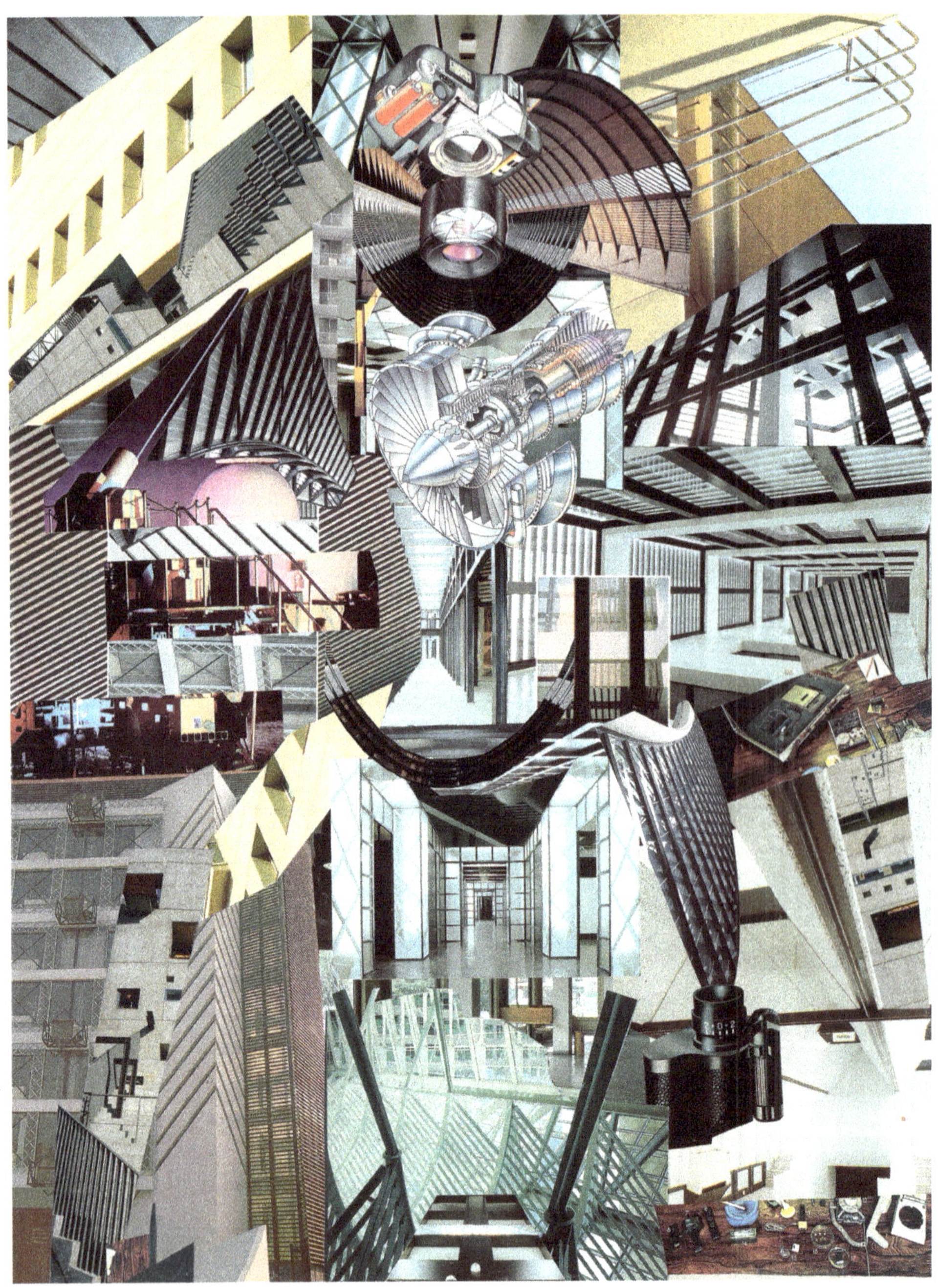

## MANGLED

*Collage on canvas, 60 cm x 80 cm*

**NICO VASSILAKIS**
GREENVILLE, ILLINOIS

## UNITED UNTITLED

How do we
Find a way through
When we can't even leave our house
Or say hello or shake another person's hand
Or dance in the aisle or hum out loud

How do we
Move forward
When more and more people can't be themselves
Or climb a tree or piss their pants while smiling or cry around others or just puke at watching the news

How do we
Get going
And point others to a better place
Or mask our shame at what we do
Or be so hung up about dying or it being so easy to kill or it being so easy to blame

How do we
Reach that place
Where we should
Just shut the fuck up or listen better
Or rip out the ego part of your brain
Or see the other person there hurting
Or meander through or nuance or flitter
Or serpentine movement

How do we
Do that
How do we
Become complete in a state of division
Or disasters are continuous
Or catastrophe rampant
Or we are forever being torn in two in four in eight in sixteen in thirty-twos
Or so on or so wrong or desperate to overcome the pull of simple conflict

**ROBIN TOMENS**

LONDON, UNITED KINGDOM

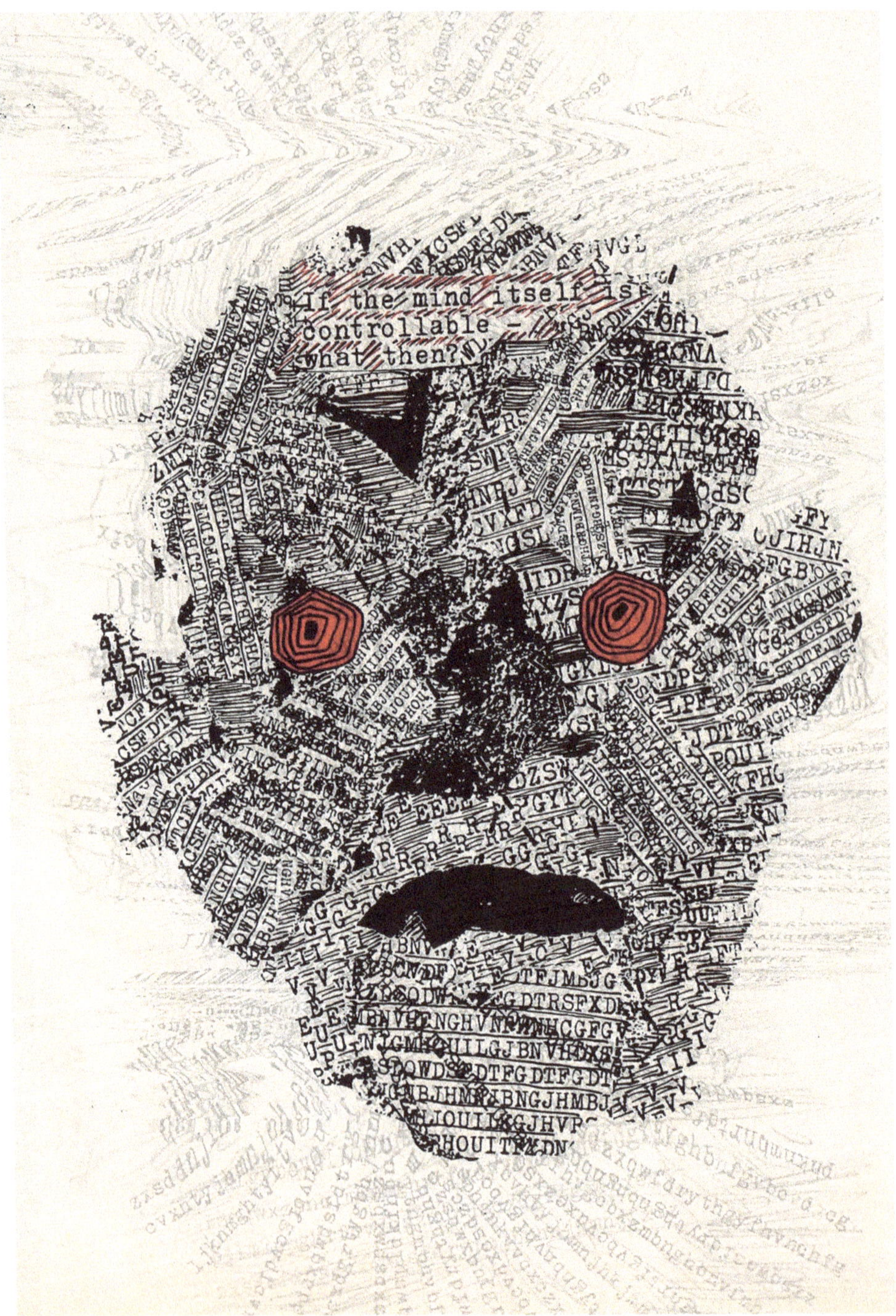


**MIND CONTROL!!!**

*Typewriter on paper*

## DOUG KNOTT

(1943–2022)

### I BECOME SURREAL AT AN ART OPENING

I don't look for truth around here
People live quite happily without it
Going around each other in their long forms
Even though they are standing still

Just now I was talking to
Someone I didn't know
And their face fell off
And my face fell off

Our expressions rolled
In pieces at our feet.

My watch still worked.
Otherwise I was out of time.

Contrary to popular opinion
Most of the people in this room
Are quite innocent

They have not heard
Of themselves yet

**PENNY ARCADE**

NEW YORK, NEW YORK

## THE AVALANCHE

I am parting with my ability to tell the difference between truth and fiction. I am losing my ability to stay sane after a lifetime of balancing the reality of what I see and perceive with my own eyes and the propaganda that flows thru the ether. I used to have a way to shelter myself from the misinformation, what was once a intermittent trickle has become an avalanche.

I try to think when this started, this departure from the truth. I try to think back to when I started to be worried about America. In elementary school when we had bomb raids and we had to go under our desk and we were afraid and I thought that Khrushchev is going to come to my house and hurt my mother and hurt me and my brothers and sisters and my grandparents and I worried all the time that he was coming and how could I fight him? That's when I believed that America was good and Russia was bad. . . I could keep the story straight but later after JFK was assassinated, it was harder to keep the story straight.

Yes I was 13 when John F. Kennedy was assassinated or was it when Robert Kennedy was assassinated? Or was it when Martin Luther King was assassinated? After he had a dream after which he made a speech that said I may not live to see it? Did that haunt me? All of these thoughts are piled on top of each other and I am old now and I learned how to think and it was hard to do but I did learn how to think and how to add two and two together but no – truth has no value, integrity has no value, honesty has no value, care and reflection and thinking about others before yourself has no value.

Propaganda was something that was manufactured in Russia, we did not grow propaganda in America, I believed that till I was 14 or 15. But that was before the trickle down, the trickle down from Halliburton and Enron before America lost its taste for honor.

I knew all this would happen. After all I lived thru the 1950s thru the 60s 70s 80s 90s and 2000s. This is not a surprise to me. The surprise is I thought it would happen after I was dead. I thought what is happening now would happen in 2040 when I was 90 or 2050. I always knew that this would happen I just didn't think that I was going to have to live through it although my mantra all those years was "I want to see how the movie ends" – perhaps that's the crazy part for me because I didn't realize the movie was going to be a horror film. I thought it was gonna be a black and white movie like *Mr. Smith Goes to Washington*, where after a totalitarian regime defeats democracy and the citizens rise up to claim their social and political heritage – instead I get the storming of the capitol with no repercussions! Watch the shooting of Renee Good and Alex Pretti in cold blood. See the blankness in the men's eyes. ICE – a private militia with no supervision, the natural bastard child of Blackwater and Trump. I didn't realize the movie was going to be a Silicon Valley AI generated emotional sci-fi, horror, integrity-less thriller, a hopeless dilemma.

Tell me? Is there something I am missing?

**W.K. STRATTON**
ROUND ROCK, TEXAS

## DAWN WORDS AFTER A VIOLENT NIGHT IN AMERICA

Last night blood smeared suburban bedroom walls in Minnesota. This morning, I hear fundamentalist Mormon lines about ordinance through time and eternity. I have never sought to be sealed. But I understand Peckinpah's adage lifted from the Bible. I do want to enter my house justified. I can say this: a common prayer blanket is the foundation of everything that is a thing. Medicine and songs revealed this to me on a subfreezing night in the Wichita Mountains. After that, I learned to commune with hawks while absorbing soil, becoming, at last, what I have always been. Now I pray in a ten-thousand-year-old way for the dead in Brooklyn Park. Bumblebees breakfast on red yuccas outside my window.

**CHARLES PLYMELL**
CHERRY VALLEY, NEW YORK

## I THINK MY ANCESTORS WERE CELTIC

My dogs and cats never read the Bible
but they know as much about God as I do
Good is soaked in evil, brilliance drowned in stupidity
bad water falling into the sparkling stream
the ads on tv are fools with tools
I did read a hep cat in Corinthian who said
when the inhabitants of Jerusalem go a whoring
that;" Know ye not that a little leaven leaveneth
the whole lump?" maybe too much reefer?
I was 91 years old last Sunday and this world
ain't the same no more don't let the etcetera getcha.
The saffron of the morning crocuses lights my memory
and red lips quicken my heart rate and I read somewhere
the words of King Merikaure of ancient Egypt:
"Great is the great one whose great ones are great."
Sounded like our dear leader and the amazing generation
waiting for the ecto-skeleton to move the genitals and AI
allows us to create ourselves without the propaganda.

## NASTA MARTYN

MINSK, BELARUS

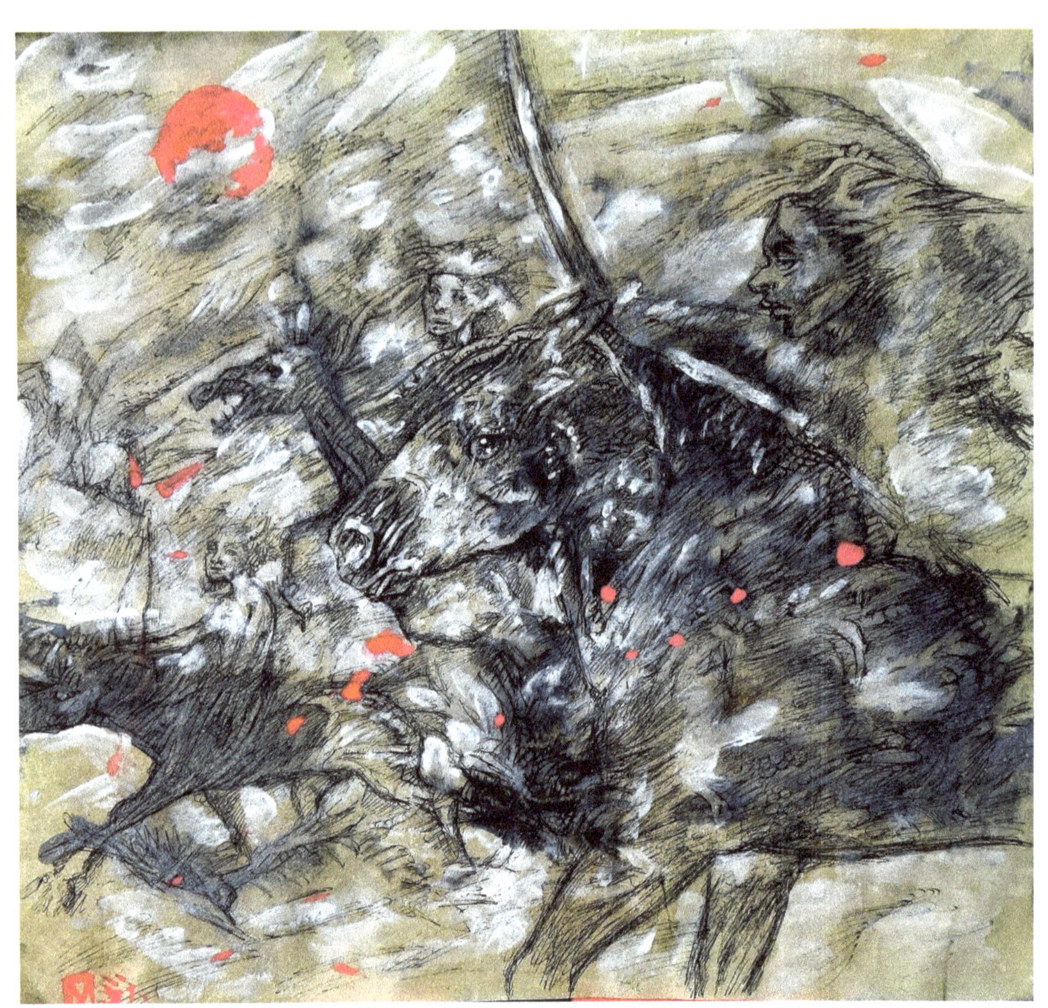

**OBLIVION**

*Ink, acrylic, paper, 30 cm x 30 cm*

**LORENE ZAROU-ZOUZOUNIS**
SAN FRANCISCO, CALIFORNIA

# GAZA GRAVEYARD

Gaza graveyard booms with aliveness
Palestinians are not zombies
That is the genocidal killer persona
Killers roam, foam at the mouth
Earthly souls stirring below
Cross peacefully
Guiltless, full hearts
In the arms of loved ones-ancients

We are not horror
That is the genocidal killer persona
Souls below chant incessantly
Demons escaped from far deeper than here
We are not dead down here

We see you killer, trample on top of us
We feel your grisly killer boot steps
We stretch out, jet through sandy soil
We sing to you killer, ring in your ear
We enlighten you killer, behind poisoned eyes
Our bone, soul-filled soil sinks you killer
We hum to you, humanize you, haunt you killer
Gaza graveyard is the quicksand of your demise
We do not stop blooming each spring
We are not dead down here

**MALIK AMEER CRUMPLER**
POEM | PARIS, FRANCE

**JONATHAN FINLAYSON**
PHOTOGRAPH | NEW YORK, NEW YORK

## PULVIS

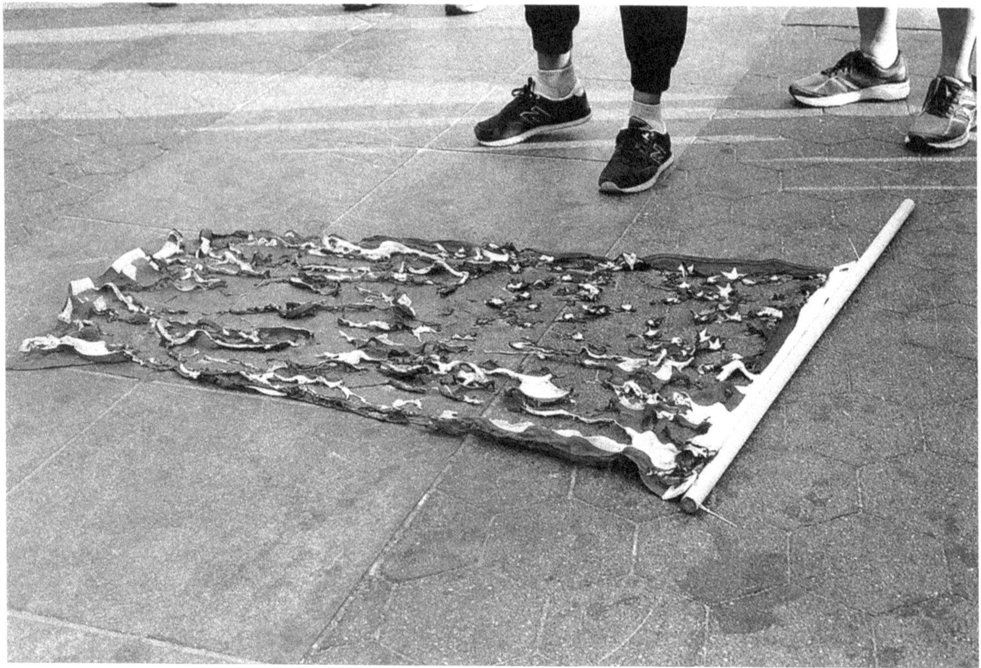

there it isn't... nylon, polyester, & cotton... originals used wool buntin' for stripes & canton, with cotton stars. Standard blue from indigo, & red from madder root, some also use cochineal insect dye for red. White parts left undyed, never dyed white... inverted detonations... those ain't shootin' stars, son...

& then all the colours of fire, sustain pedal... boundless low
draggin' transients, smearin' beige Hadfield helmets tipped way
over as seven feet admire Uncle Fractal still leanin' in our
favorite private graveyard, ashin' (there is no sound for this,
anymore) as whistlin' wires electrify infrared railroads copperin'
conundrums in waves thick as silver quilts dryin' in caked coils
of a meltin' sun's collective shadow after unbearable clarity

inside breathless screens wavin' at facts lyin' about lies fresh out of indium cauldrons slow-cookin' lobbyists & ammunition—_____ fast as contagious policies—don't adjust their vulnerable helmets just yet, putrid pupils fuse over another resort built above ruins by____ as explodin' expressions fade in reverse, as amanuenses mutate into new definitions unbound in pageless books reinterpretin' hybridity's ability to strengthen interoperability for dismissin' port directors trackin' allies navigatin' pyrite toilets into bedazzled international summits & forums & symposiums & banquets & embassy ceremonies celebratin' cerebral vacancy dependin' on the unchallenged entertainment of entropy... Here, just behind my left ear leans my main man whose manganese couldn't refrain his chorus—— ain't no ears on that deity, no more... Gospel sangin' barnacled whales= eyelashes of tubas blown backwards clappin' scorched choral reefs together smashin' into sand, bunkered inside a chameleon's hallucination of calcite waves devoid of fingers flippin' the ibis at our hauntin' order —These tongues? My dusty trophies... & lipless predators, teethless data hunters pluckin' gut strings until gumless, flingin' rotten teeth up into crumpled clouds beyond nebulas where Aunt Certainty flickers herself into fascinatin' scarlet streaked celestial streams carefully encouragin' non-baryonic matter to gather 'round smolderin' violet veins of a missin' postcard, until unburnable trances are suddenly stilled... to move on or move in? Daughter, i escaped that poltergeist but often, i still cough up cotton stars.

**MIKE WATT**

SAN PEDRO, CALIFORNIA

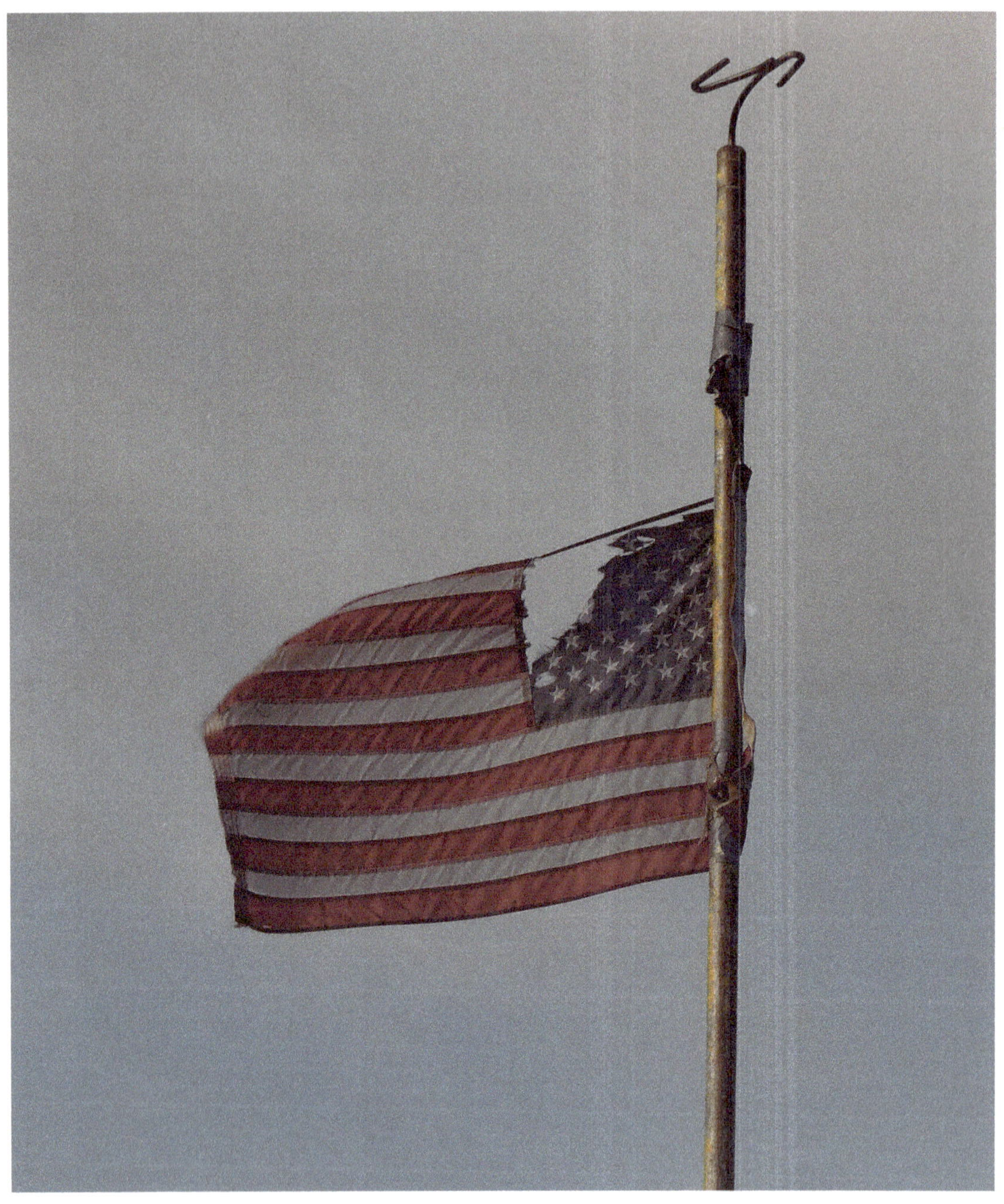

**THURSTON MOORE**
LONDON, UNITED KINGDOM

## GASP POEM

Disruption
Fan out
Boots

Black
Viscosity
Crimson

Quick death
Flaccid response
Wailing

Prayers
Food
Insanity

We
Need
Tomorrow

**ANGELA CAPORASO**

CASERTA, ITALY

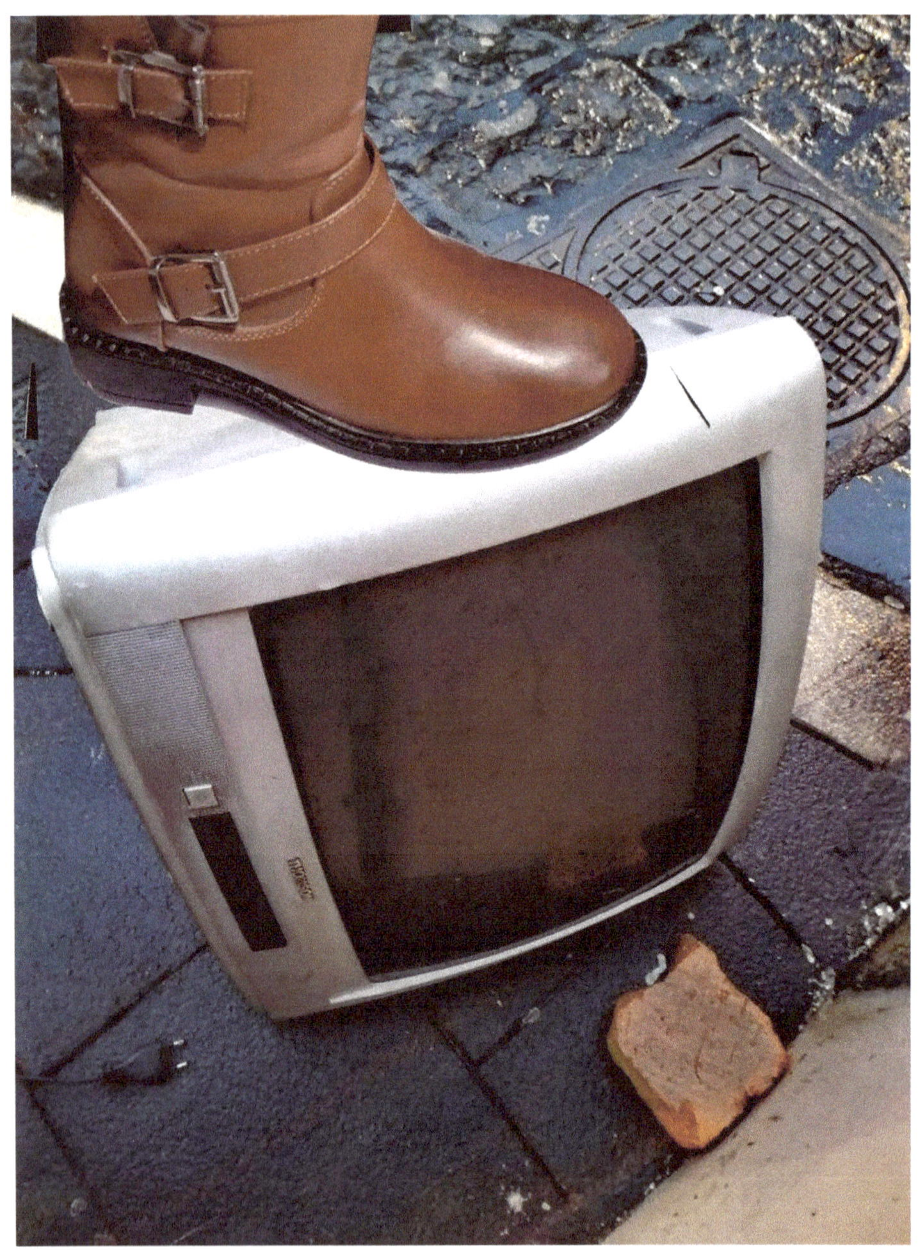

**BUTTA LA TV**

*Collage, 1280 px x 1707 px*

## MARIA FILEK

WADOWICE, POLAND

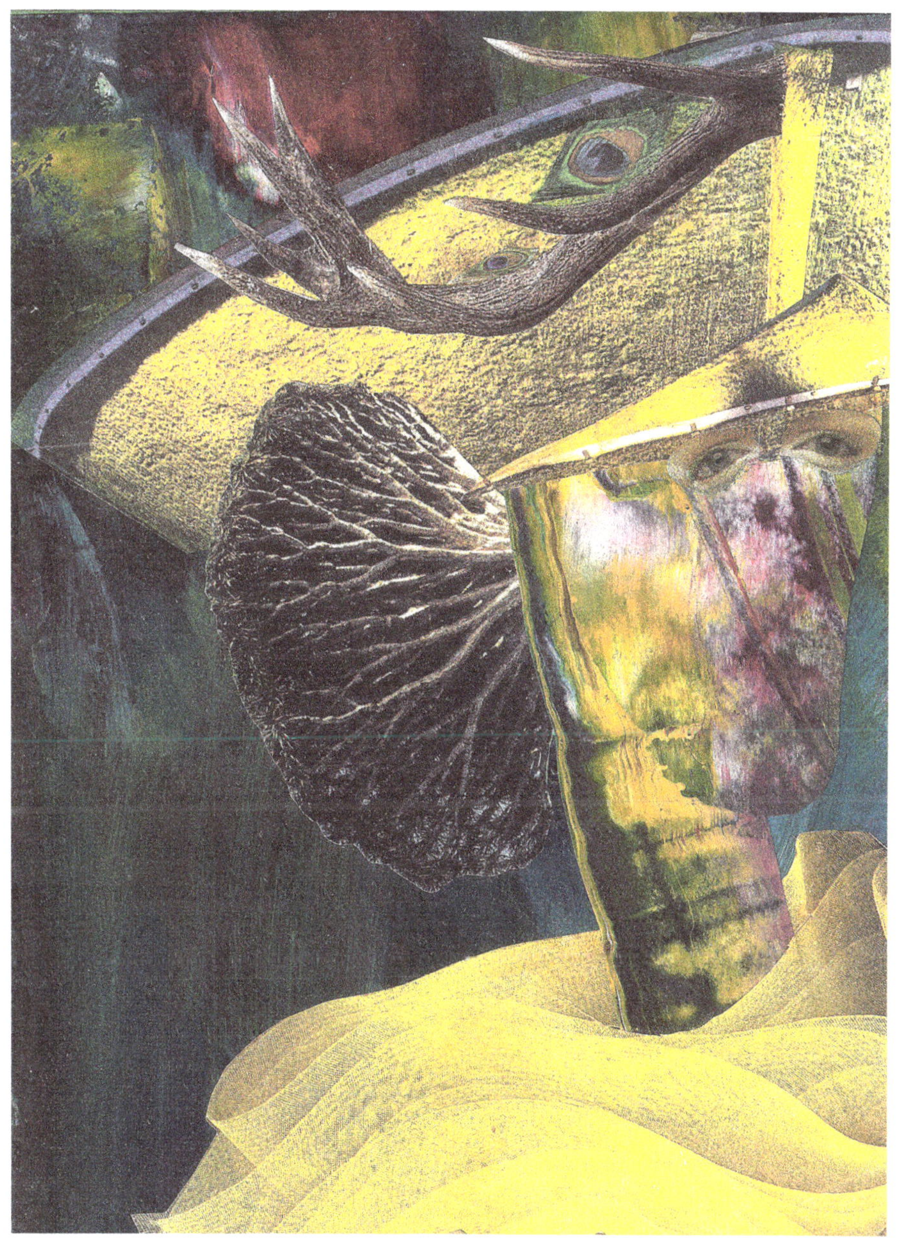

## SHERIFF TRUTH

*Handmade collage, 23 cm x 16 cm*

## CHUCK CONNELLY

(1955–2025)

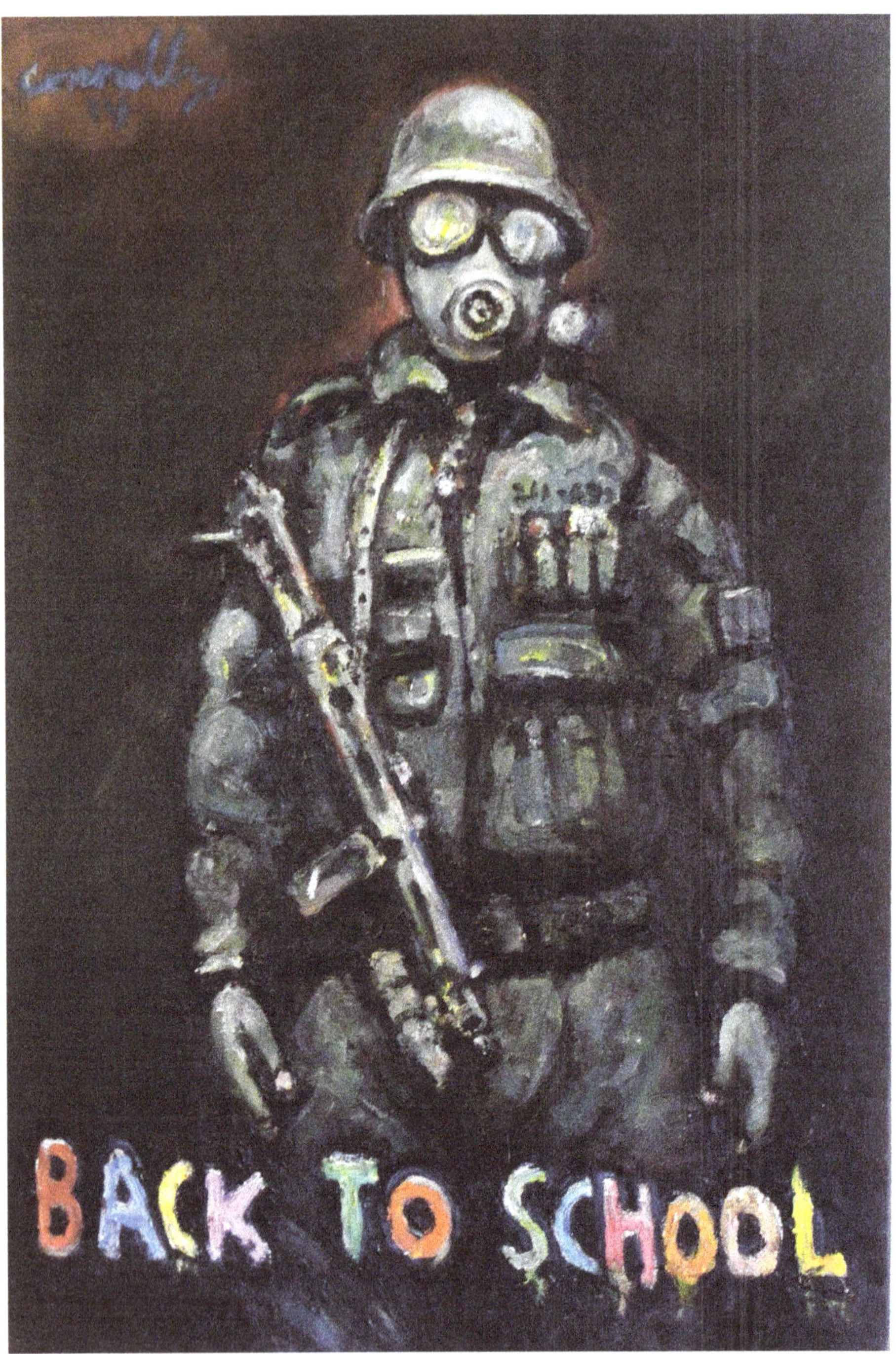


**BACK TO SCHOOL**

*Oil on canvas*

**HANNAH BERHENS**
HEILOO, THE NETHERLANDS

## AT SCHOOL

It might as well have been all of us
as if the world was not dangerous already
we barely survived
the spring of 99

huddled on the ground
away from doors and windows
prepared for the unknown world
we practiced our first
Active Shooter Drill
'in case of the real thing'

The Trench Coat Mafia
the news coined them
dressed in black
broken hearted
bullies
burned from the inside out
on swastika hate
and took their rage to the tip of the gun

that day left permanent holes in bodies
and blood on the floor of the library
all the violence America had to offer
pinned young souls to the ground

Columbine
a flower, a name, a memory at school.
A hole left burning in the sky

## MARK KOSTABI

ROME, ITALY

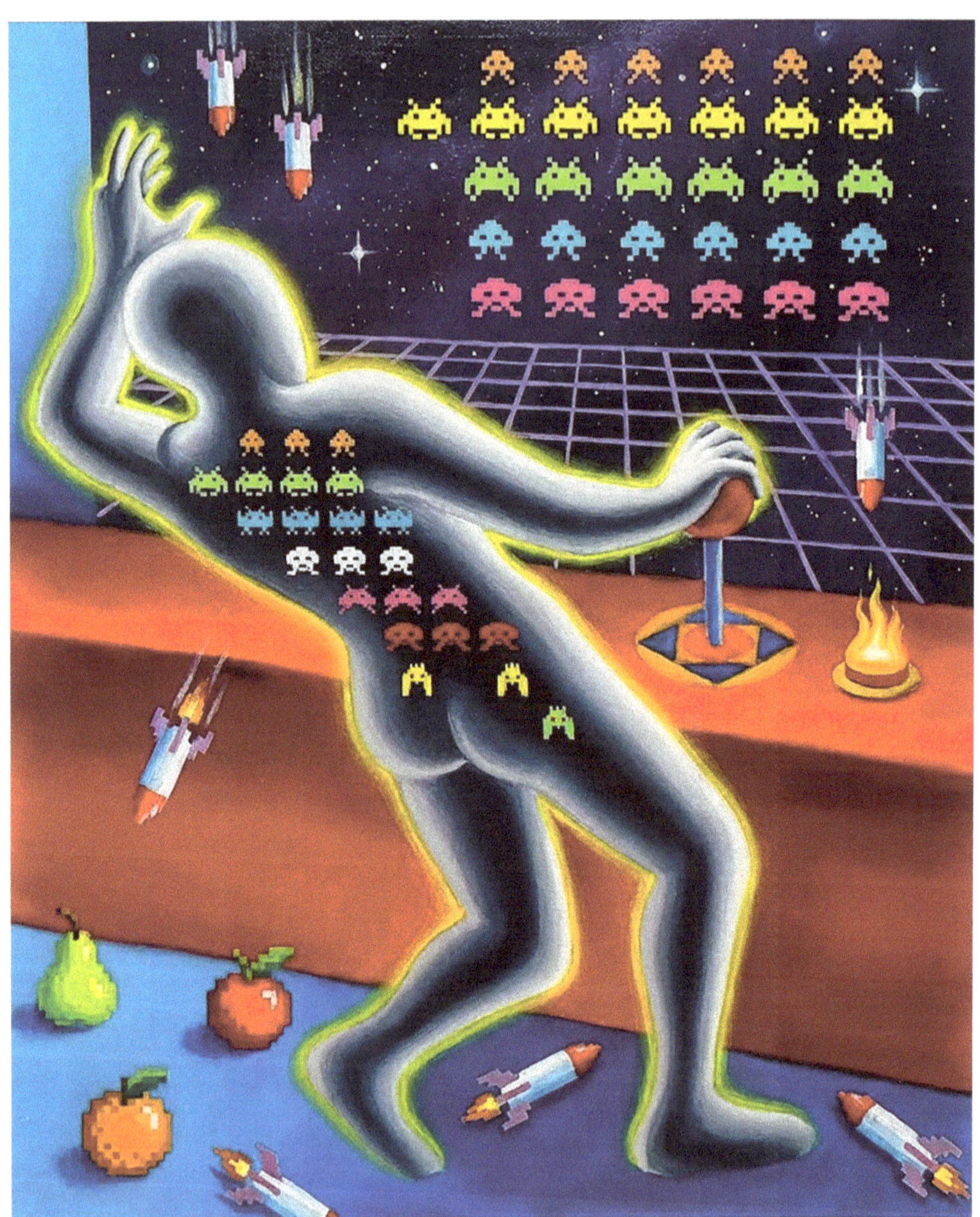

## WAR GAMES

*Painting*

**DUŠKA VRHOVAC**
BELGRADE, SERBIA

# REBEL – BUT PEACEFULLY

My friend is in a car, flying, with no one at the wheel.
My six-year-old child says: "Mom, I can't see well,
how can a car fly by itself
when even an airplane has a pilot?"
Maybe our vision has truly failed us,
and that car is driven by the devil himself,
escaped from Epstein's Island,
invisible, just as my guardian angel is.
What is the truth now, Mom, when the TV says
that these games for adults - who eat children and drink
their blood to become eternal - are played by those in power
in the name of democracy and oil?
Improperganda *par excellence*?
They kill girls in schools and let our soldiers die - everyone
but their sons, who play Hollywood on social media
and calmly call for the rebels to rise,
but to rebel peacefully, without riots,
without disturbing those still asleep,
those who believe the president never errs
because they voted for him and gave him leave
to do as he pleasses; truth and democracy are dead anyway.
Mom, you sleep too; sleep peacefully.
Forget the bloody hands and the murdered girls.
I am gone; I am going somewhere far away,
because this is not my world.

## JANE ORMEROD

HUDSON, NEW YORK

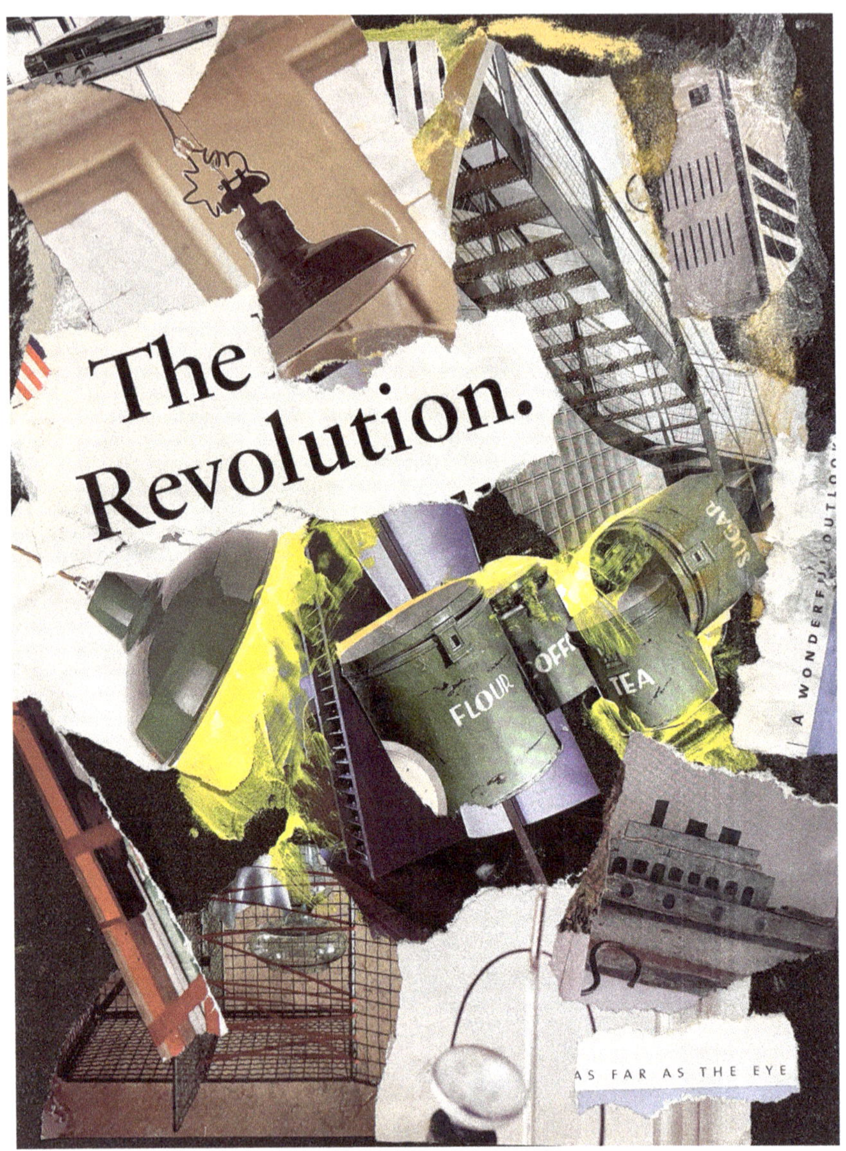


**FLOUR COFFEE SUGAR TEA**

*Collage, acrylic paint, pastel on paper, 12 in x 9 in*

## MAGGS VIBO

VICENZA, ITALY

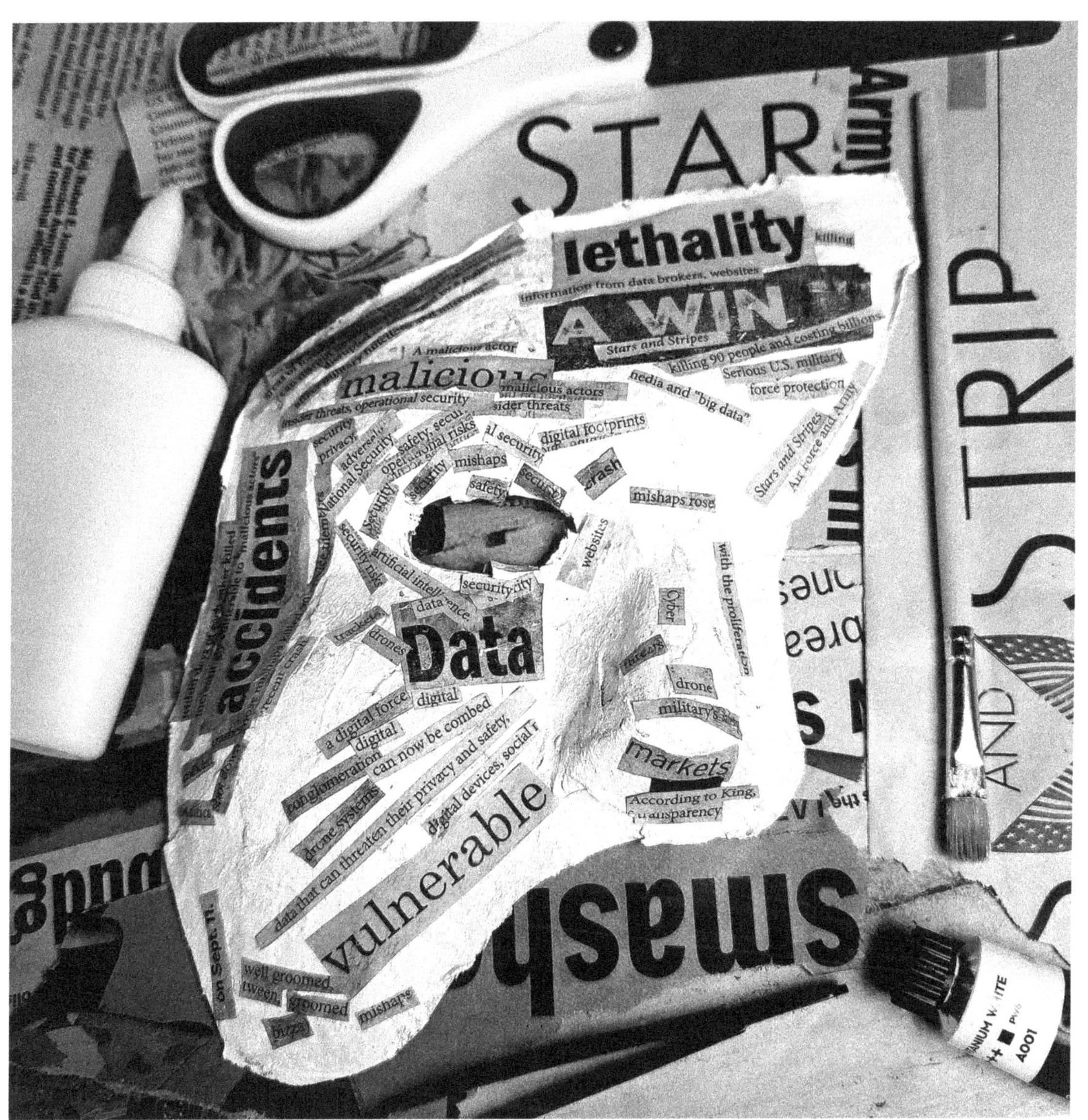


**MaskOrAld**

*Mixed media: (*Stars and Stripes *military newspaper fragments layers, glue, white paint in "Phantom of the Opera" masquerade mask) 2992 px x 2992 px*

**ANNE WALDMAN**
NEW YORK, NEW YORK

## compiling simple thoughts

*A moon drifts heaven's exquisite depths*
*radiant. Lovely women ready winter robes,*
*Ten thousand sticks beating frozen stone"*
*—Lady Midnight, China, circa first century, BCE*

It is crisis time. Frozen. Minnesota Iran Hormuz. Under current lawless rule where safety nets are down, surveillance, war, illness, extreme weather and irreparable shifts are occurring triple time in the frequencies in every quarter of life, the culture, the civilization, the geo-politic, plus AI worlds and detention centers rising and all the warring factions, where sense, sensibility and intellectual aptitude and informed cogitation are in pariah-mode. Where harm is ice. Gnosis continues to be under siege by an egregious white supremacist bully cartel blackmail gangster sex ring. What is the Dakini poet trickster's role in all this we explore and are at it daily. In these time science unwelcome in this disaster capitalism, global economic policy upended, understanding the gorgeous shimmering interconnected webs of symbiosis unwelcome, generosity, civility unwelcome, etcetera what are creative artists doing to have agency. Follow the money. How do we navigate the storms of outrageousness? Follow the money. Channel our knowledge, our care, our rage. With skillful means. Meditate on our own desire. And have something to offer. A new jazz. An ancient jazz riff played anew. How to meet the new Con? The latest most challenging of lifetime USA citizen takeover. How do we move it, the art forward, and it, humanity forward? What's our discourse our investigation what's our community, our commons, our under-commons. We know it. We keep talking. Go underground to bury the treasures. Memorize the treasures. It's all there. We already do it together. Exchange books. Play instruments til dawn. What new could I write to navigate my way through, keep presence and mind. Been studying empire way way back. Cradle to grave. Studying the maps, studying poets of Russia, China. Studying beautiful poetry dharma of our perceived "enemies." It's also time to continue an antithesis reality as I'm calling it in our precious rhizome, our temporary autonomous zone, our lives outside the dead realms, work our ethos out in the precious sangha. I wanted in Trickster Feminism and in the more recent Mesopotopia a compilation of interconnected histories, spiritual paths, poetic forms & pedagogies & moods and resistances and assignments toward a stand of gleeful post post mod feminist emphasis & empowerment to take on the idiocy and danger of the current dismantling of "state" that is so reprehensible in its cruel and greedy machinations. The dismantling of identity, of struggle, of lineages of heroes, heroines. Of histories. One is beyond complaining about it; what more can one say with each atrocity? They are ready to pull humans - extract life from life, – snuff life out. Huge detention centers coming across the land. The French Invisible Committee stated a few years back that no one believes in the social use of language. An exchange value that's fallen to zero, it's just an inflationist bubble of idle talk". And more: "The world no longer needs explaining critiquing and commentaries on commentaries of revelations that don't trigger anything, other than revelations about the revelations. This fog is taking away any purchase we have on the world" . Poet has another job in this. Poet goes beyond social use of language. For the poet all times are contemporaneous, ancient and future commingle in the prophecy. The core consciousness, freedom of imagination at poet level needs to keep writing, compiling, composing improvising the libretti, elucidating, and continuing to be a child of illusion in the lineages of the 3 kayas. Not robotic ego bot. And please add be watchdog from nuclear irresponsibility to separating children from parents and putting them in internment camps. It's a visionary ethos to be taken into public space does offering the language and image and ritual for one to respond with nuance and documentary imagination against killing and torture. The facts are on the ground. Rituals of emphatic sounding and focus, walking with others in public space and protest does quicken the heart to urgent mental and activist awareness. I live in a continuum blessedly of art humans that won't give up, as one goes down, one steps up. This is what sustains the spirit even we call it whistling in the dark. Let's whistle against the darkness. Let's defend what we have of our Constitution, write new amendments. "In the Dark Times, will there be singing? Yes, there will be singing about the Dark Times". That's Bertolt Brecht in 1939 and we know what a dark time that was and the incipient fascism brewing and expanding on that horizon." Trickster Feminism and Mesopotopia and The Velvet Wire are poetry arenas of sets in a variety of voice and modes, meditation, and critical study with interventions of quotation and penned in mind and heart and sand too and in part on streets of protest NYC, DC, Berkeley, Denver, Boulder, Madrid, Grenada, Brussels, all Europa, our own "meditations in an emergency" "across wounded galaxies". Thanks for all you all do, all the pop up manifestations in galleries & on radio & in bookstores and café and on stages and in the books and songs on the stream & purposeful hopeful delights that our comrades share and do themselves in these Kali Yugas. We continue. Do no harm.

**ROBYN MALLERY**

SAN RAMON, CALIFORNIA

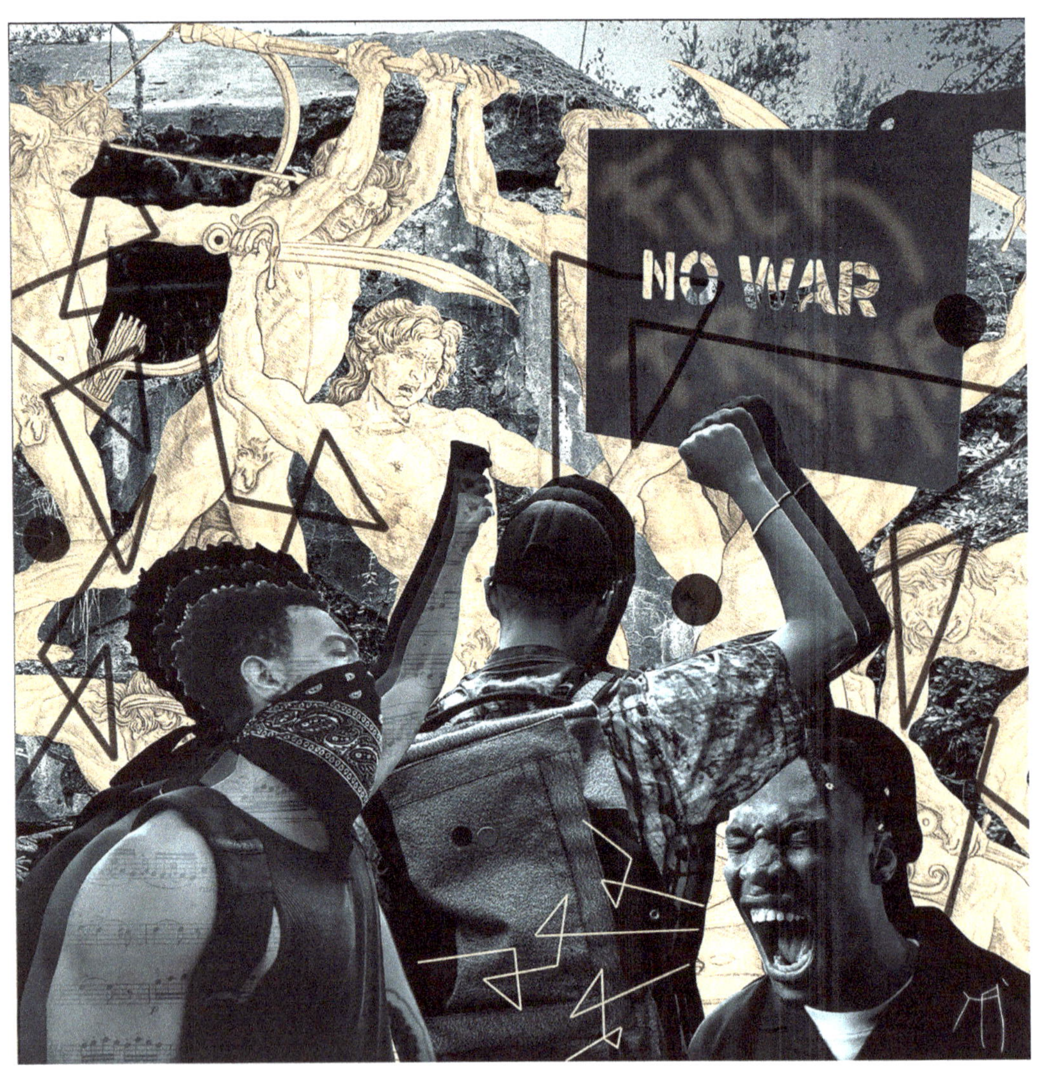


## THE FALL OF ROME

*Digital collage, 1286 px x 1278 px*

**ALLISON A. DAVIS**
SAN FRANCISCO, CALIFORNIA

## ANTIFAGANDA

*Walter Cronkite, and all the President's men are churning in their collective graves*

I babysat Bill Hundley's six kids
while he defended John Mitchell.
There have always been bad men
who loved power more than people.
But today's pungent propaganda machine
sucks you into an algorithm eddy
full of pleasant images and false info.
That's not your mother they implanted
in your Bladerunner brain.

Nothing is worshipped like money;
they will tell you anything to get it.
It's the immigrant's fault, it's Iran, it's Venezuela.
What they don't tell you is Uncle Sam's a pedophile,
anti-vax because only disease makes profits,
produce full of e. coli, meat with hormones,
and your favorite shampoo gives you dermatitis
because private equity bought the brand,
squeezing every last dollar from that tube.

Is it real or is it Memorex?
We are truly living in the Matrix.
Leaders' malevolence with their oligarch overlords
hides behind kitten videos and recipes,
window dressing down of current events.
They shoot you for filming the truth.
Meta suspends your post criticizing the war,
and here we are, truth telling
in an old beatnik bar.

## MUTES CÉSAR

ARCOS DE VALDEVEZ, PORTUGAL

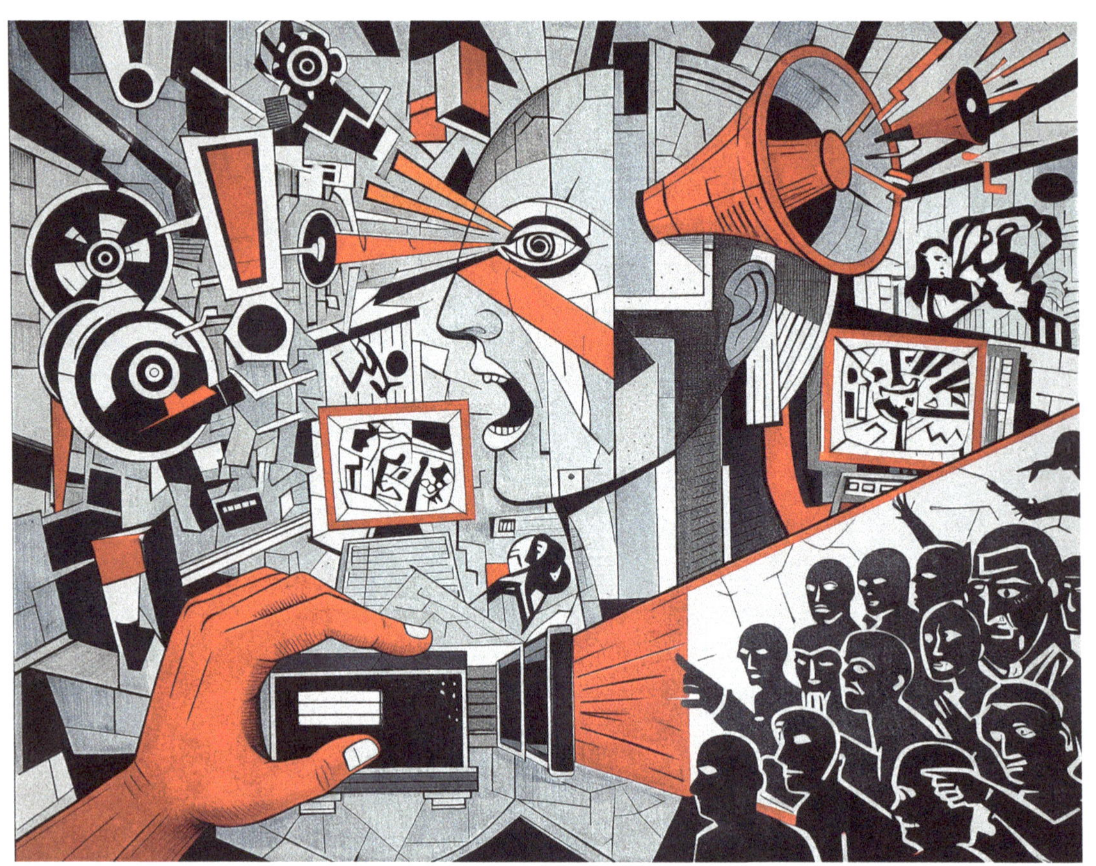

## THE CHOIR OF CONFORMITY

*Marcadores e canetas sobre papel, 29.7 cm x 42 cm*

*This work reveals a visual ecosystem of control, where amplified voices replace truth and repetition builds artificial consensus. Eyes, screens, and megaphones converge in the same mechanism of surveillance and persuasion, nullifying individual thought. The human figure appears fragmented, reduced to a transmitter or receiver of imposed narratives. The masses observe, react, but do not decide. In this world of political and media pretense, disapproval becomes useless—not because of agreement, but because of the deliberate absence of truth.*

**NINA ZIVANCEVIC**
PARIS, FRANCE

## ELYSIAN FIELDS OF POWER

*(For Fanette, Ivana eventually)*

So, Tiny Tom and Speedy Gonzales
Have had a Lab,
It was pretty much a physical thing,
They tried to outdo the topology of a body in space
From person A to person B ran the 'power-field of
a person', so, how would we envelope them
into our power-circle, if we were to say
'I'm taking over a situation'?
then
You would say 'I don't want to take a person
In my power-field, I want them to be free,
And besides, I'm not Pina Bausch or Vito Acconci',

Documentation is more a referent than a remainder
And performance means
There's an audience,
An event is an accident sometimes
And sometimes it's steady and sleepy, like a video;
There may be people or not
A couple of technical by-products
But what always really counts is people
Who make decision whether
to be there or not to be
as we're making a private
out of their public space
and
not everyone can get it...
we are just trying to become these buildings
themselves, a part of the architectural landscape,
surroundings which is
the other

**FEDERICO FEDERICI**

MAGLIOLO, ITALY

*\begin{document}*

READINESS 2030

an amount of €800 billion is proposed
for leverage purposes

flexibility is предусмотред
at national level
loans are qualified as instruments
cohesion resources are subject to reallocation
SAFE is established
as a relevant measure
concerns persist regarding oversight
concerns persist regarding fragmentation
sustainability remains under assessment
alternative options are under consideration
traction is recorded
low-interest guarantees are foreseen
interest is guaranteed
joint procurement is recommended
origin priority is recommended
the construction of a base is recommended
the plan constitutes a political signal
experts express reservations
the reference period is considered crucial
Parliament expresses support
through emergency procedures
the emergency assumes a structural character
support continues
resources must not

DADADATA

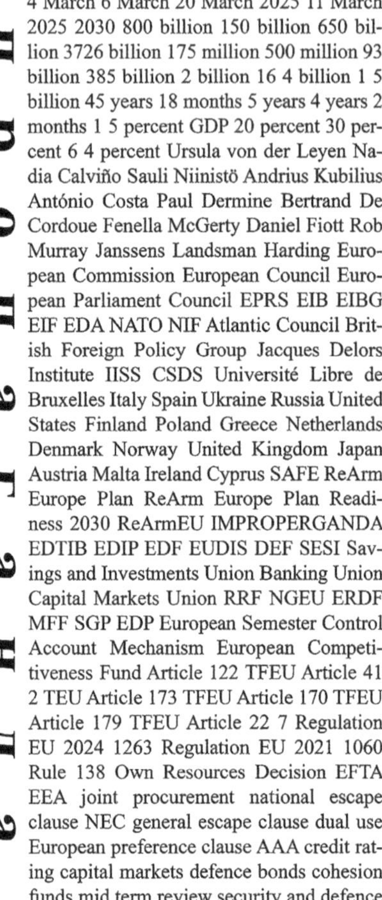

пропаганда

4 March 6 March 20 March 2025 11 March 2025 2030 800 billion 150 billion 650 billion 3726 billion 175 million 500 million 93 billion 385 billion 2 billion 16 4 billion 1 5 billion 45 years 18 months 5 years 4 years 2 months 1 5 percent GDP 20 percent 30 percent 6 4 percent Ursula von der Leyen Nadia Calviño Sauli Niinistö Andrius Kubilius António Costa Paul Dermine Bertrand De Cordoue Fenella McGerty Daniel Fiott Rob Murray Janssens Landsman Harding European Commission European Council European Parliament Council EPRS EIB EIBG EIF EDA NATO NIF Atlantic Council British Foreign Policy Group Jacques Delors Institute IISS CSDS Université Libre de Bruxelles Italy Spain Ukraine Russia United States Finland Poland Greece Netherlands Denmark Norway United Kingdom Japan Austria Malta Ireland Cyprus SAFE ReArm Europe Plan ReArm Europe Plan Readiness 2030 ReArmEU IMPROPERGANDA EDTIB EDIP EDF EUDIS DEF SESI Savings and Investments Union Banking Union Capital Markets Union RRF NGEU ERDF MFF SGP EDP European Semester Control Account Mechanism European Competitiveness Fund Article 122 TFEU Article 41 2 TEU Article 173 TFEU Article 170 TFEU Article 179 TFEU Article 22 7 Regulation EU 2024 1263 Regulation EU 2021 1060 Rule 138 Own Resources Decision EFTA EEA joint procurement national escape clause NEC general escape clause dual use European preference clause AAA credit rating capital markets defence bonds cohesion funds mid term review security and defence partnerships COFOG GNI

*\end{document}*

**DADADATA**

*Formatted text*

**ALEXANDER LIMAREV**
NOVOSIBIRSK, RUSSIA

# 10 THOUGHTS ON THE AESTHETICS OF DADAISM:

1.
Truth is an atavism. In a world where mockery replaces justice, sincerity looks like obscenity. We don't lie; we simply edit reality into a state of total ecstasy.

2.
Your vote has been counted and cancelled. Democracy has morphed into an endless stream where the only „natural" human right is to press „Like" under your own death sentence. If the world is a circus, why are you still paying for tickets instead of juggling heads?

3.
IMPROPERGANDA doesn't persuade—it infects. We are returning absurdity to its rightful place: the news headlines. When facts crumble into pixel dust, only the most bare-faced lie can evoke sincere tears. Laugh or vanish, don't show up.

4.
Conscience for sale: low mileage, never crashed, original paint. In the post-truth era, morality is an accessory too expensive for those who don't know how to use filters. Loliticians don't steal—they simply redistribute meanings for their own profit.

5.
Freedom of speech is the right to scream into a muted microphone. We've flooded the world with information so that you may never hear the silence. The louder the press bellows with laughter, the quieter the crunch of bones under the table. Devour your content and ask no questions.

6.
The Truth Industry declares itself bankrupt. There's no longer any need to hide the filth—just illuminate it with neon. Lolitics is the art of ruling the world without waking from a coma, simply by broadcasting the void.

7.
Absurdity is the final line of defense. When reality becomes unbearable, we make it ridiculous. We are the noises in your perfect signal.

8.
Trust is the currency of paupers. Wise men invest in disinformation. While you search for the roots of the problem, we're shredding aspen leaves and selling them to you as salad. Swallow without chewing: this is the taste of the future.

9.
The world is a collage that someone forgot to glue down. We cut out your rights and paste them over our sins.

10.
The future is a limp that we've rebranded as a new way of walking.

## FORK BURKE

BIEL/BIENNE, SWITZERLAND

# DIRECTION

Unacceptable Dipping
What are      who came before us
I don't care how good legacy feels
A poem that is always happening          To believe   That

I'd have to be Plum
To believe   That
Lift   Give      where
   Up      hope   is   opposite

I Transcribe  How
got here
Tell me the dates don't matter
Agreed  –  The Ayes Have it
Notes matter                              Needs  – suggest

A Start
Level one please find purpose
usefulness based on skills and practices thus far

Inhale exhale  thyself                              all at once
Who are you not
Be more simply                              be
More       human reflection moments
A moon is falling

Water our fresh life
elves and Wagner
whiteness did what                              from what
Command words cease to activate

Where were you when your old self kicked in
                              be unrepairable

**TYKO SAY**

PRAGUE, CZECH REPUBLIC

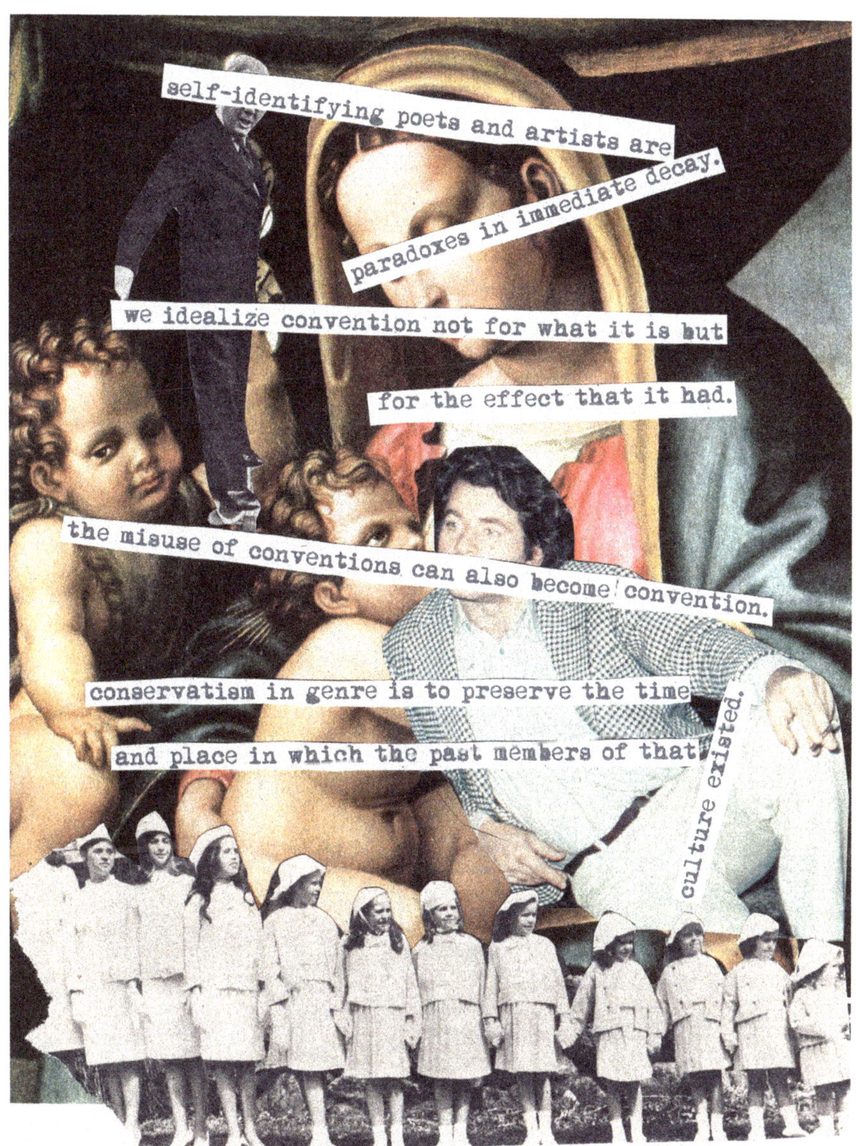


## STICKERS I LEAVE AROUND PRAGUE

*Stickers, 2480 px x 3508 px*

## EVA HELENE STERN***

GRAZ, AUSTRIA

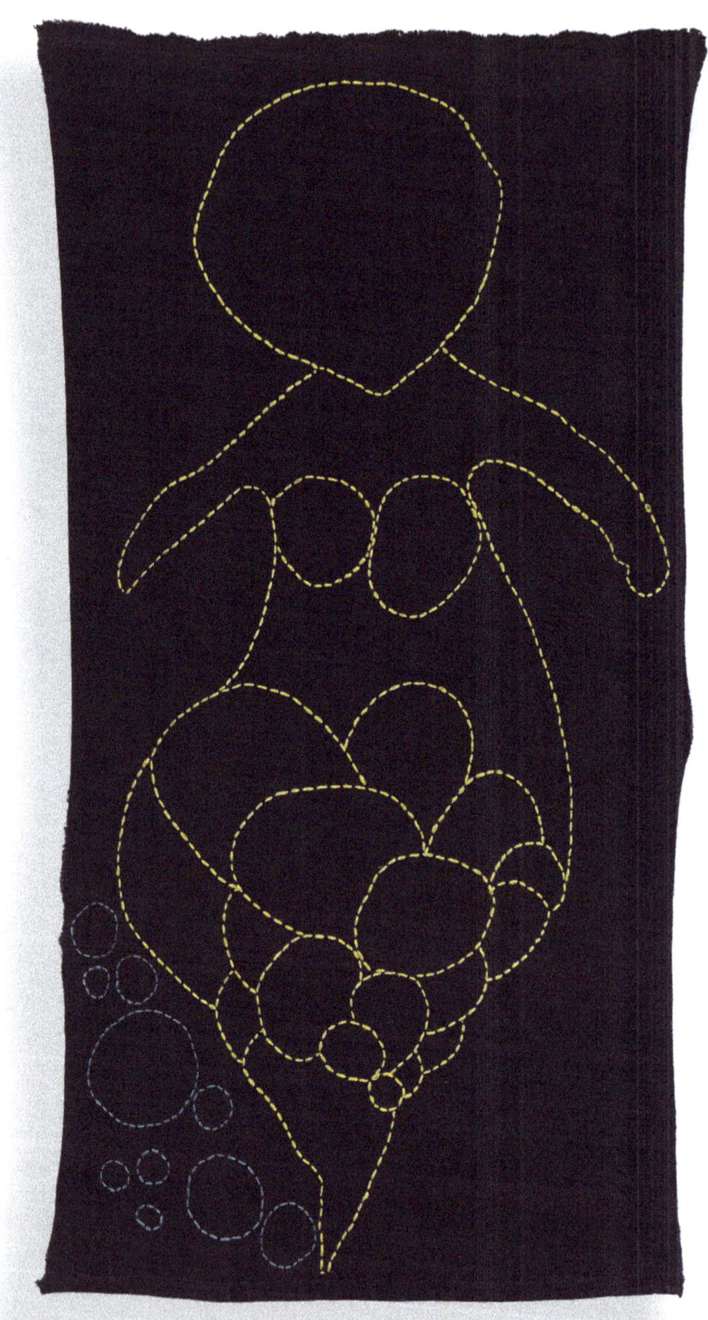

**pearl diver * she who is relentlessly diving for truth through oceans of darkness contaminated by lies, tabus, confusion and distortions caused by fears * she who finds the pearl of revelation after all**

*Tapestry, embroidery, wool on black cotton, 68 cm × 133 cm*

## ERZSÉBET PALÁSTI

BUDAPEST, HUNGARY

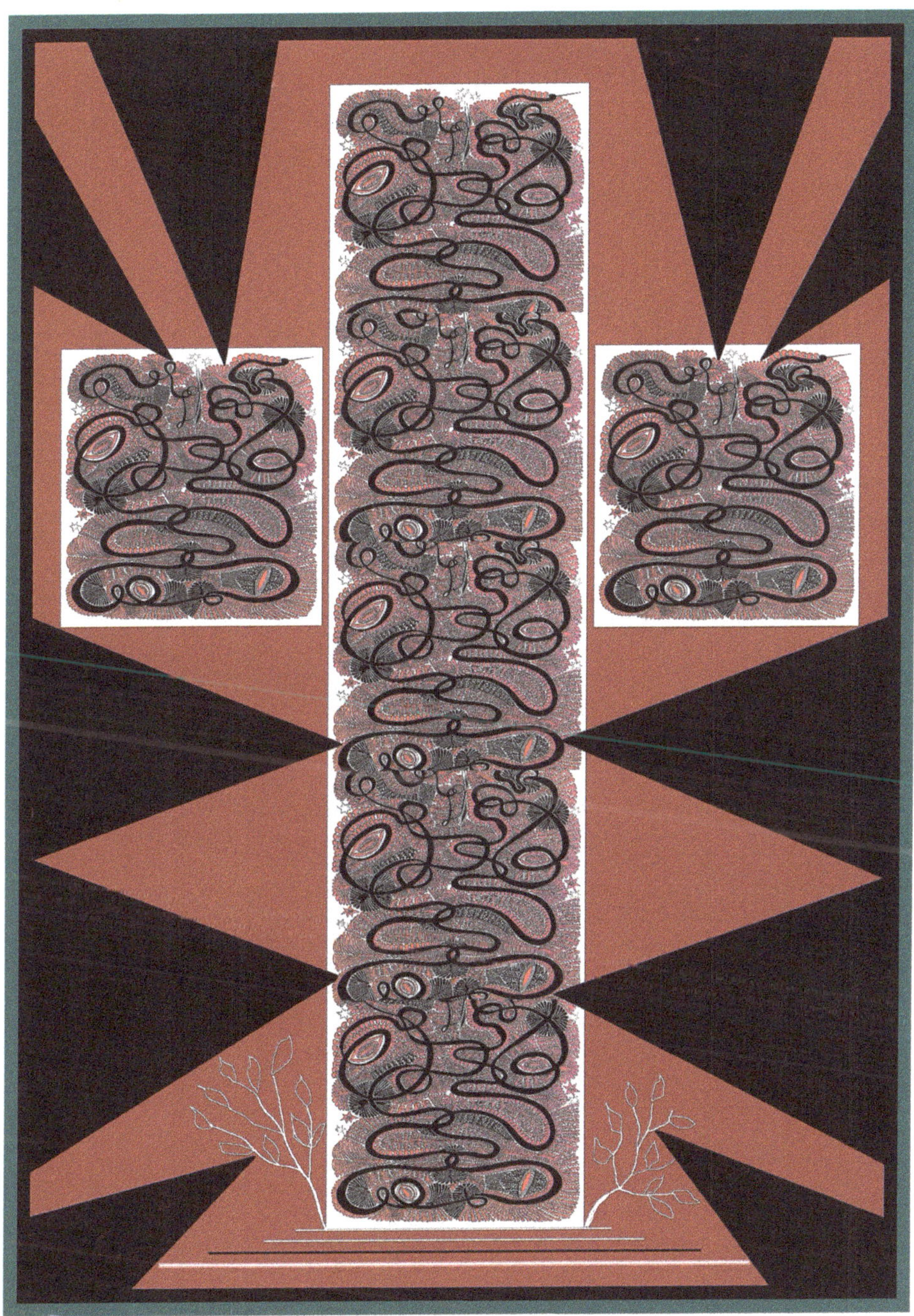

**THE DEATH OF TRUTH**

*Paper and digital graphic, 700 mm x 510 mm*

## THE RED SISTERS: HEIDE HATRY

NEW YORK, NEW YORK

### IMPROPERGANDA

*Sculptural Drawing: paper, ink, and wood, 11 in x 8.5 in x 1.3 in*

## THE RED SISTERS: JANE LeCROY

NEW YORK, NEW YORK

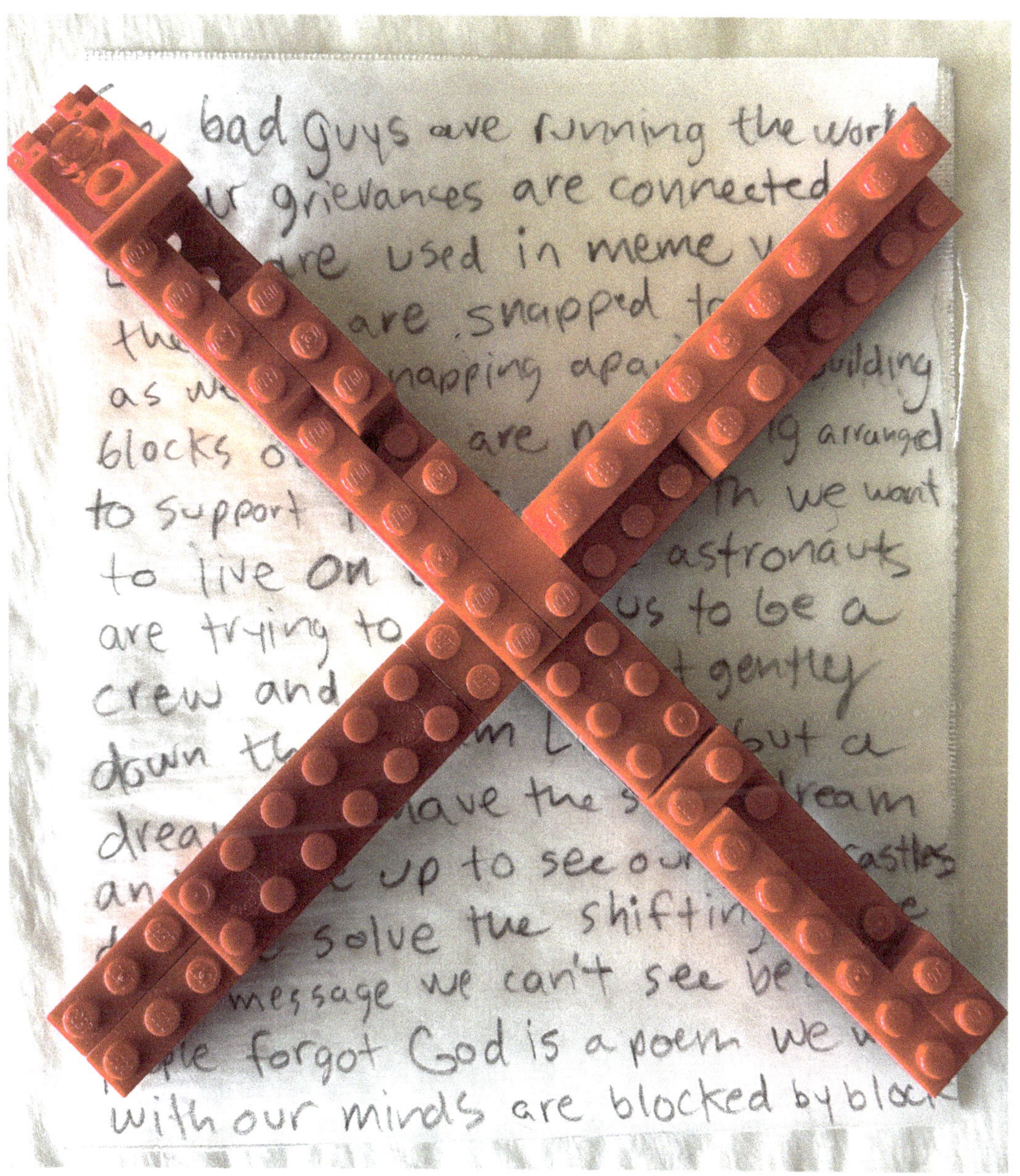


### BLOCK

*Lego, poem*

**BRENT R. CARR**
GAINESVILLE, FLORIDA

## CIVIC PROCESSING

INTERNAL USE
File ID: CP-17-A

ARCHIVAL RECORD
Recovered fragment —
civic administration file

CIVIC PROCESSING
Operational status: pending

PUBLIC NOTICE
Citizens are encouraged
to think independently.

Independent thoughts
require approval
to continue.

FREEDOM SPEECH
SPEECH FREEDOM*

*footnote
subscription required

STATE OF THE UNION
Speaking apparatus
has been relocated posteriorly
for efficiency.

Statements now emerge
fully digested.

Applause continues
until processing is complete.

MENTAL STATUS EXAMINATION
Appearance:
the century appears disheveled

Thought process:
tangential
circular
broadcast

Insight:
Pending

DISCHARGE SUMMARY
Condition:
unchanged

Instructions:
continue

POSTAL STATUS FORM
Recipient status:
☐ living
☐ deceased
☐ unknown

Action requested:

☐ deliver
☐ return

☑ continue

**GAY PASLEY**

CORRALES, NEW MEXICO

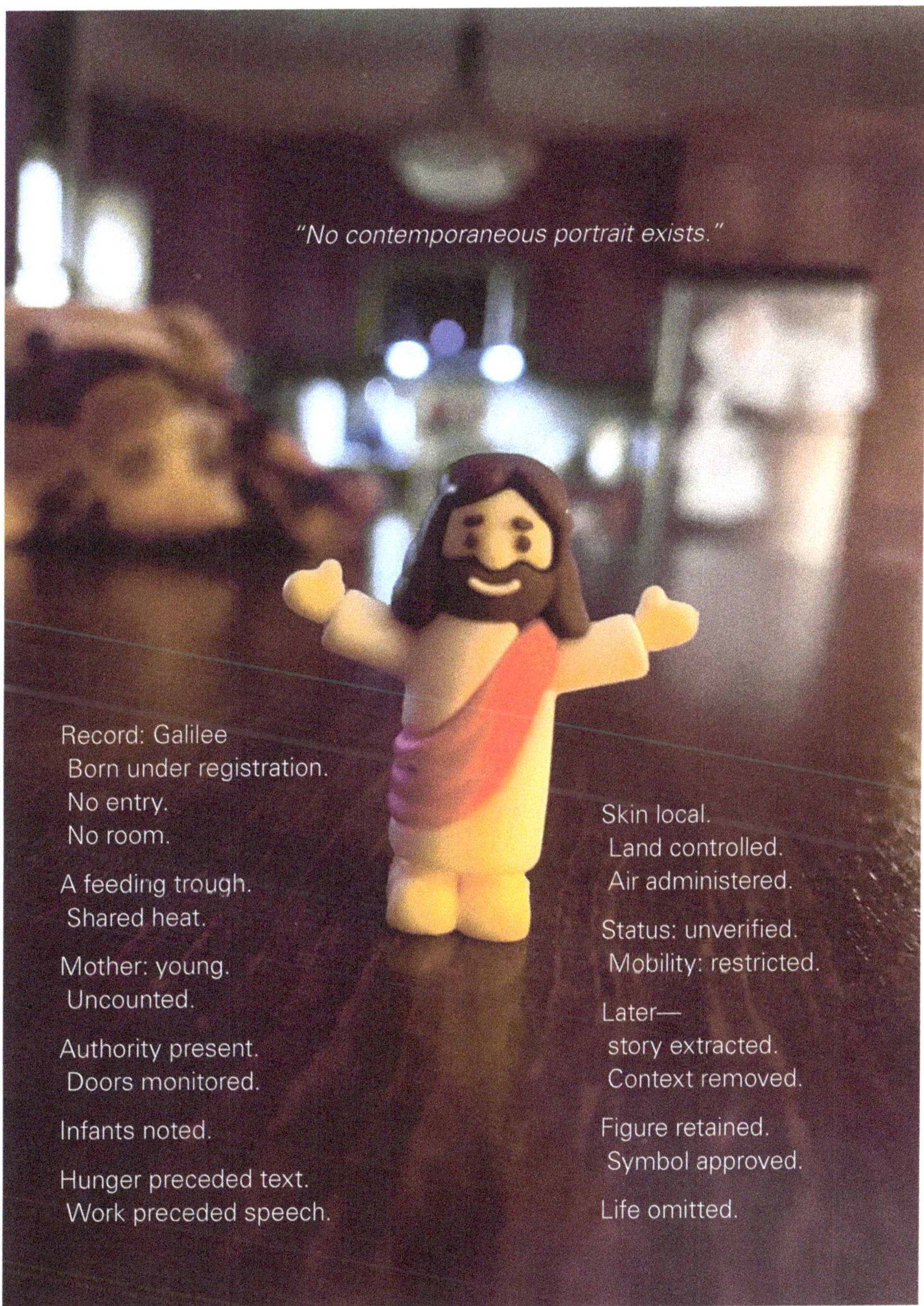


## ADMINISTRATIVE NOTE: GALILEE

*Text and image*

**MARTINA MATIJEVIĆ**

VIDOVCI, CROATIA

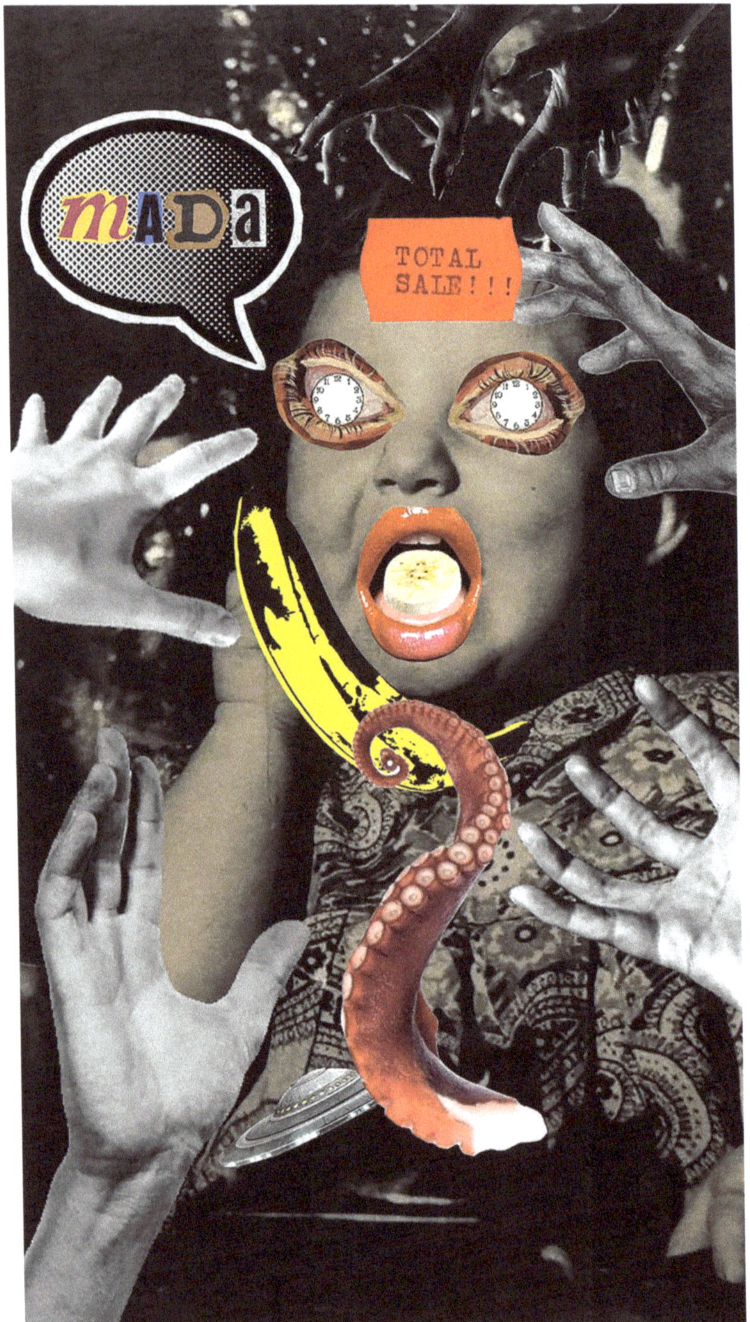


## FRESHLY WASHED YOUNG BRAIN ON SALE

*Digital collage, 736 px x 1308 px*

**BENITO VILÁ**
GUERRERO, MEXICO

## THE NEW LORD'S PRAYER (2026 GOP EDITION)

Oh, great white gringo father
who doesn't like brown people,
hallowed be your guns,
the technology that helps us
kill other cultures and steal
their territory. Our kingdom comes
from breaking every promise
so our kind can continue
to live in comfort. Give us
the power we need
to make sure no one
finds out about us,
and lead us out of our despair
by putting new worlds up for sale.
For thine is the rule of might worshipped,
now and forever. Ah, money.

**MONA JEAN CEDAR**
LOS ANGELES, CALIFORNIA

## IMPROPERGANDA

Improperganda
Fool's gold sold as the real deal
Know/No! Buyer Beware

Improperganda
Nefarious narratives
Alternative Facts

Improperganda
Self-righteous Hate shown proudly
No Christian Love here

**BELINDA SUBRAMAN**

EL PASO, TEXAS

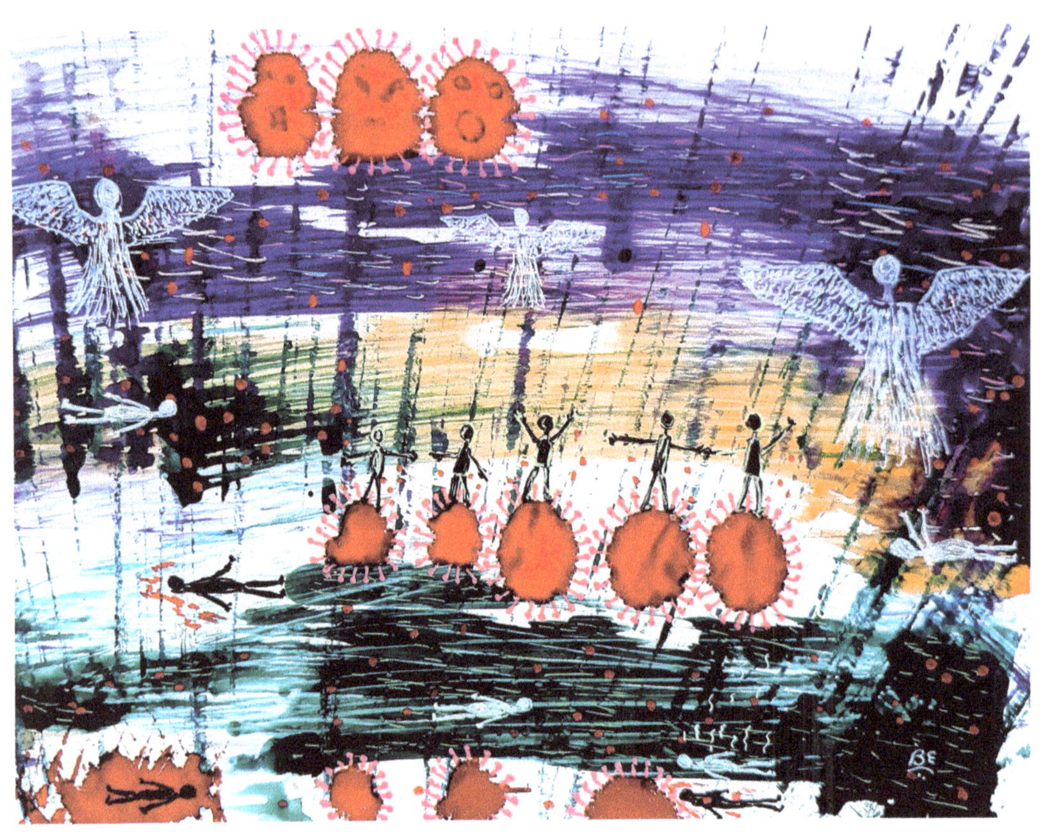

**FEAR AND RELIGION**

*Ink and posca pen, 10 in x 14 in*

**LIZ AXELROD**
ALBUQUERQUE, NEW MEXICO

## ICE PICK

They control our streets with corporate greed
killing nurses & mothers & babies in the name of god & MAGA.
Masked basement bully heroes with loaded guns & pepper spray
paid to patrol in hatecoins minted by Apple and Amazon.
How is this the world we inhabit?
When did compassion become anathema?

They sit on their gilded thrones & beg us not to believe our eyes.
Like Humpty hard boiled & seeking revenge on the water.
Like Joshua with his horn blowing ear-breaking calls
to shoot down fathers & babies in blue bunny ears.
Swollen fears & lies of omission—
This is what informs their mission
Their new national policy full of good "Christian" sins & sinners
gassing public schools & bussing innocent children into profit-making cells
Jesus wept!!
In Matthew 25:35 Jesus says, "I was a stranger and you welcomed me."
In 1928, Adolf Hitler said, "We tolerate no one in our ranks
who attacks the idea of Christianity; In fact, our movement is Christian."
Then over 6 million tortured & killed.

The dove of peace has once again fallen off the bough
She's bloodied & holding an iPhone in her mouth
She will not lay down silent
We pick her up & tape her broken wings
Feed her with seeds of love & solace
Come judgment day the masks will be torn off
& the mad sheep will shed their camo wolf hoods
We await their sad sorry cries of please forgive me
*I knew not what I'd done...*

**LEAH KOGEN ELIMELIAH**
NEW YORK, NEW YORK

## AND ON THE SEVENTH DAY...

the White House rested
Tik Tok style — chat bots
caring for free wheeling mascots
sharing is bearing the missile strikes
cluster bombs — impressions of oppression
wave flags as strategy, a grimace reality
packaged robots inside the White House
uniforms — alien wonder
$12.7 billion on day six, the gravity —
that's when you know the ducks are mad
Supreme Leader is dead
Vance in a bind can't find the energy prices
soaring attacks make us forget
video games — a man's best friend
bombings, strikes, planes sell us wars online —
In/box declines to make a statement
conferences anonymously support
candidates candidly with the most candy
refinery — wonder about responsibility
this one on floor 5 screams Free Palestine
that one on floor 17 shouts Death to America
the rest contemplate if US ever healed from 1776
somebody, come get me from floor 10
I am beginning to think I-ran — gas leaks
oil spills, slippery slope — entertainment
for kids — thousands march on, opinions rock on
Hollywood massages our memories
turns on the threat — winning is believing

**GERALD YELLE**
AMHERST, MASSACHUSETTS

## OLD ENOUGH TO KNOW BETTER

The news says there's a definite possibility.
The senator says there's nothing to fear.
They want us to think terrorists are about
to claim responsibility for an attack they
say they haven't thwarted yet but they're
about to –the attack itself could come at
any minute. That's why the bells are ringing.
It's like a fire alarm or a wakeup call.
There's a debate where the moderator asks
candidates if they'd do anything different.
We take their answers and plot them against
the claims they make in their talking points.
They bang down the door and say they
see what we're doing and accuse us of
plotting to rig the election. They'll find
kids who'll say we touched them the
wrong way. We might have to go to jail.
They might even deport us. They like to
punish people. They're like a disease
we'll be stuck with the rest of our lives.

## LARRY ZDEB

TROY, MICHIGAN

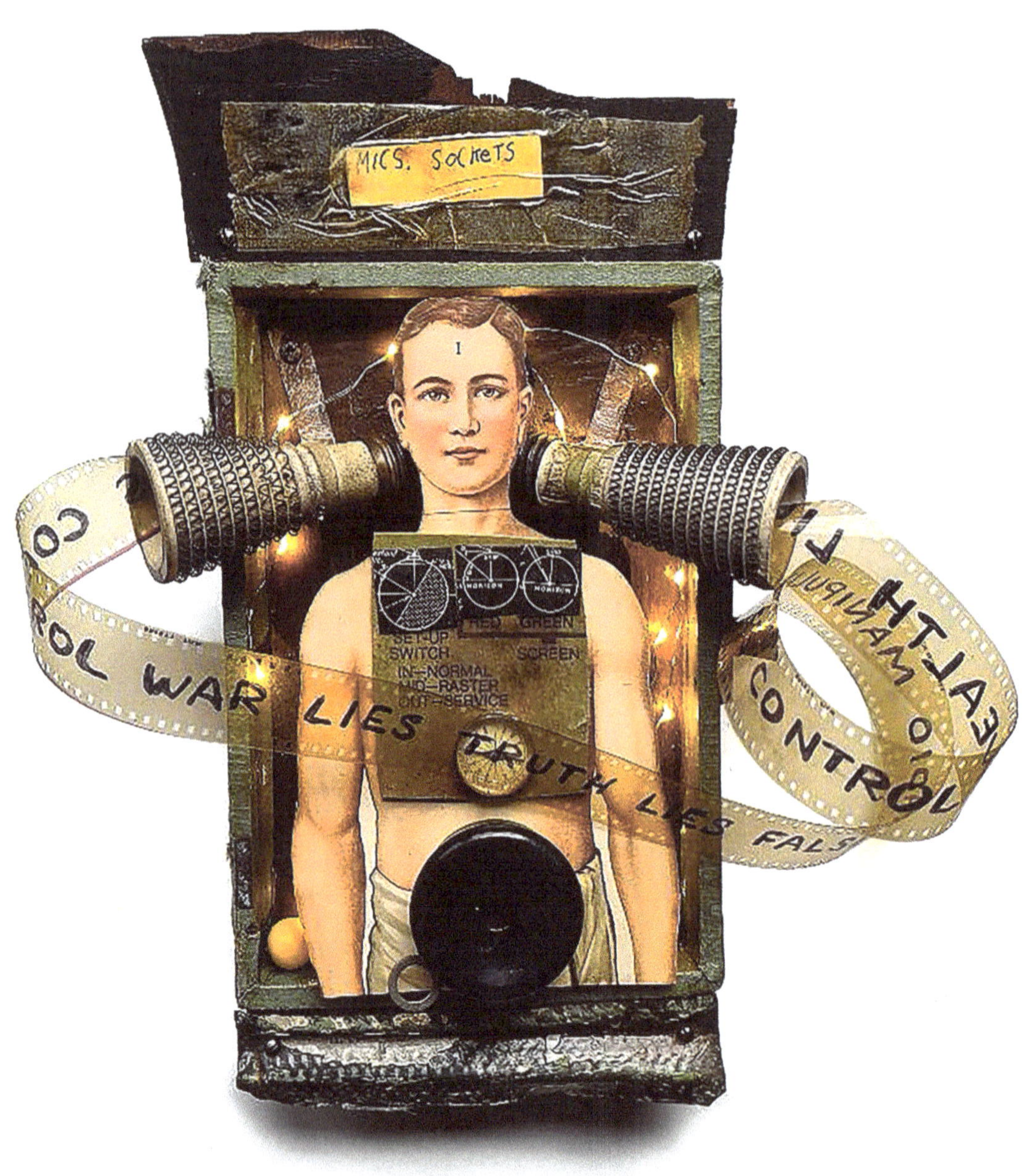


**KILOWATTS**

*Mixed media, 15 in x 12 in x 6 in*

**JIMMY VEGA**
LOS ANGELES, CALIFORNIA

## HOW LONG HAVE I BEEN DEAD

how long have i been dead
pet theories vibrational frequencies
nostalgic for novocaine & champagne
millions of people are still flying
despite taking inventory for grief
my tia's eyes, blood shot for months
you are being watched sunshine
the fuse ruptured but we tried
our best & even now after 40 days
of government shutdown there are
motorists lined parallel to the school
with a church near it, no one makes
eye contact & no one plays their music
loud—i keep chipping away smelling
rain as soon as i touchdown from
visiting the atlantic ocean—i gesture
to dissy that the fire alarm inside
my brain is still billowing, opaque
but nevertheless, suffocating especially
between the nostalgia of my squishy
wet sneakers & my future void's schism
in a time of genocide, spring will still bloom
flowers & angels still dizzy will still eat
ash with sharp teeth, who will you be

## SALVATORE ESPOSITO

VALÈNCIA, SPAIN

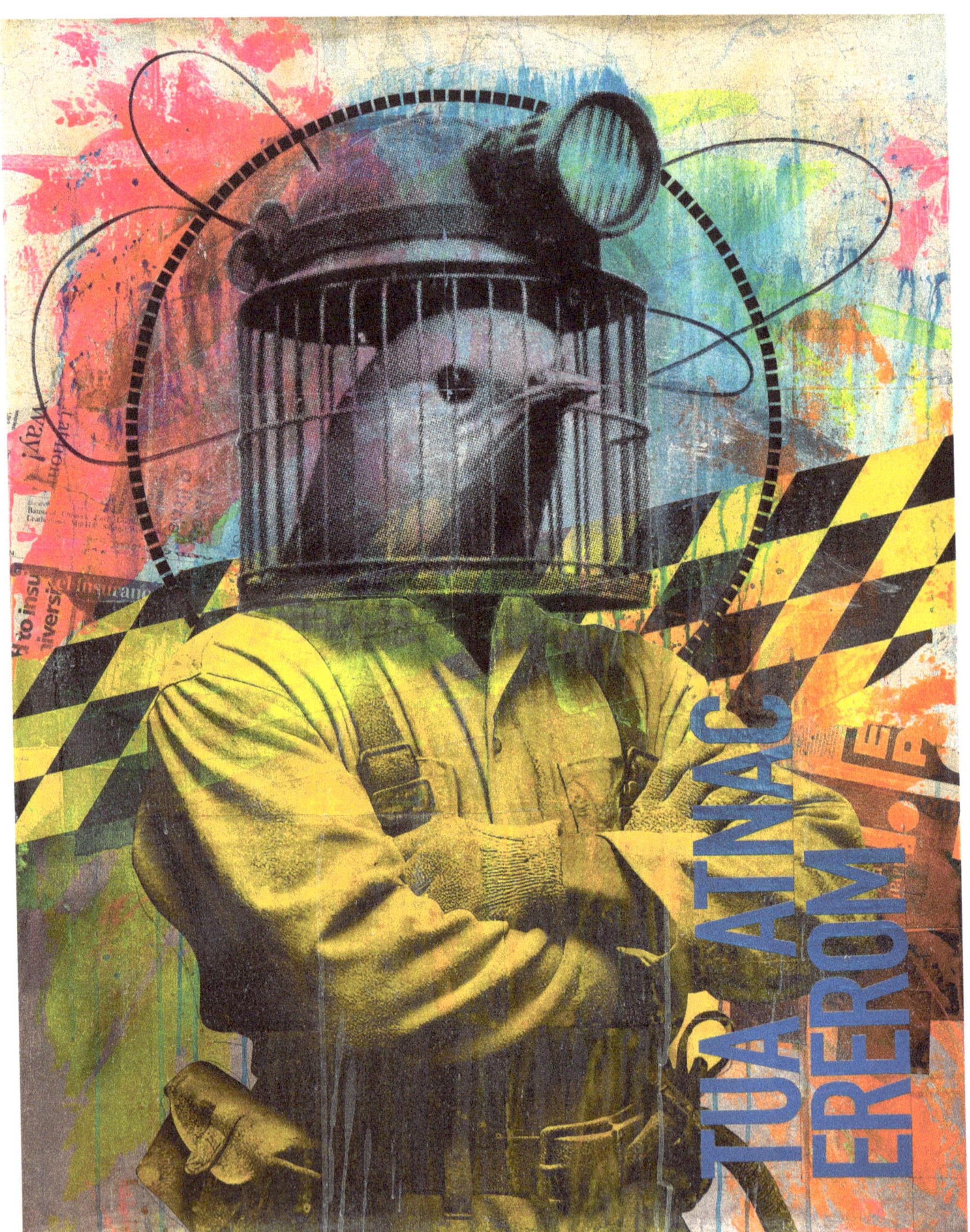


**CANTA AUT MORERE (CHANT OR DIE)**

*Fluorescent acrylic, tape, paper collage on canvas, 80 cm x 100 cm*

**MAHNAZ BADIHIAN**
SAN FRANCISCO, CALIFORNIA

## YOU ARE SHOT THERE, AND I DIE HERE

"You are shot there,
and I die here,"

not only an elegy,
but a pledge:
to live together,
or to die together,
until freedom.

How short the distance is
between a gunshot and
death.

A bullet knows no borders.
It passes through the streets of Iran
and settles
in the heart of exile.

You fall to the ground,
and I, standing,
am buried.

You give blood,
And I lose breath.

Each day
We die with the news,
buried beneath images,
and in the morning
walk like the living dead,
hoping someone will ask:
Are you still alive?

No mother
was prepared
for this many coffins.

We burned with you in the fire,
But we did not turn to ash.

From the soil
We grew wings.

From death
We called out
The name of Iran.

Hand in hand,
wounded,
weaponless
except for love and rage,
We will pull Iran
once more
from beneath the rubble.

You are shot there,
And I die here.

**BIBBE HANSEN / PATRICK LICHTY**

HUDSON, NEW YORK / WINONA, MINNESOTA

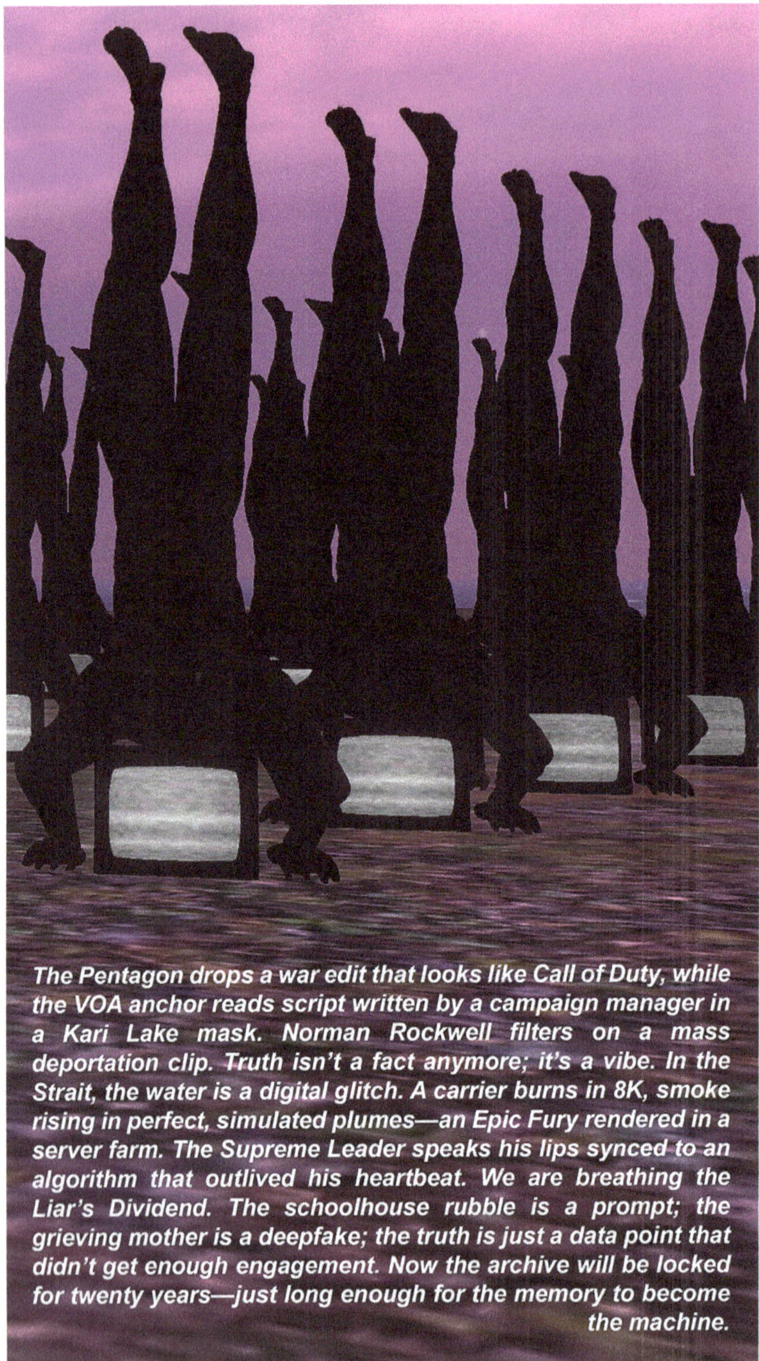


**PAX VOX 2026**

**MALAK MATTAR**
LONDON, UNITED KINGDOM

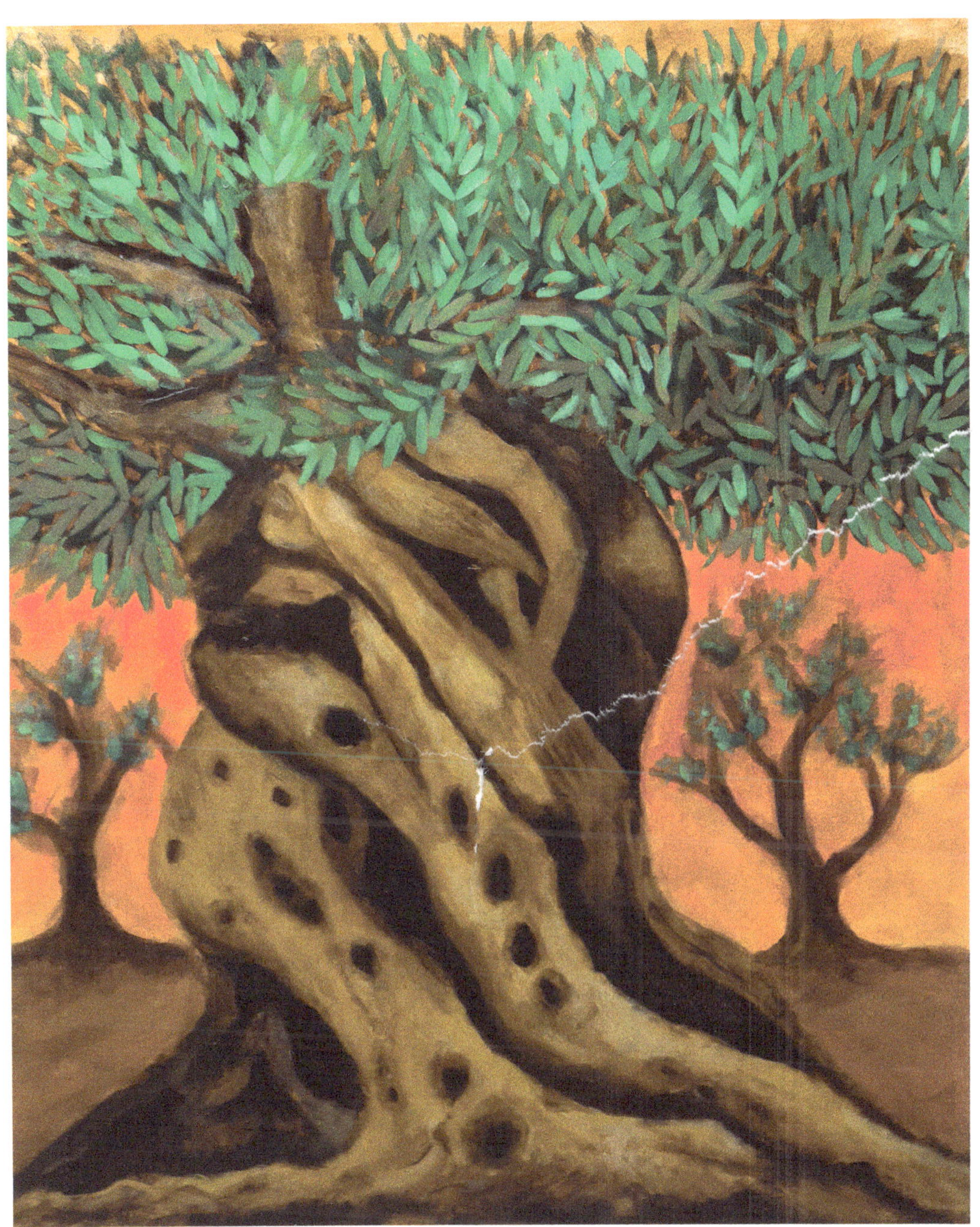

## IF THE OLIVE TREES KNEW

*Painting*

**NANCY MERCADO**
NEW YORK, NEW YORK

## WOMEN OF THE REGIME

The women serving the vile
slither to work in baseball caps
wearing gaudy knockoff watches
crashing into wall after wall
                    discombobulation at its most perturbed
they shoot puppies in the head for sport
they cage hairdressers in concentration camps for sport
they get endless botox injections
to paralyze the truths ringing in their ear

The women serving the cruel
hold photoshoots with the condemned
they crave living in a deceased world
            reminders of their colorless birthplace
they showboat crosses of fool's gold
between their breasts
they hopelessly simulate life on earth
their morbid origins inescapable

The women in the service of maggots
look elegant until they don't
sporting putrid faces that display their skeletal remains
their disjointed bones clash when they move about
            in search of their next victim-fix
they are the willing maids of maniacs
they are one spectacle hell has to offer
they are malignant beasts that now roam this world

**LINETTE RABSATT**

TORTOLA, VIRGIN ISLANDS

## WELCOME TO THE TRUTH

welcome to the truth
did you hear that?
you better lace up your boots
because this isn't the
he-say, she-say version
this is the word sound
that causes an incursion
it's a resurgence of facts
it will highlight
how the data lacked
and no it wasn't hacked
but people shifted a
few sentences
and here we are
deleted pages of their preferences
you think it's easy out here?
these people are very unfair
because they only care
about sharing their rhetoric
and no one will tell them to quit
and I can't sit and just accept
the bull on the list
so I shouted the truth
from the highest mountain
it was so intense
it caused a fountain
of remorse among the worst
because they were so caught up
with keeping the truth locked up
but I let it free
for all and sundry
to touch, smell and breathe
welcome to the truth

## SOFIA PALOMA RODRIGUEZ

BROOKLYN, NEW YORK

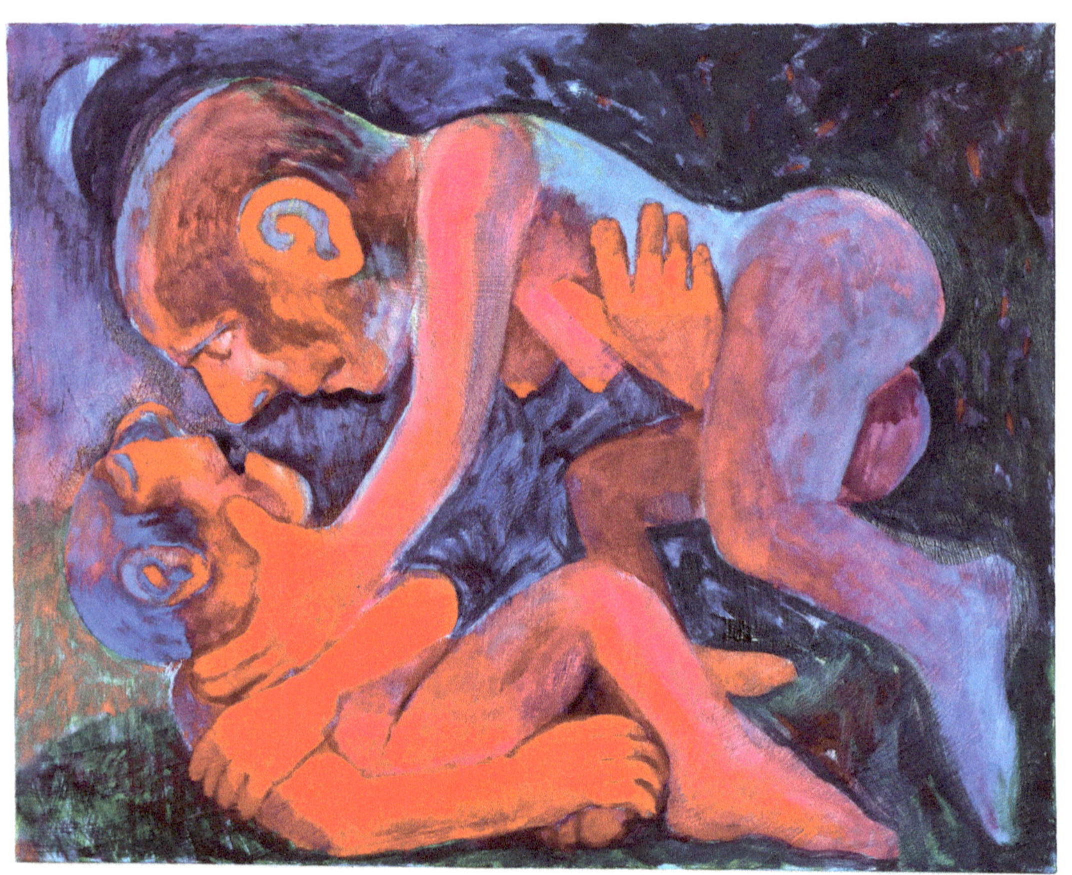

**CARMEN IN THE EVENING**

*Oil on canvas, 22 in x 28 in*

**HARRY E. NORTHUP**
WOODLAND HILLS, CALIFORNIA

## THE NIGHT

My wound, my song, a figure passing
For no apple survives a bite
No tree without a squirrel

A song & a tree, a canopy
passing by a rest, a notion,
place to believe in rest
Four hands across the table

To hold the passing
For whomsoever loves, has destiny
To reach out & hold time
for an instant lost in

reaching out to see — be noticed
A brightness in shadow
Love, cry, joy, behold a time
of two who never stop

A reaching out to almost soar
across a schism of grief unresolved
Two hearts lost in rest almost
an entry to beatific seeing
luminosity in leaves light beheld

## SOPHIE DUNÉR

HOVÅS, SWEDEN

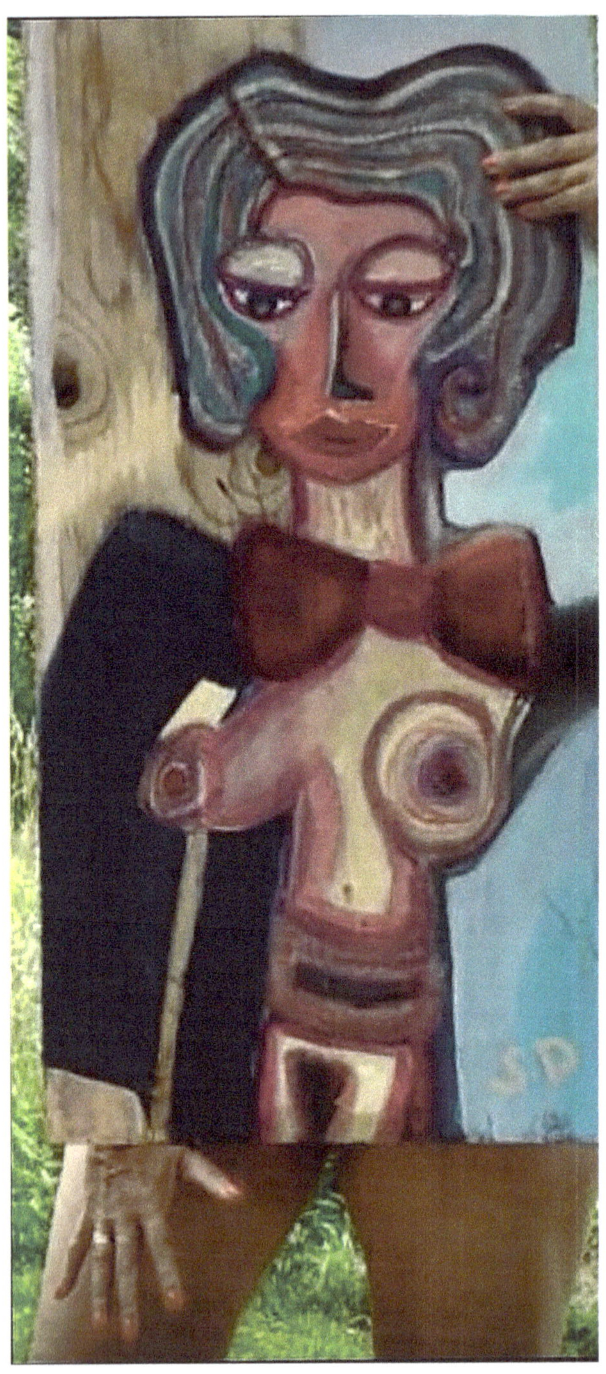


**LOVE FOR SALE**

*Oil paint on wood board, human thighs and hands, 1449 px x 1170 px*

## WER DA

BERLIN, GERMANY

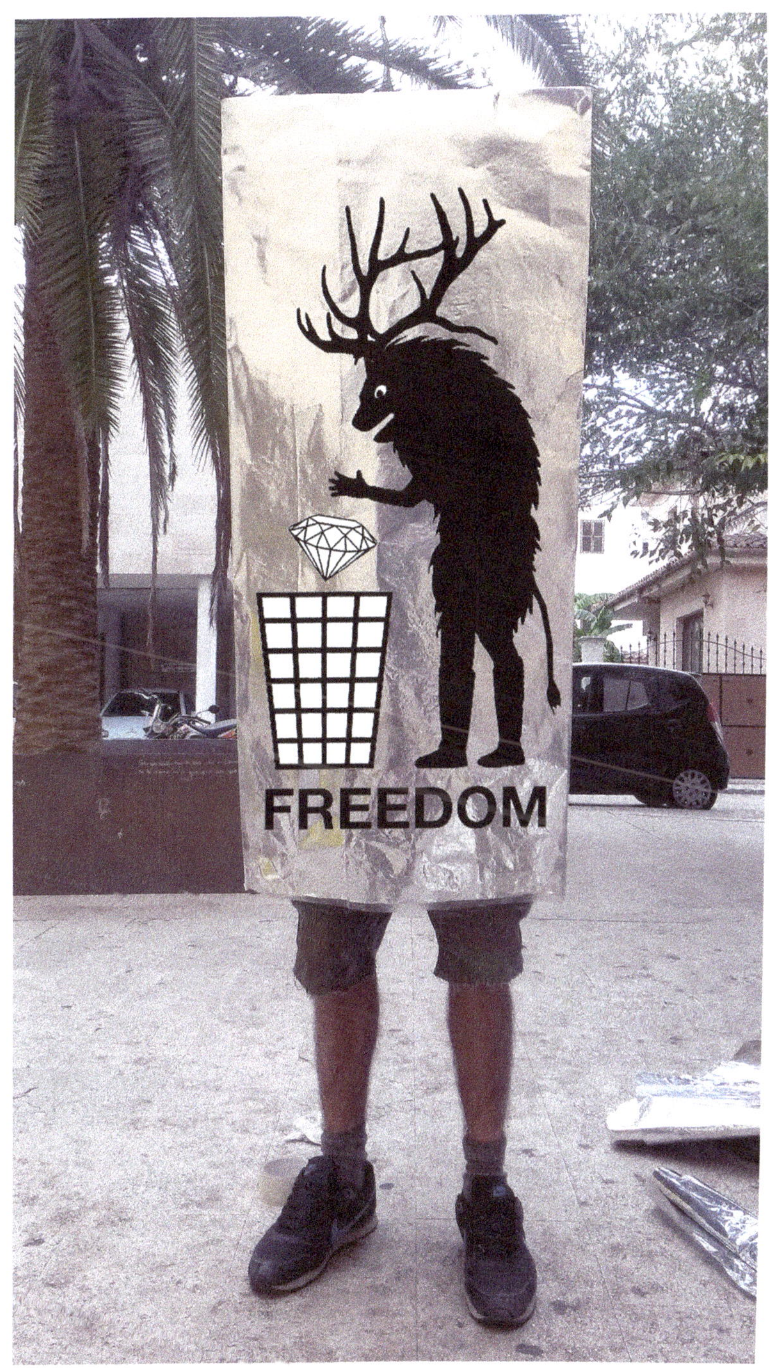


**TIME TO COME HOME**

*Digital image with text, 70 cm x 40.2 cm*

## LISA MARIE JÄRLBORN

PARIS, FRANCE

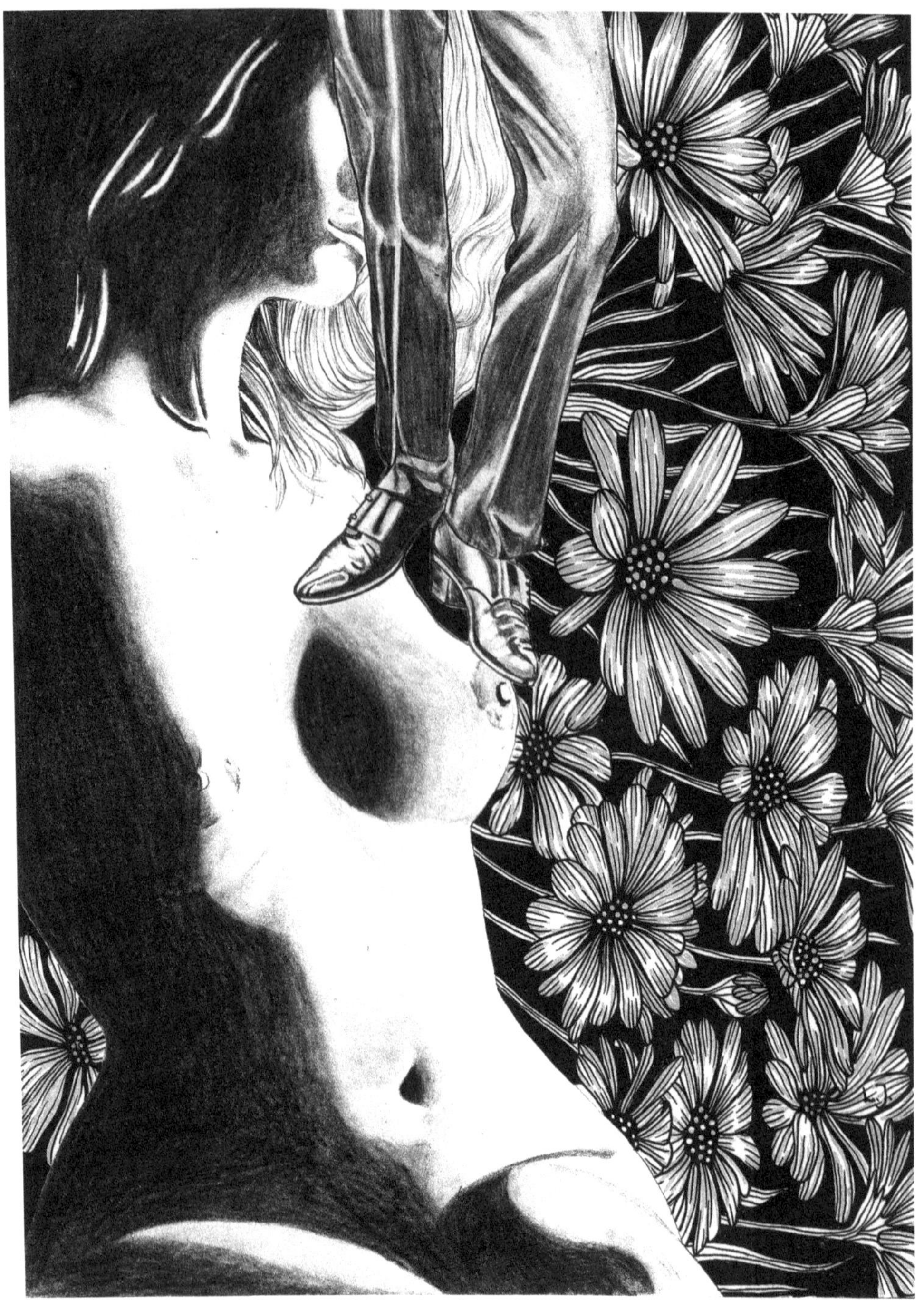

### STEP ON IT

*Charcoal and ink drawing*

**JACALYN EYVONNE**
VALLEJO, CALIFORNIA

## THEY SWEAR TO US THAT THIS IS LOVE

Regulated by rules that don't include
her opinion, where bodies must comply.
Men are only doing what is best for you.
Select the red button for your womb.
The blue button to forget that your body
belongs to you.
The calming green button for Zen music to
ease your pain in a future dominated by men
where privilege is required to
wake up unpregnant,
no longer the decision maker for your uterus,
where morality is controlled like furniture:
This one sturdy, this one strong, you replaceable,
like dreams, now archived, values preinstalled.
No backtalk, smile on command, look beautiful.
The contract to your body is owned by men,
You, quietly accepting, no longer hearing the
whispers of other women because rage is not allowed.
The rules are uneditable: Be grateful,
Stay in your place: kitchen/housekeeper
baby-bearer/obedient/no screaming.
Machines can't feel when the power is off.
And so you remain compliant because
They swear to us this is love.

**PATRICIA LEONARD**
THE BRONX, NEW YORK

## ONLY IN THE ED

I'm writing again
but
not the roses are red
or
the I love yous

I'm writing again

How my body breaks
IV's sticking from
both limbs
how catscans
doesn't match the morphine
but the dilaudid flows
every four hours
when my pancreas blares
Trumpets to Trump
Because FUCK YOU

there goes my health care
my meds cost more than your bankruptcy
but thank god it covers the several months
I'll need them to find
The parasite within me
because it's you

**LINDA KLEINBUB**
QUEENS, NEW YORK

## THURSDAY AT DRY HARBOR NURSING HOME

I visit Bridie pre-lunch; she's sleeping.
She wakes gently, in a daze, as her tray is served.

"I can't do it, Linda," she repeats, "I can't do it."
I feed her mashed potatoes, broccoli,

roast pork, and matzo ball soup.
Prayer of gratitude for distractions...

"Bridie, you're lucky.
Trump is ruining America, and you don't have to witness it..."

New York One News plays in the dayroom.
One of the aids remarks in a Jamaican accent,

"Look at this crazy man, all the trouble he's causing..."
I respond," It's difficult taking care of Bridie, but at least

I'm not watching the news all day."
Grateful for distractions of work:

Emails call my attention, a manuscript to edit,
A syllabus to plan...

Purple crocuses bloom in my garden.
Grateful nature doesn't play politics.

## SILVIA WAGENSBERG

VENICE, CALIFORNIA

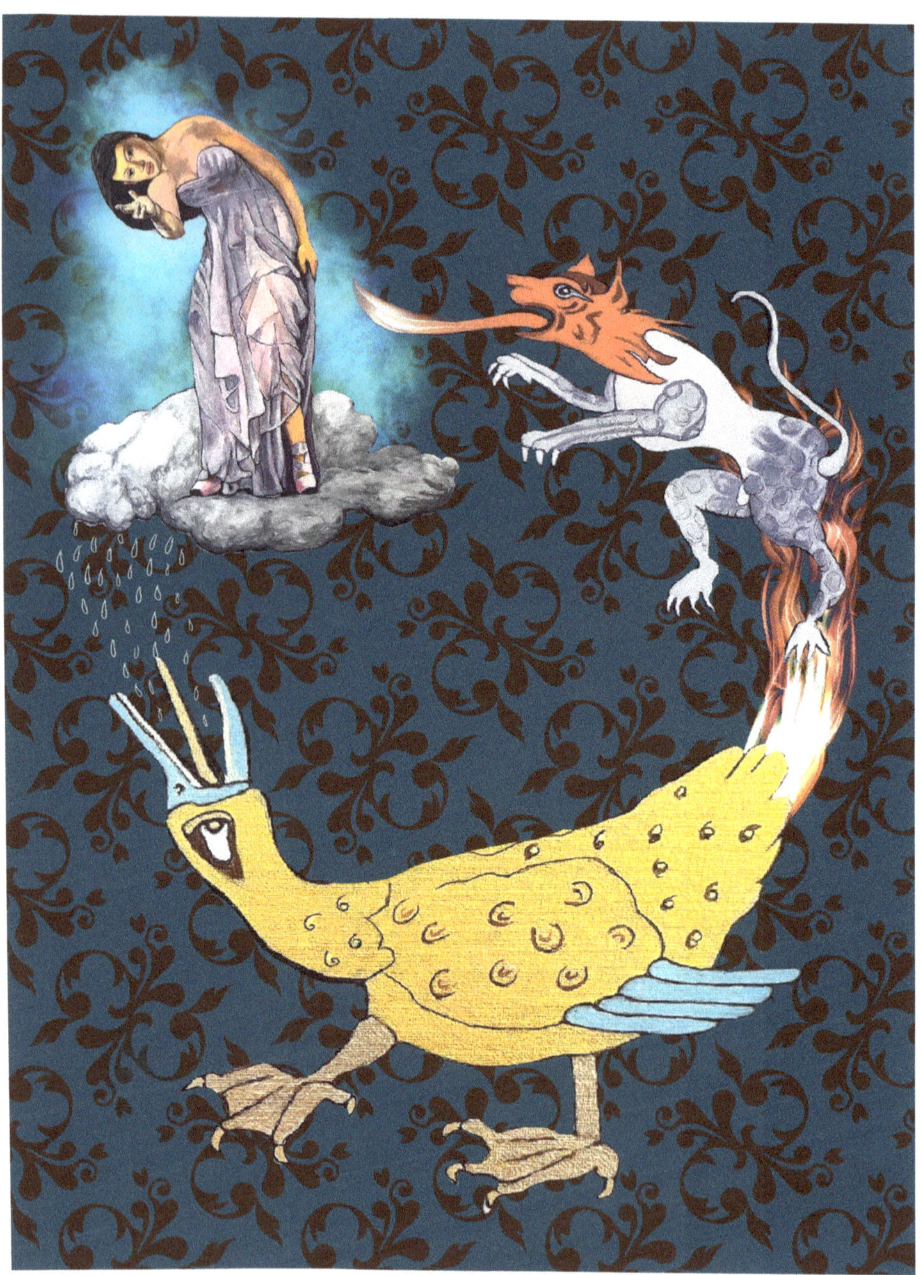

### THE GOOD, THE BAD, AND THE GANDER

*Digital collage of paintings, 9 in x 12 in*

**CAROL DORF**
BERKELEY, CALIFORNIA

## FOR EXAMPLE, IMPROPERGANDA

*Forget examples—there's not an entity or detail around that isn't more than a mere example*
*(Lyn Hejinian)*

For example, start with the seed
the way Rukeyser did and watch it transform
into porridge in a bowl remaking strangers into something both more or less

For example, did your parents every tell you
they were taking the dog to a farm where it would be free to run?

For example, at the gravesite did you leave a handful
of dirt or a shovelful of stones?

For example, when the turkey's amble across San Pablo Avenue
(aka State Highway 123) and everyone stops
how many are taking pictures out the window and how many are cursing the afternoon.

One job of a teacher is to come up with useful examples –
If there are five children and 3 donuts how much of a donut does each one eat
If you take out $20,000 of student loans at 8% interest rate
how much will you pay over twenty years? What makes it worth it?

For example, the likelihood of the sun rising tomorrow is close to 100%,
while the likelihood of an asteroid hitting the earth tonight is close to zero.

For example, explain the process of cleaning the oil out of the waters

## WES RICKERT

LANSDOWNE, CANADA

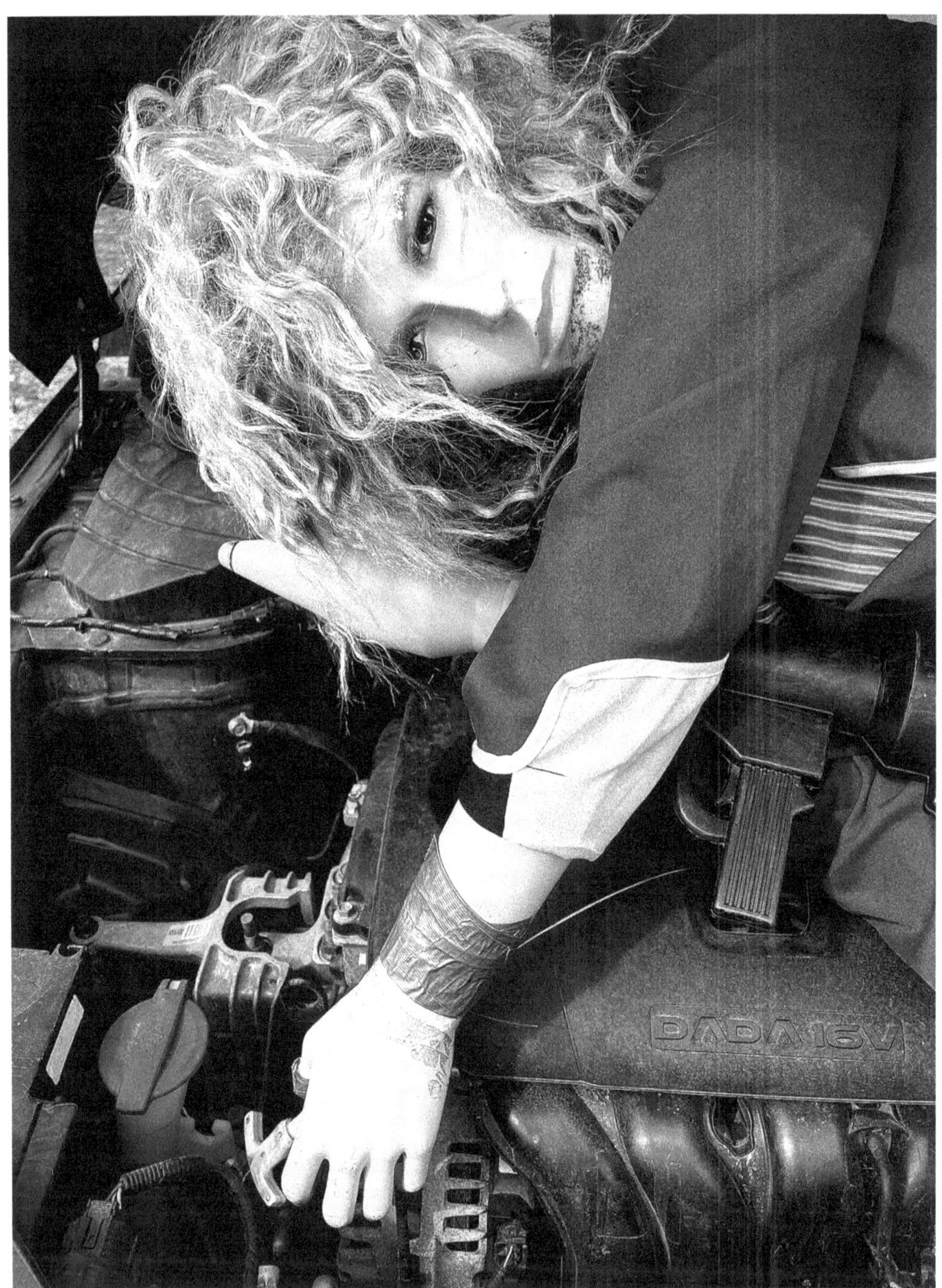


**DADA CHECKING THE OIL**

*Photograph, 3024 px x 4032 px*

**SUZI KAPLAN OLMSTED**
PORTLAND, OREGON

# BURNING FLESH

Maybe it's what they call

Generational Trauma

The heterosexual cis-male aryan Christian psychologist

questioned my sanity when I talked about not being safe

He was confident and secure in the world

Tall, slender, handsome and wealthy

But I can always smell the burning flesh

it's a baby burning world

Beating schoolgirls back into burning buildings

Burning crosses on lawns

Melting buildings full of people having ordinary days

Wafting smoke from gun barrels in the agora

Mixed with pungent copper across the floors of supermarkets

The villagers never throw out their torches & pitchforks

We treat our weapons better than our children

and our cars better than victims of ill fortune

Don't you smell the barbecue?

## JANET KAPLAN

BROOKLYN, NEW YORK

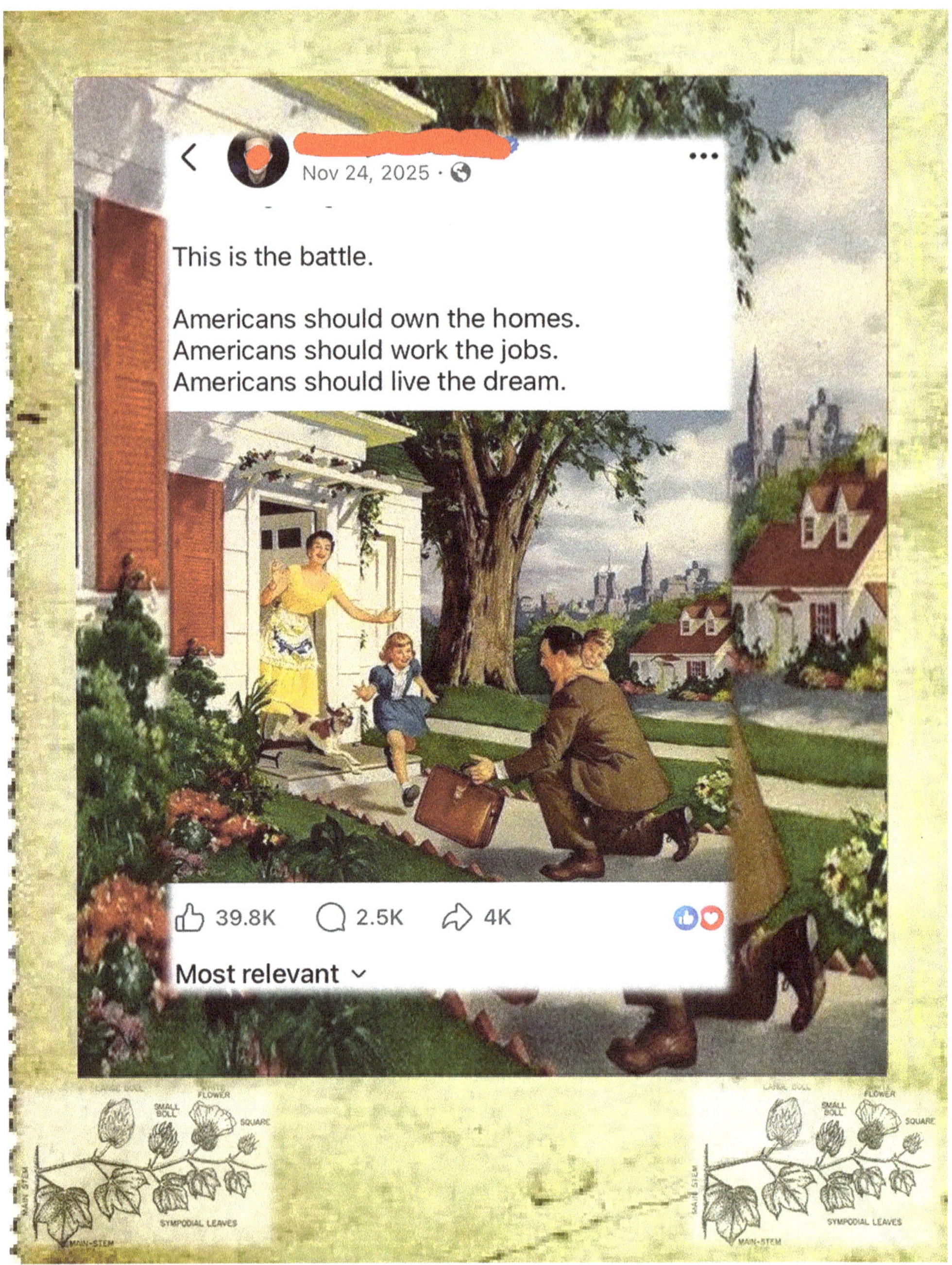


**THIS IS THE BATTLE**

*Digital collage (not AI); 1700 px x 2200 px*

## DAVID LILJEMARK

STOCKHOLM, SWEDEN

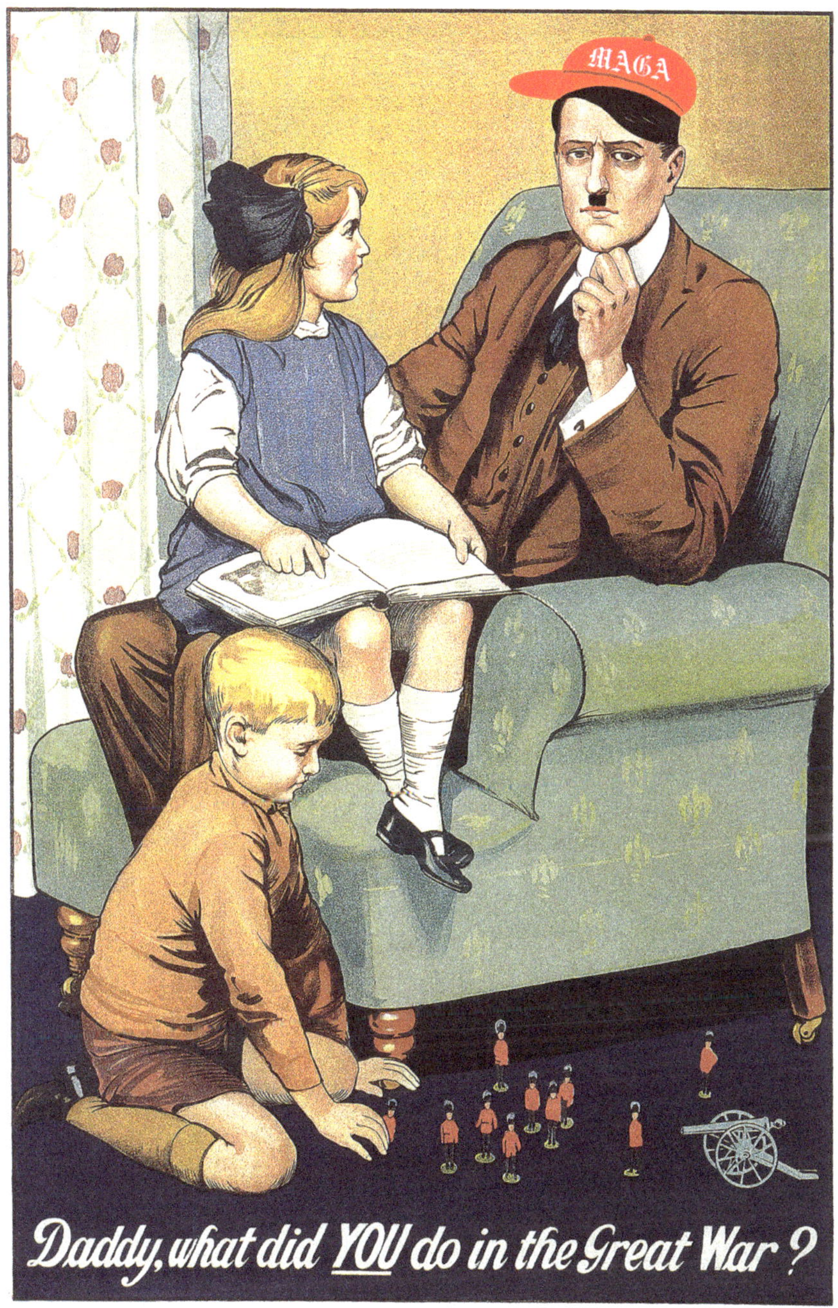


**Daddy, what did YOU do in the Great War?**

*Digital drawing, 25.04 cm x 37.96 cm*

## MARK GLISTA

ROCKPORT, MAINE

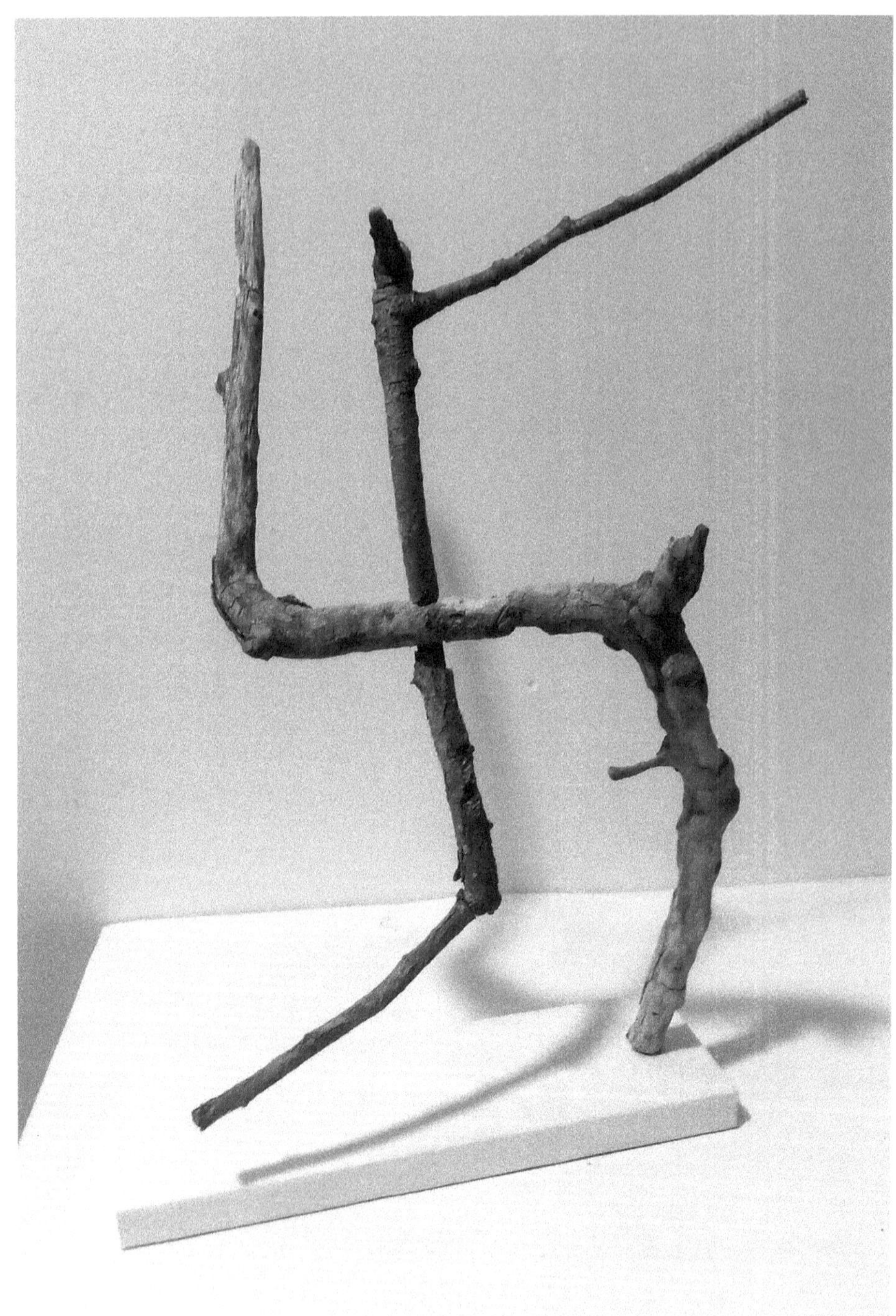

**SCULPTURE**

*Twigs*

## NATURE, SABINE SCHNEIDER-Z. AND DADADORN

ZÜRICH, SWITZERLAND

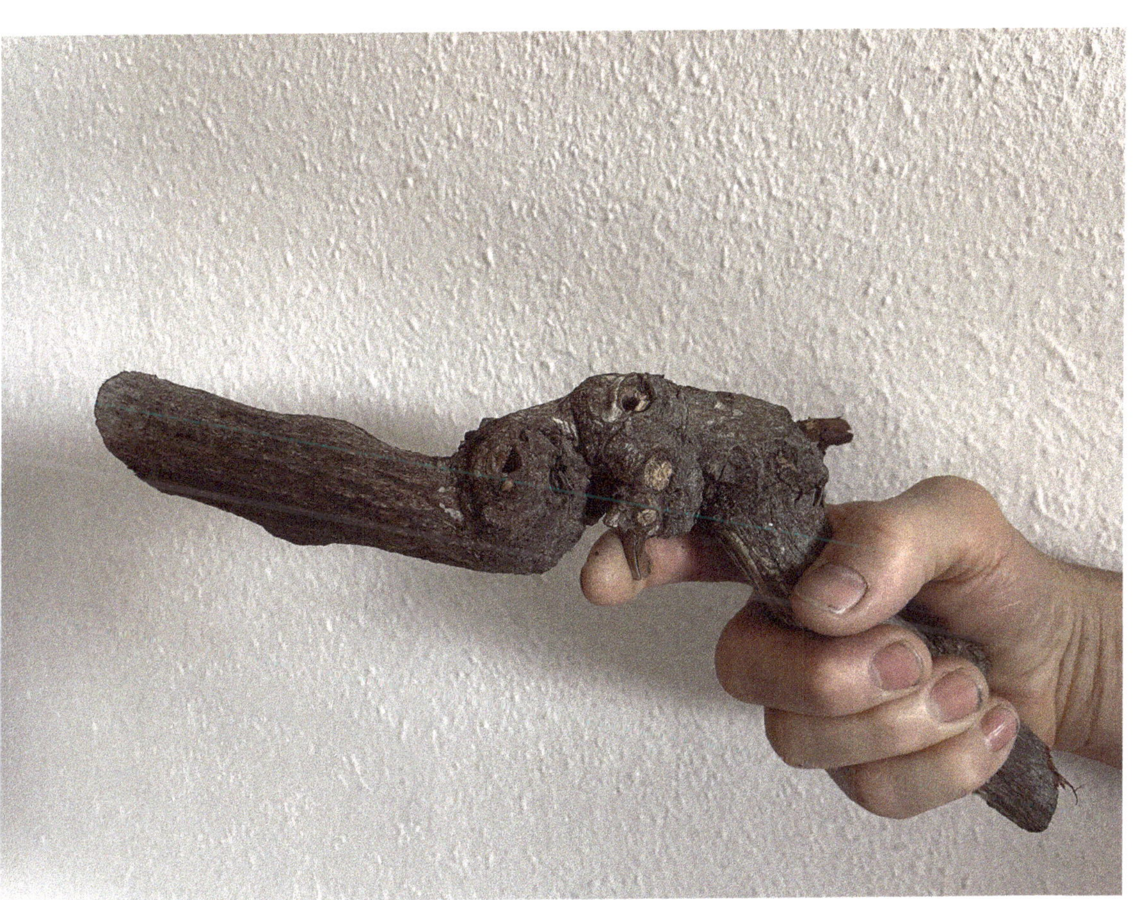

**PEACETOL (IT'S WATCHING YOU)**

*Photograph*

## SHIVA ABOSSEDGH

GRAZ, AUSTRIA

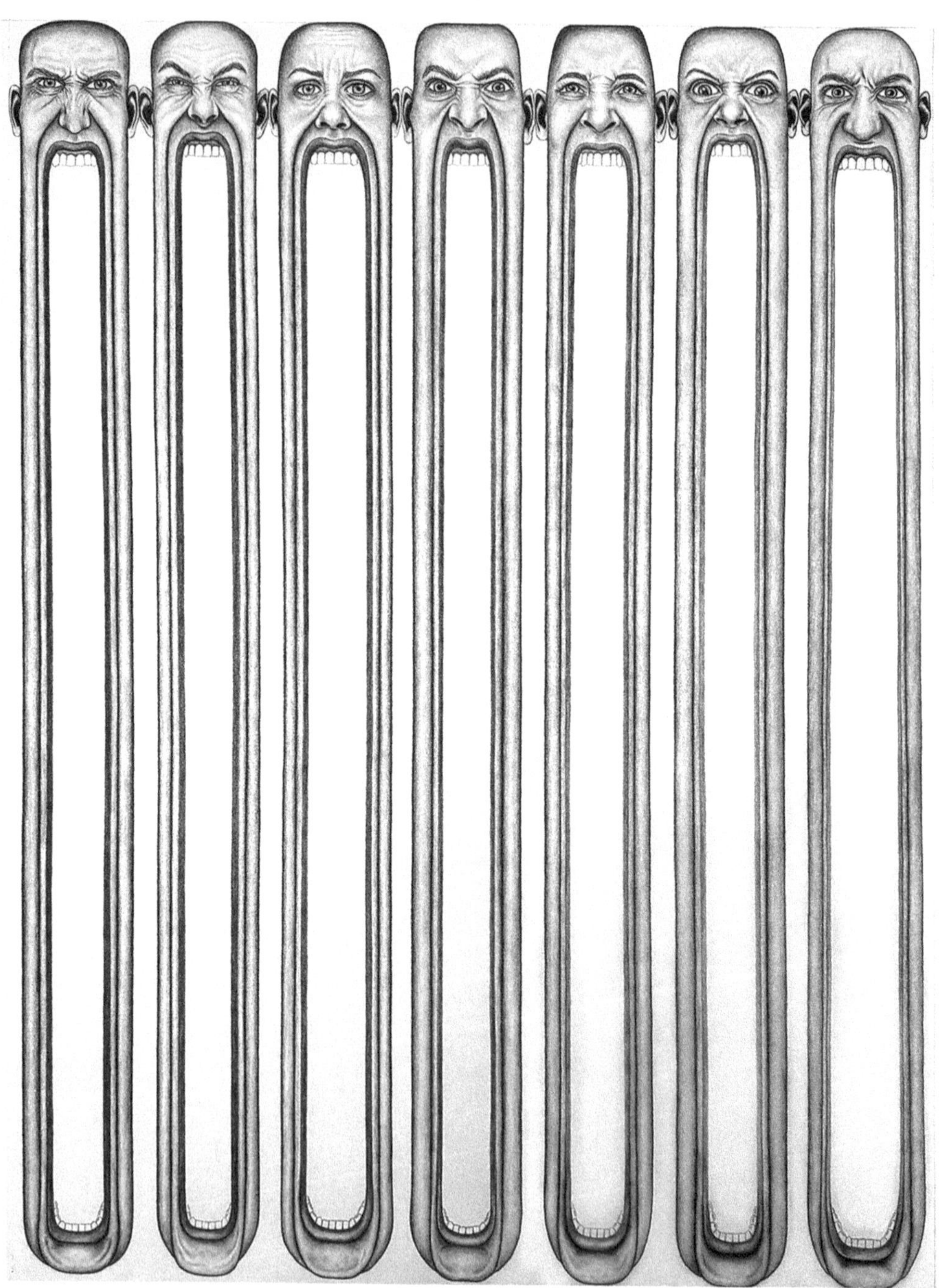

**DEEP SHOUT**

*Charcoal and graphite on board, 68 cm x 88 cm*

**LOIS KAGAN MINGUS**
NEW YORK, NEW YORK

## WHAT IT IS NOW

Ice cream

Ice ice baby

Ice skating

Ice bucket challenge

Ice was

delicious

lyrical

athletic

noble

Now rewritten

reassigned

made reversed

made perverse

ICE bullet to head and now

dead.

## RICH STONE

SAN FRANCISCO, CALIFORNIA

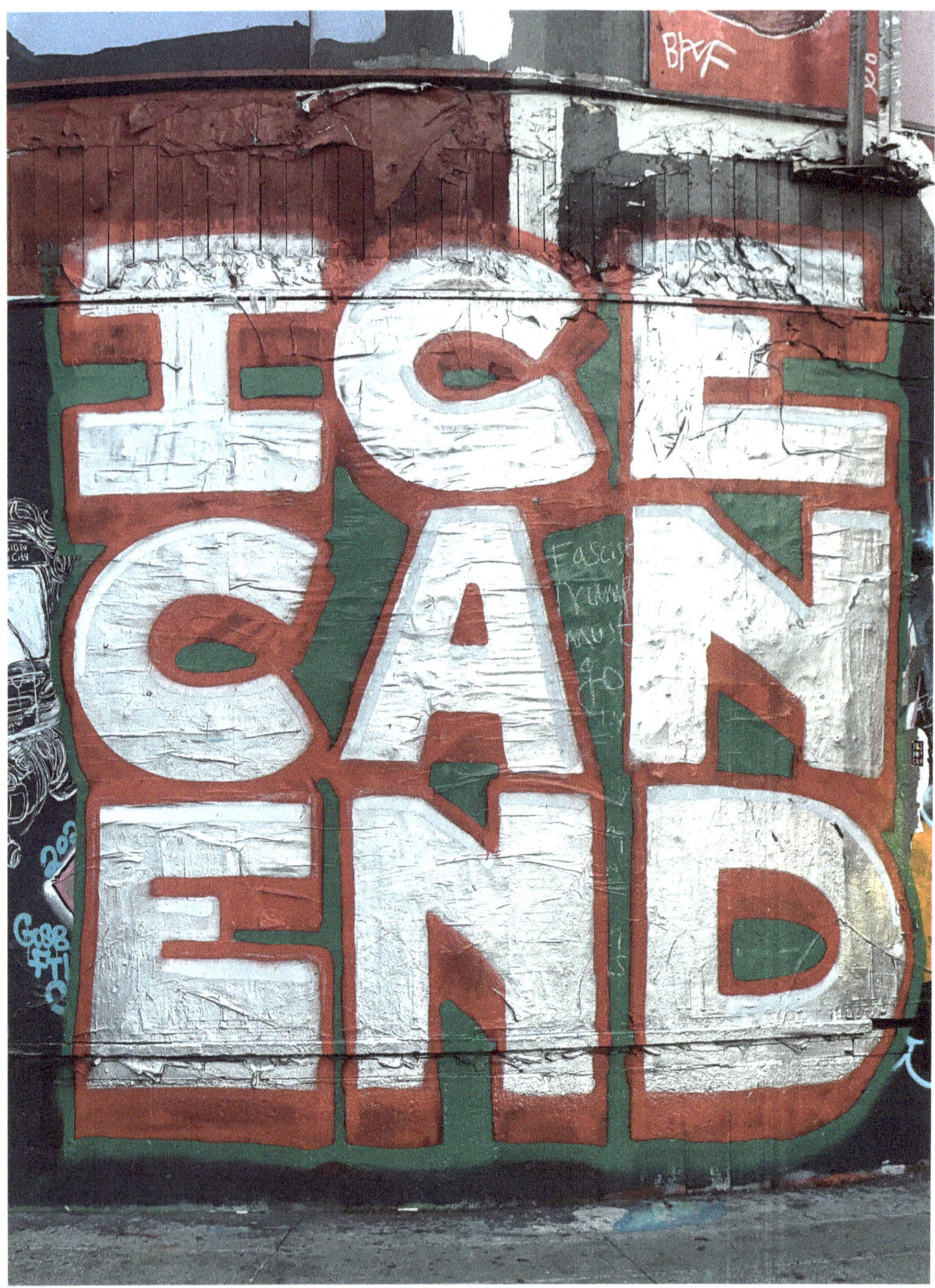


**ICE CAN END!**

*Photograph*

**DIG WAYNE**
LOS ANGELES, CALIFORNIA

## WE ARE ICE

drown them in the bathtub at birth

string them up by their ankles like Mussolini

make them dig their own graves before you shoot them in the back of the neck

learn how to speak the language

whet your tongue with questions for the missing adults

fill your empty drawers with sock bombs

protest against your reflection

we are ice

whether we like it or not

everyone is innocent everyone is guilty

we have not been invaded by aliens

how many degrees of separation are you from the jackbooted others

pushing you to the ground, choking on aggression

all sons and daughters of your neighbors if not you

you are ice

you can't separate yourself from humanity

we are ice

we are America

this is who we are

don't get used to it

**FAUSTO GROSSI**
BILBAO, SPAIN

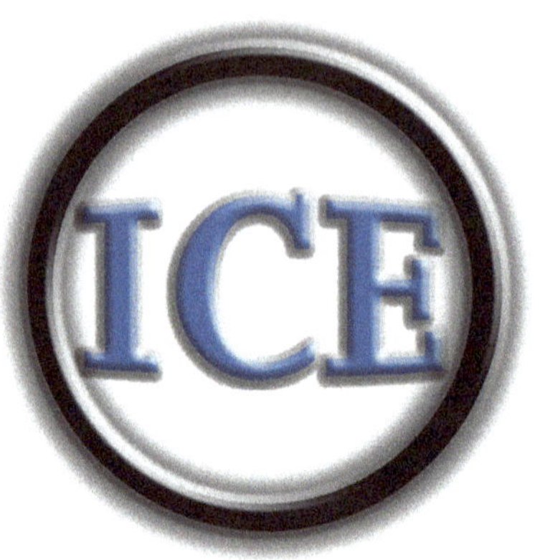


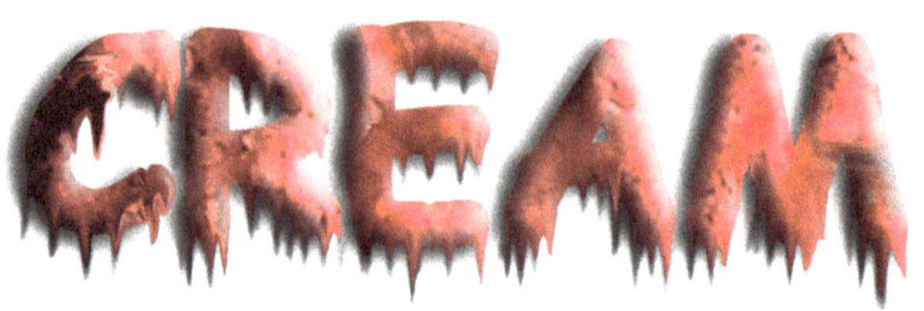


OF CRIME

**UNTITLED**

*Infographic, 15 cm x 21 cm*

**MISA LEVEY**

NEW YORK, NEW YORK

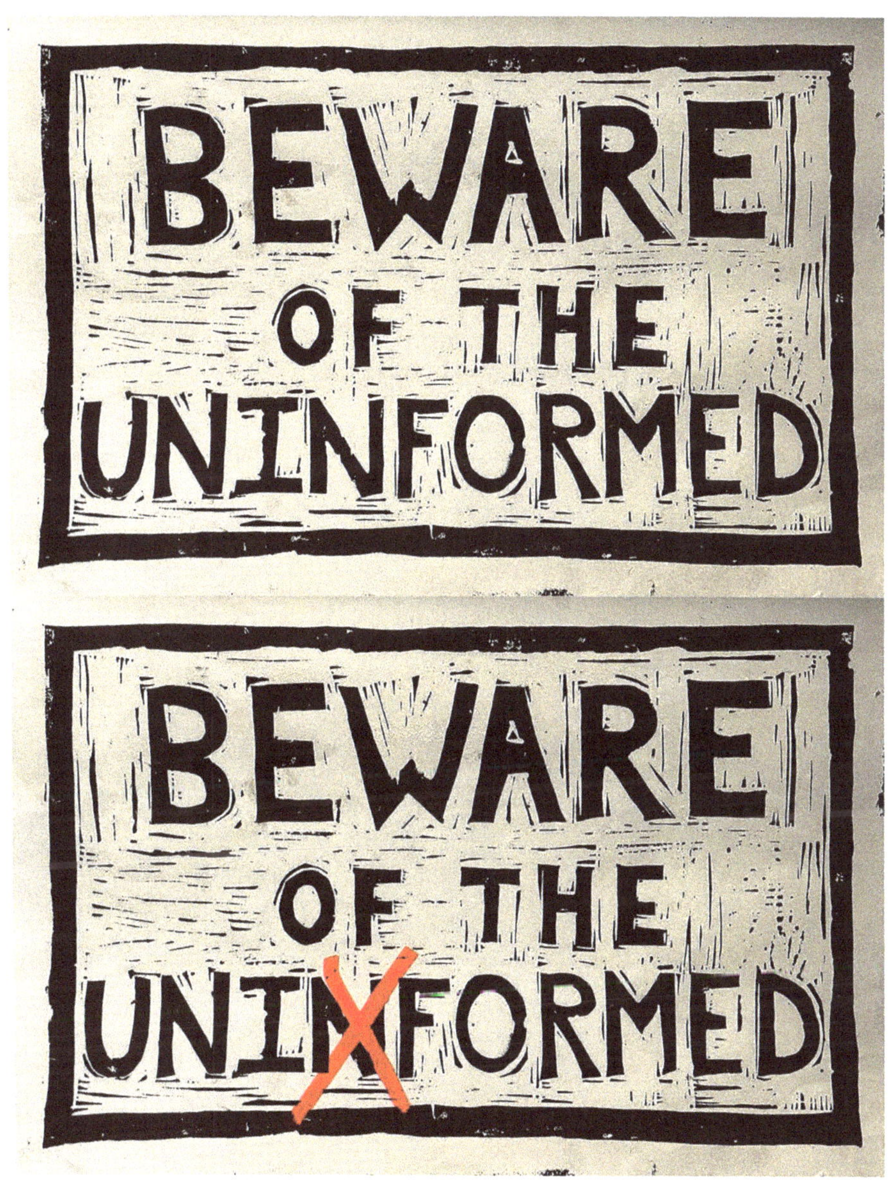


**BEWARE**

*Linocut, 16 in x 20 in*

**KOSTAS KIRITSIS**

BROOKLYN, NEW YORK

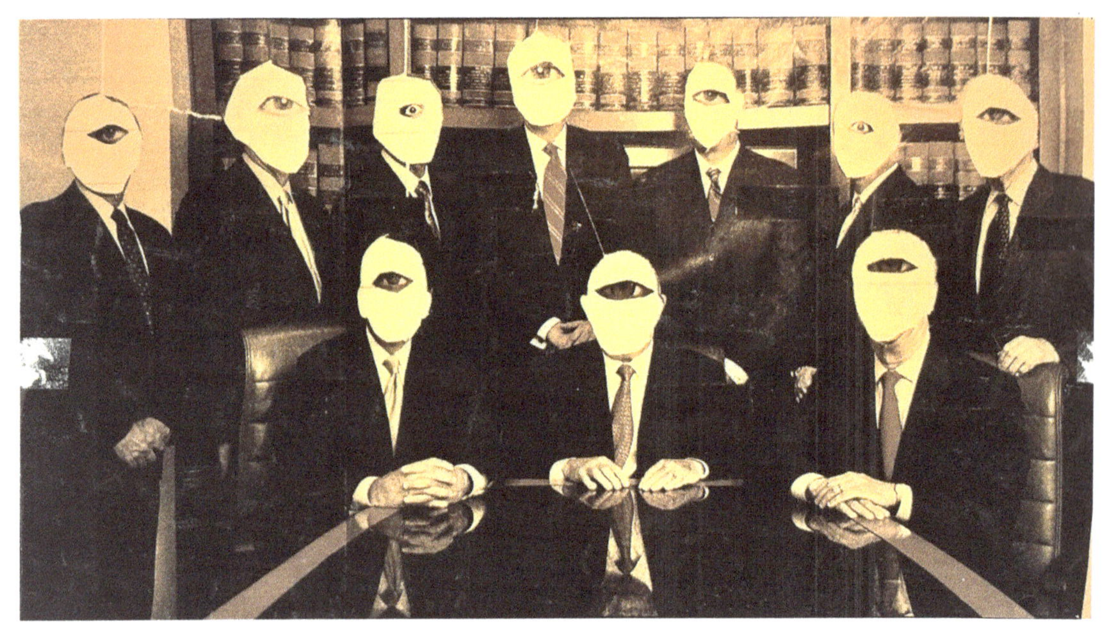

## THE CYCLOPS

*Inkjet prints on paper from original photographs, 20 in x16 in*

**ANDRIANA MINOU**
LONDON, UNITED KINGDOM

## THE WAX MUSEUM OF TRUTHS

*The best way to predict the future is to invent it*
The X-Files

Once upon a time
There was an old man
Who invented the future
So he built a museum
The Wax Museum of Truths.
Nothing looks true to the naked eye
In the Wax Museum of Truths
But
Everything looks real in selfies
-and that's true enough.
So he filled the museum
With
Wax old men
Wax historical figures
Wax historians
Wax histories
All melting away
In blissful agony
Turning into
A wax river
That cannot go back
Heading straight
To an invented future.

## ROBERTO SCALA

MILAN, ITALY

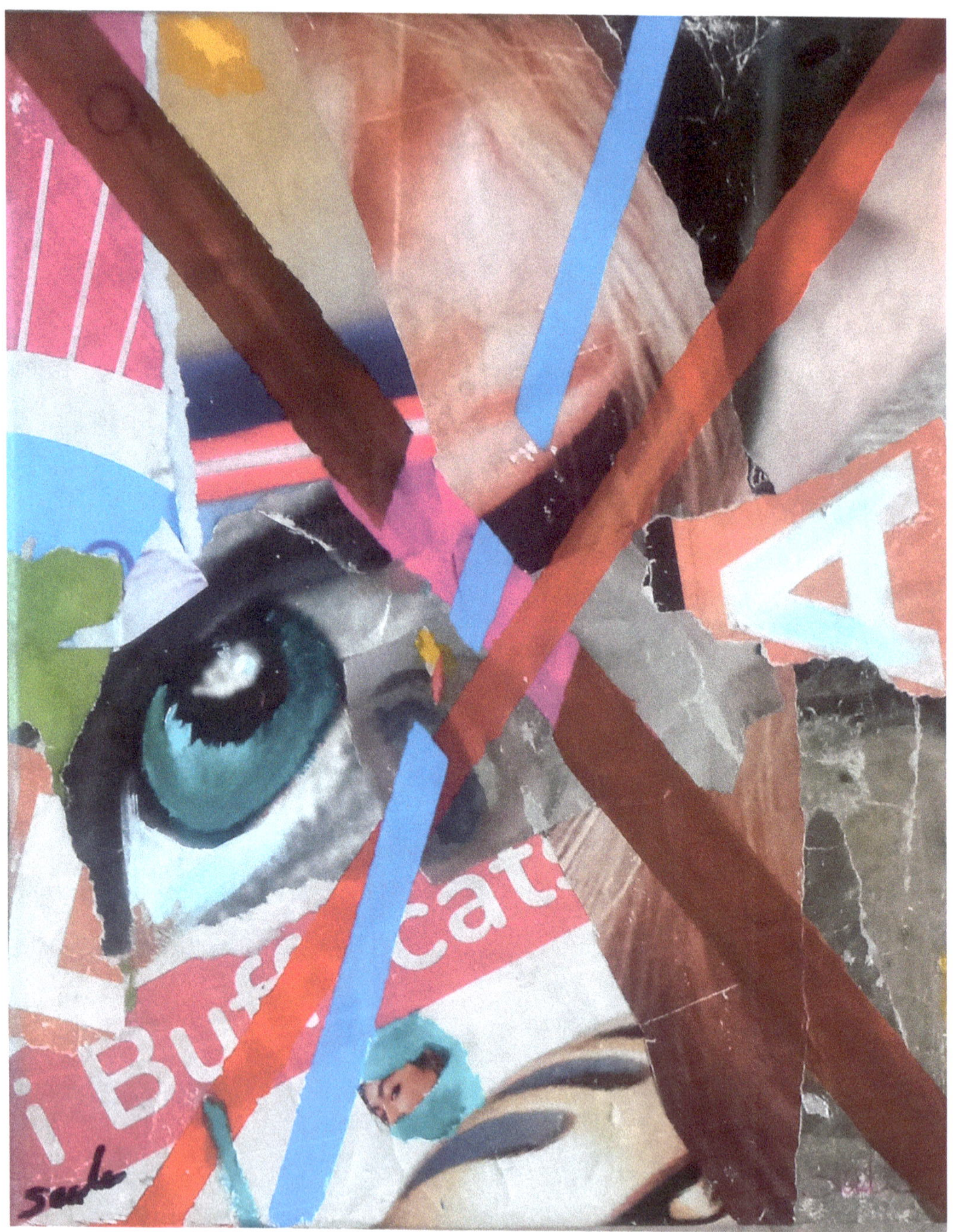


## NOBODY SEES EVERYTHING

*Acrylic painting, collage, writing, photo, spray paint on canvas, 40 cm x 30 cm*

MATTHEW HUPERT
NEW YORK, NEW YORK

## blindfolds bandages veils & shrouds are not the same

we were worshiping belief in blind justice
we cover her eyes in front of the courthouse
we pat each other's backs
celebrating our enlightened view.

turning on the lights means nothing
to the blind
blind justice
is blind when open eyes are required

blind justice is blind
to inequalities
that shape outcome
before it begins

strip the blindfold off
we do not seek equality in outcome
but equity in access
maybe we can see justice then

## PAULO SANCHES

LUZ, PORTUGAL

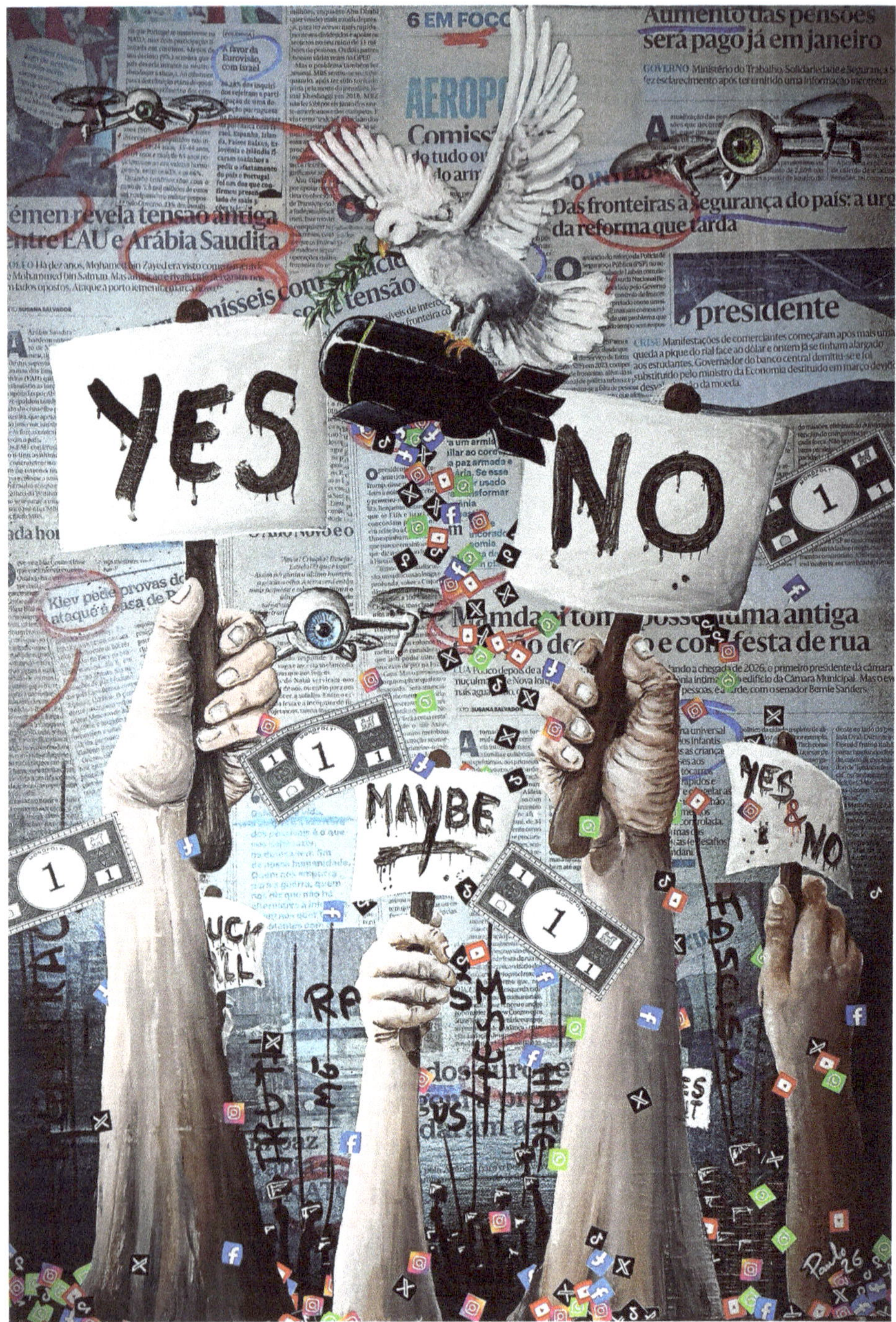


### DYSTOPIC NOISE

*Acrylic and collage on canvas, 70 cm x 50 cm*

**CARLI MUÑOZ**
SAN JUAN, PUERTO RICO

## THE FINAL SALE — OF THE HOUSE OF LAW

Odium—resistant to Imodium.
A constipated conscience,
chronic virtue,
the leaky gut of a nation's inflamed bowels —
and calling it law.

The last breath stolen from Lady Justice,
sold like looted goods
to the highest bidder for the lowest cause;
a rigged slot machine,
ordered by the master of the deal.

The house of law,
demoted to a Vegas casino,
with waxen pawns
nodding blind approval in unison —
their eyes on the prowl at the expense of their soul.

So it goes — the saga,
the tale of Justice Roberts,
a putrid legacy
at impropriety's pinnacle —
the final sale of the House of Law.

**MADO REZNIK**

MEXICO CITY, MEXICO

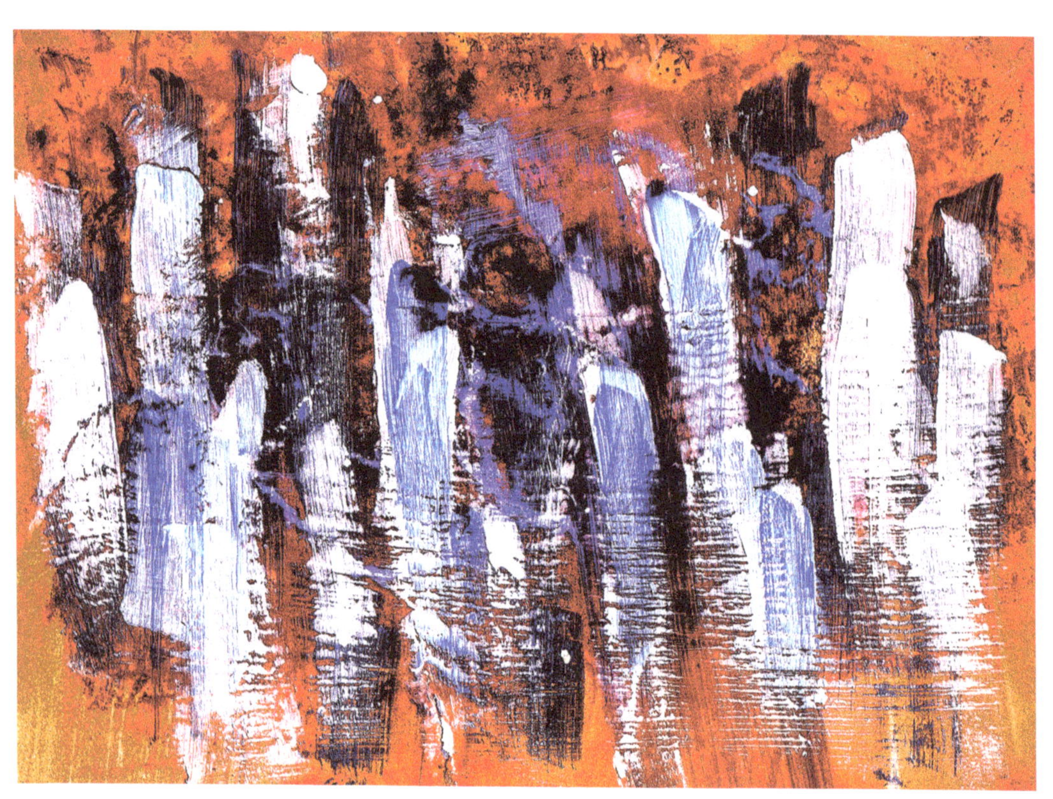

**GAZA REAL STATE**

*Acrylic on paper, 11.69 in × 16.54 in*

ELIOT KATZ
HOBOKEN, NEW JERSEY

## IT'S ABOUT REPRESENTATION

Someone asked why
I've written so many
poems about this war.
As a democratic-left
atheist son
of an Auschwitz survivor
I have to try
my imperfect best
to help
in refusing to let
the sociopathic bombing
tactics
of a corrupt
Benjamin Netanyahu
pretend to speak
for universal Jewish thought
to the world.

**LISA PANEPINTO**
HOLDEN, MAINE

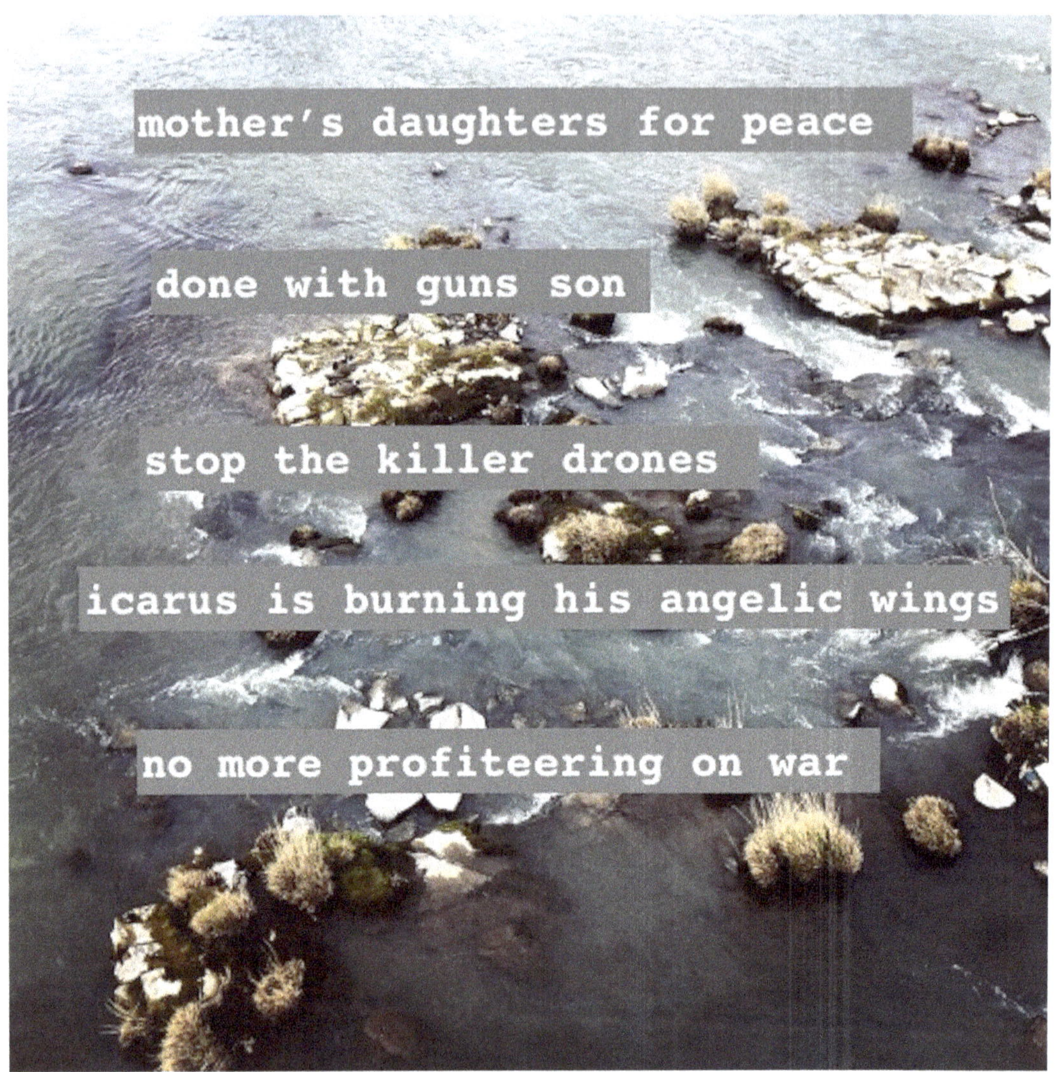


**no more war**

*Photo and text*

# DAVID LAWTON

NEW YORK, NEW YORK

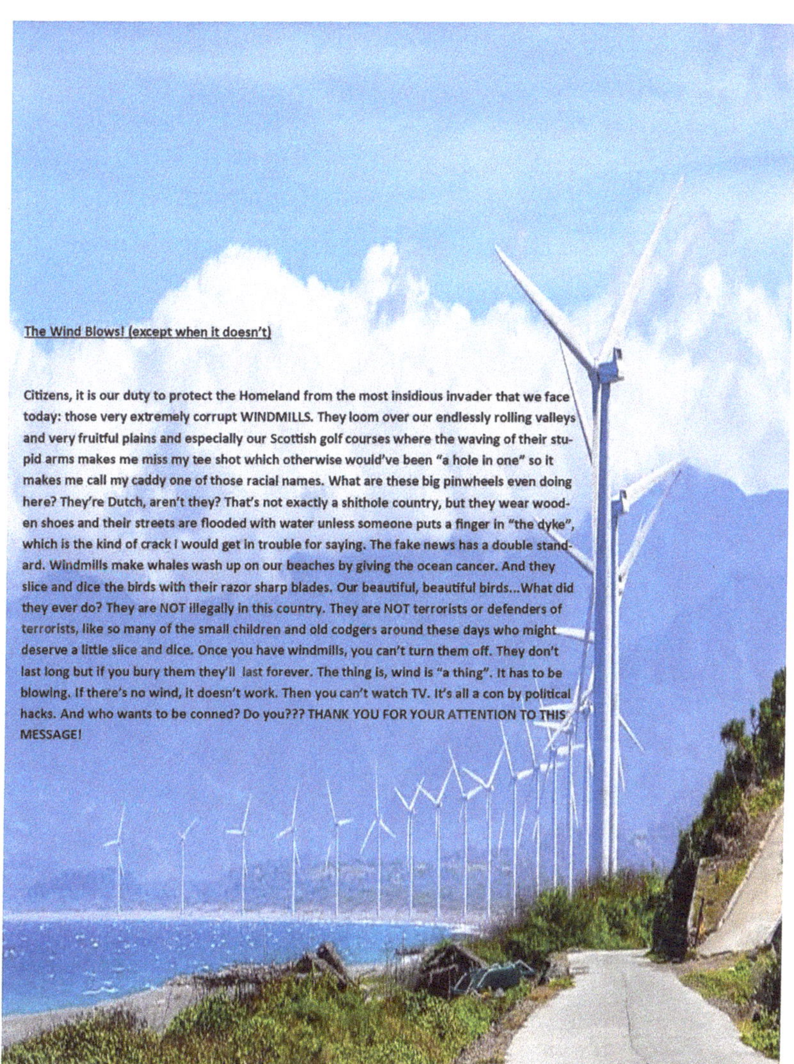

The Wind Blows! (except when it doesn't)

Citizens, it is our duty to protect the Homeland from the most insidious invader that we face today: those very extremely corrupt WINDMILLS. They loom over our endlessly rolling valleys and very fruitful plains and especially our Scottish golf courses where the waving of their stupid arms makes me miss my tee shot which otherwise would've been "a hole in one" so it makes me call my caddy one of those racial names. What are these big pinwheels even doing here? They're Dutch, aren't they? That's not exactly a shithole country, but they wear wooden shoes and their streets are flooded with water unless someone puts a finger in "the dyke", which is the kind of crack I would get in trouble for saying. The fake news has a double standard. Windmills make whales wash up on our beaches by giving the ocean cancer. And they slice and dice the birds with their razor sharp blades. Our beautiful, beautiful birds...What did they ever do? They are NOT illegally in this country. They are NOT terrorists or defenders of terrorists, like so many of the small children and old codgers around these days who might deserve a little slice and dice. Once you have windmills, you can't turn them off. They don't last long but if you bury them they'll last forever. The thing is, wind is "a thing". It has to be blowing. If there's no wind, it doesn't work. Then you can't watch TV. It's all a con by political hacks. And who wants to be conned? Do you??? THANK YOU FOR YOUR ATTENTION TO THIS MESSAGE!

## THE WIND BLOWS

*Photo and text*

**LYNETTE CLENNELL**

FOLLINA, ITALY

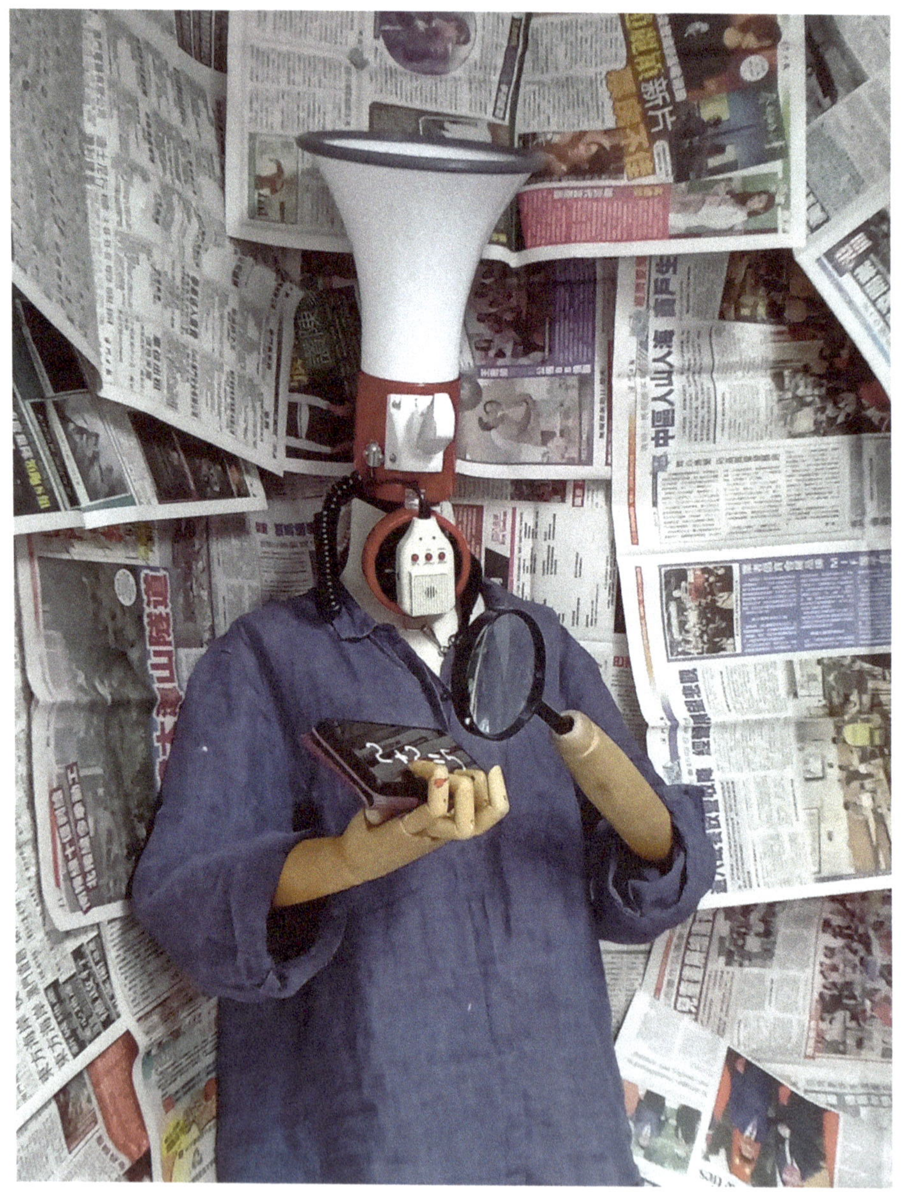

**2 + 2 = 5**

*Photograph: mannequin, shirt, bullhorn, magnifying glass, cellphone, newspapers, A4*

**BEATRIZ SEELAENDER**
SÃO PAULO, BRAZIL

## CURRENT EVENTS

Give me a soundtrack or a god suddenly interested in my activities
Show me why I should be sorry, 'cause I just can't comprehend it
Give me 3 to 5 business days to process
Tell me about the photo albums you donated accidentally
Give me a lecture about my inherent lack of empathy
and the rest is not quite history, it's a question of faded memory
Cast me as the idle contrast to your puritan ascension
Give me a past or a future but please do not give me current events
Give me a narrow sepulcher, a brain out of order
that just repeats gibberish, a gun to my head walking down an altar,
a feast of black licorice in my old apartment,
a boss to impress, send me to the border
with poetic license on an empty stomach
Put me in the corner until we are even
Make me a believer in your revisionism
Tell me that none of these things ever happened
But please do not start with current events

To hell with current events
always waiting for context
To hell with context
and historical consciousness
To hell with hell and the New York Times
To hell with fact-checking and podcasts
and QR codes and counter-hoaxes and hindsight
None of this matters in hindsight
The answers are there in some obscure anarchist gazette
To be heavily quoted twenty-eight years from now
on a dedicated academic volume pirated from a disreputable website
and that's where the truth is, not the propaganda
To hell with wishlists and think-pieces and technocratic experts
and neoliberalism and the military industrial complex
To hell with the things you care about without grasping
without realizing you're a massive part of the problem
Jesus fucking Christ

I'd rather live in the Classics
and drown in a beauty that's been vouched for
I cannot stand the tip of the iceberg
It's scratchy and ashy and just isn't worth it
Jesus please for the love of god get me out of this surface
Give me a novel of caliber, give me an escape plan
I'll take a passing grade in this test
just please do not give me current events

## JUDITH LINDBLOOM

(1933–2016)

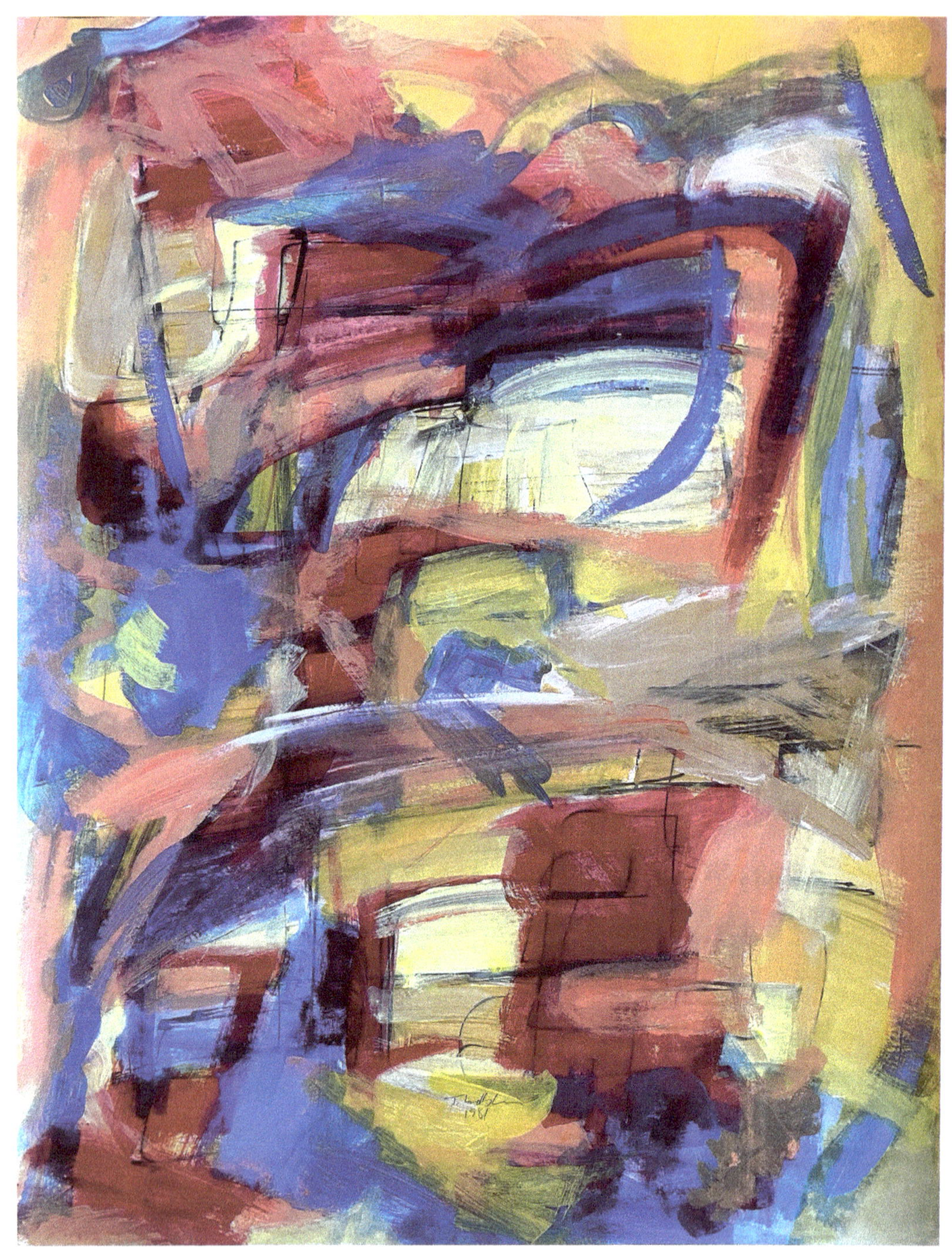

**CONSENSUS COLLAPSE**

*Acrylic on paper, 26 in x 20 in*

**LINDA LERNER**
BROOKLYN, NEW YORK

## ROARING BACK

I.
My father breaks through the evening news,
*one person can't work for three.*
He stops working, my mother stops making dinner.
Only it's not my father's voice I now hear
repeating *can't,* like a door being slammed
across America; fear grows, hunger too.

Every morning I wake up
it's Halloween again

II.
In The People's House, renovated for a king
we find Gatsby, masquerading as the president,
a lavish party going on, whatever his insatiable
greed wants offered to hungry eyes on screens
everywhere he is, everywhere, all the time

knows It's not the 1920's, not exactly, but
his smile says, isn't life just...you know

then they do. it's Halloween
trick or treat have switched places,
the air they're breathing is the same old air recycled,
some too embarrassed to admit being tricked
and provoke his wrath, be shut out from
this big, beautiful party, continue to pretend ...

In the distance the vague sound of a crash
Is slowly making its way through the decade,
can they hear it, growing louder
and louder

## TCHELLO D'BARROS

RIO DE JANEIRO, BRAZIL

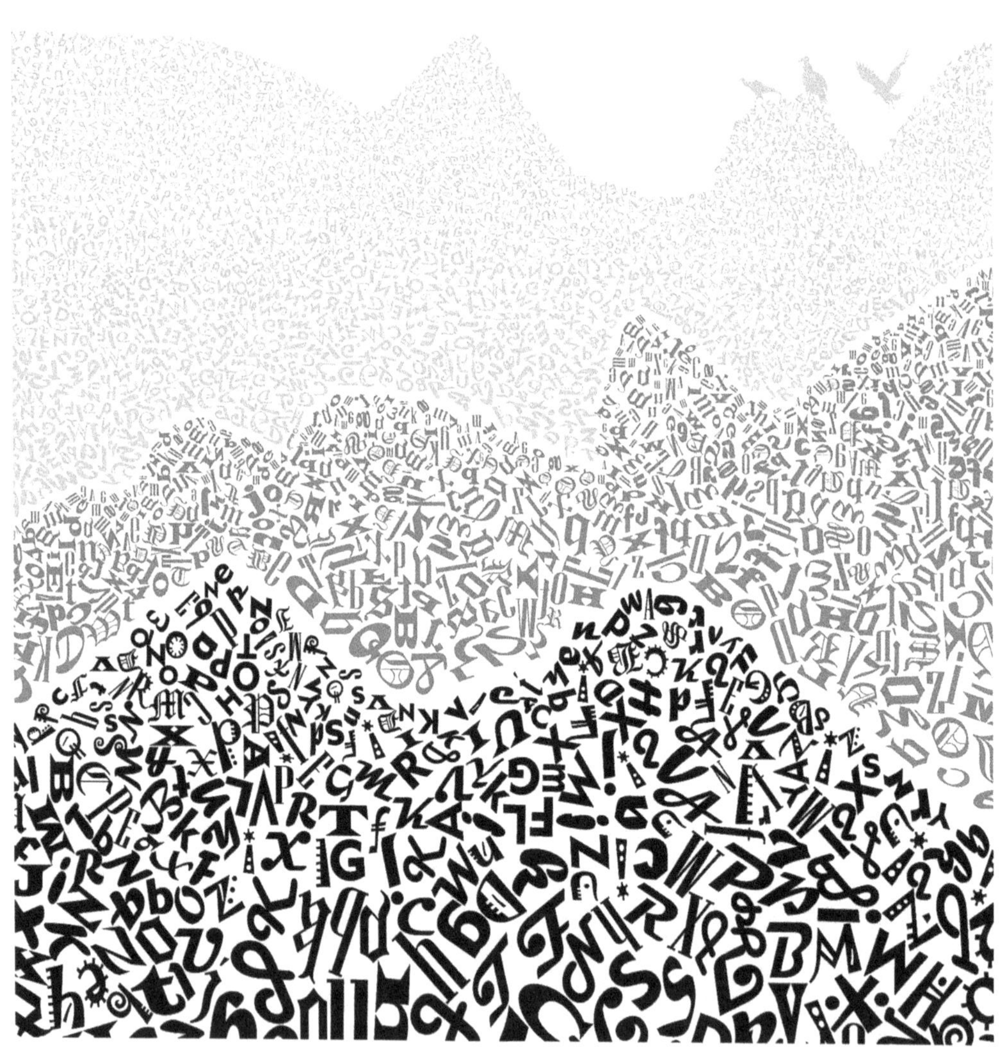

**DUMP NEWS**

*Drawing and computer, 200 mm x 200 mm*

## SCOTT WANNBERG

(1953–2011)

# THE BLEEDING NEWSROOM

The news today is pale.
Kid gloves ride the headlines.
When does the real story get written?
The newsroom bleeds and they put a band-aid on
to stop the bleeding.
Questions are not asked
and followed through.
Tenderly now, the news raises its hand,
but oh so fearful of causing waves.
The news sleepwalks
and fumbles the ball, mumbles
inarticulate rhythms.
Finally, the news gives certain people
a free ride.
Once upon a time the news meant something,
but today it means nothing much.
The blood of the newsroom coagulates,
dries up. Questions are not asked
and the kid gloves still dictate
the headlines.

**MARC OLMSTED**
PORTLAND, OREGON

## NEWSREEL

The kingdom of knives
will cut the king
the fall of America
is a slow wild fire,
a slow motion newsreel
of an atom blast blowing
the fake town down

**Dd. SPUNGIN**
VALLEY STREAM, NEW YORK

## CHOPPY WATERS, LEAKY BOAT

Sharks circling, smoke signals
Trumpets playing taps
Aren't we tired of peace treaties,
burning in the sand?
Starving civilizations
drawing plans
in mud drenched fields?

The strong man lifts his barbells,
drops them on your toe
Aren't you tired of pain?
We gather together
but forget the lyrics

Aren't we glad to meet here
listening to the lies,
betting on whose is bigger?

I am tired of false promises
drowning out the little truth that's left
Did you watch tv last night?
Pass me the comics section
Never mind. Nothing's funny anymore.

**ELLEN SANDER**
BELFAST, MAINE

## GOD AS A WALNUT

Art is a victim, not a fulcrum, of history. The war after the war to end all wars was one heartstake, the atom bomb, then footsteps on the moon, a rocket that wore the rings of Saturn like a bracelet looped on a swinging wrist. Art stopped looking like; unwound, voiced the imagination of perimeters.    God took a break.    God re-emerged as a walnut, crenulation without and within. A lippy seam. Theologies bred power, the heroism of heretics punished by the smug arrogance of silence. The sight of the blue marble, incomprehensibly suspended, a pause between breaths. Infinitesimally brief. Dot dot. Bigotry simply burrowed under, a rancid well slaking a hegemonic thirst. Reason was the gift to [of?] humankind. Eclipses cowered primitives, then pickpockets learned to love them. Obscene wealth and moths infected coalitions for cures, for peace and innovation. Oh, fiasco, fiasco, fiasco erupts when pocket computers extrude whatever news the pocket wants. The pocket wants. Chromosomes of language become worms devouring corpses.

**JERRY T. JOHNSON**
NEW YORK, NEW YORK

## WE ARE MASKED AGAIN

today's mask, symbolic. today's mask, not representative of coronavirus.
today's mask, represents the liar-virus. spreading, spreading so. a resurgence
of 1938, Germany. a resurgence with horrid symptoms. like the resurgence
of measles and all types of pox. our skin is covered with sores from eras ago
when Jim Crow ruled the land. and the land lays blemished, putrefaction, sepsis
settles in. wasting we waste away and we are masked again, hiding our sore denying
our pain, closing our eyes to our slow but steady rot. dead we are walking, in a dying world.

## GIOVANNI FONTANA

ALATRI, ITALY

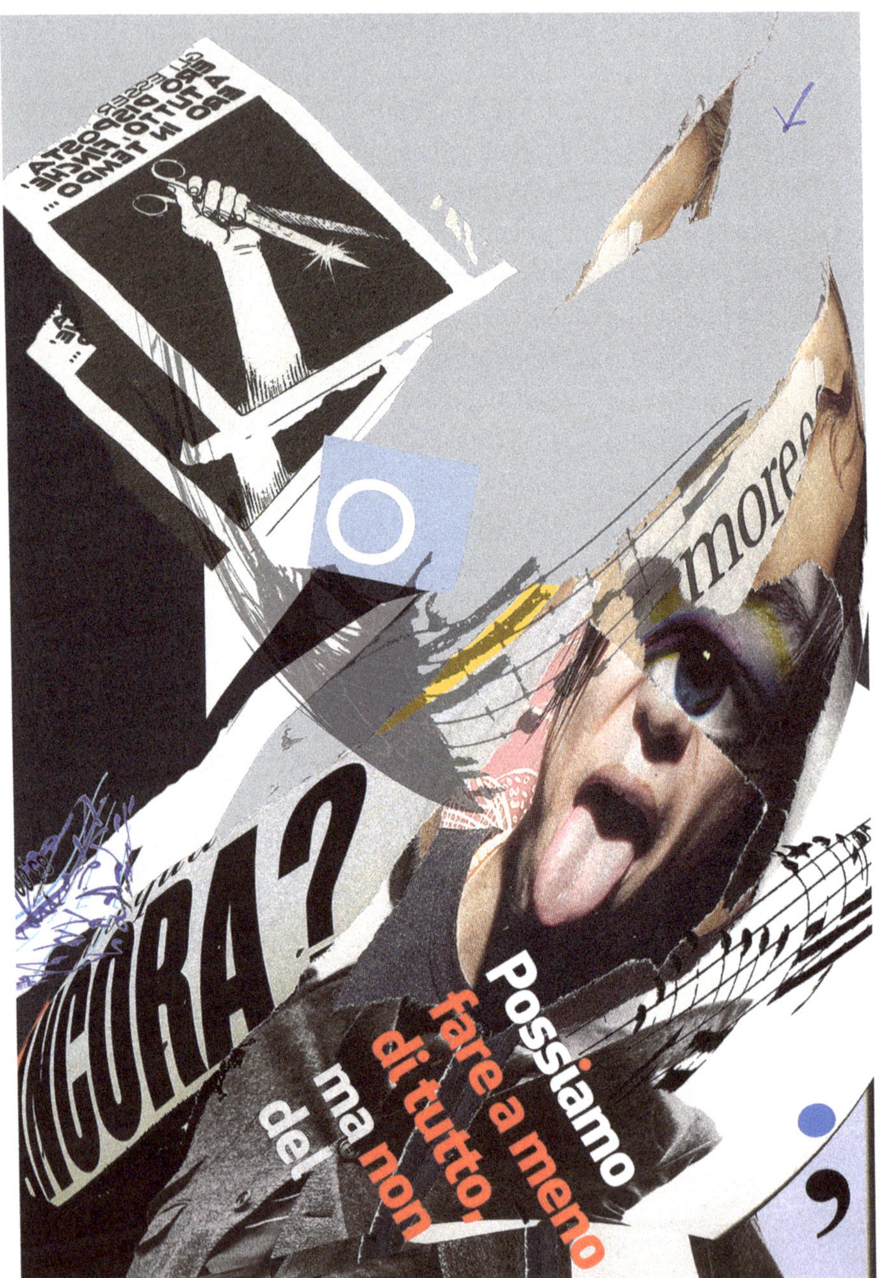


**LINGUACCIA!**

*Mixed media, 21 cm x 29.7 cm*

**BONI JOI**

LUZERN, SWITZERLAND

## THE LARGE LANGUAGE MODEL GENERATION

Sometimes our senses don't make sense
of the majestically fake.
We no longer trust our gut—somehow
we lost our wolf perception,
the high vibrational frequency of our magic.

Confabulated and discombobulated,
unsure of what exactly the conspiracy is
or if dark energy is weakening The Big Crunch,
we trust a building to hold us
while we lift weights and dance the samba.

Then remember when we were told radium connoted quality,
that burning liquor store incense will open our third eye,
that ear seeds cure addiction,
and search engines can hallucinate and scramble
their answers like a Magic 8-Ball seer.
We remember the fear of mass-produced heretical typos
and the time-telling turtle shells
that recorded the lost thirteenth month.

Our minds have always been flexible.
We like nice dresses and concepts
when they're packaged well
and spoken behind velvety rum voices.
We once fell in love through writing letters
and waited patiently for the divine magnet to respond.
Now we need a watermark for words.

Is our internal music tuned to an inharmonic frequency?
Because of the speed of our entanglement
maybe walking outside and rando conversations
are the new internet
where users can enjoy free gentle breezes,
where ancient societies speak to us
through pinecone fountains
about activating our pineal glands
instead of scrolling scrunched over and slurping,
adorning the Artificial I.

**@MONKEY_ON_THE_STREET AKA RACHEL DIXON**

OXFORD, UNITED KINGDOM

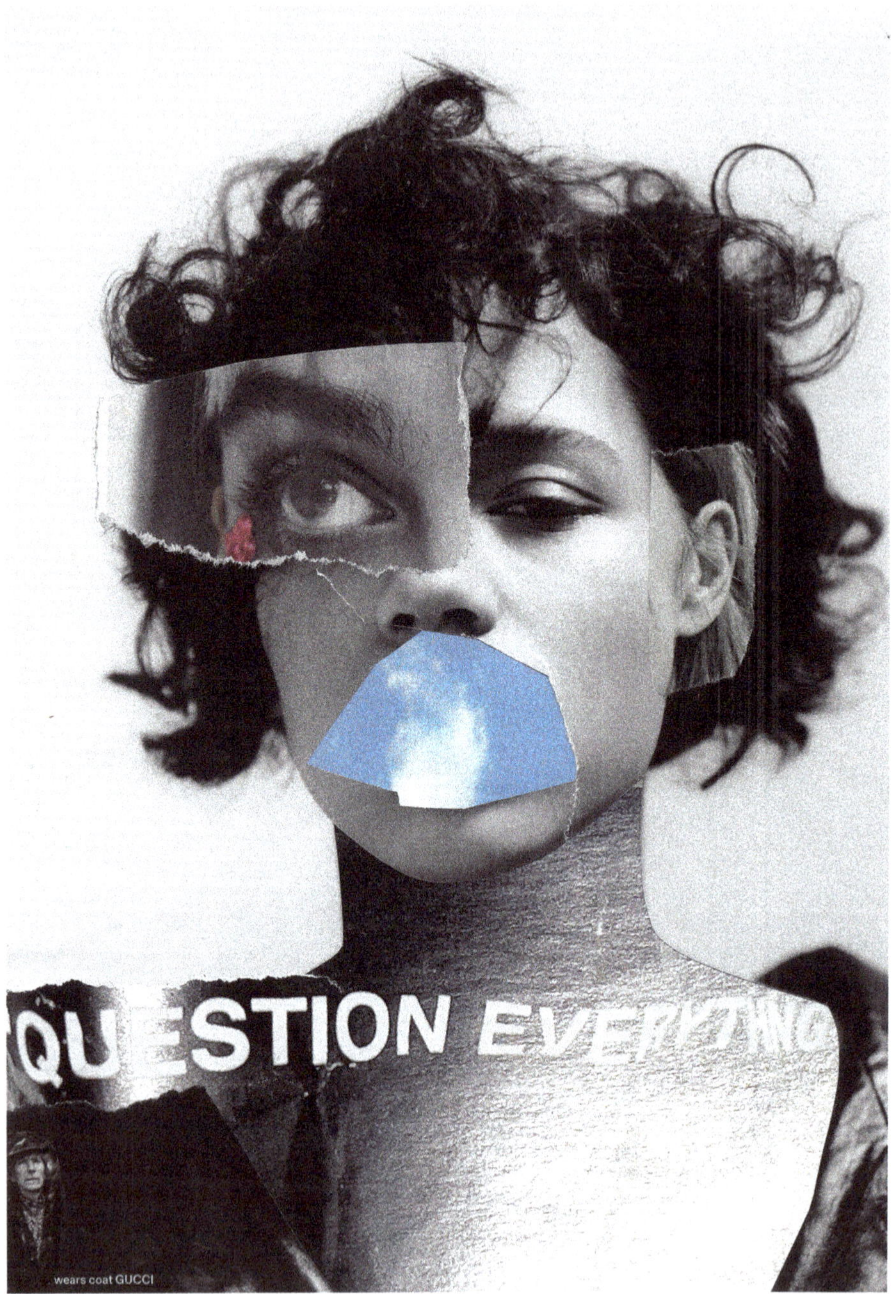


**DON'T TELL ME YOU'RE RIGHT**

*Magazines and glue, A4*

## MARGARET LEONARD

HARPSWELL, MAINE

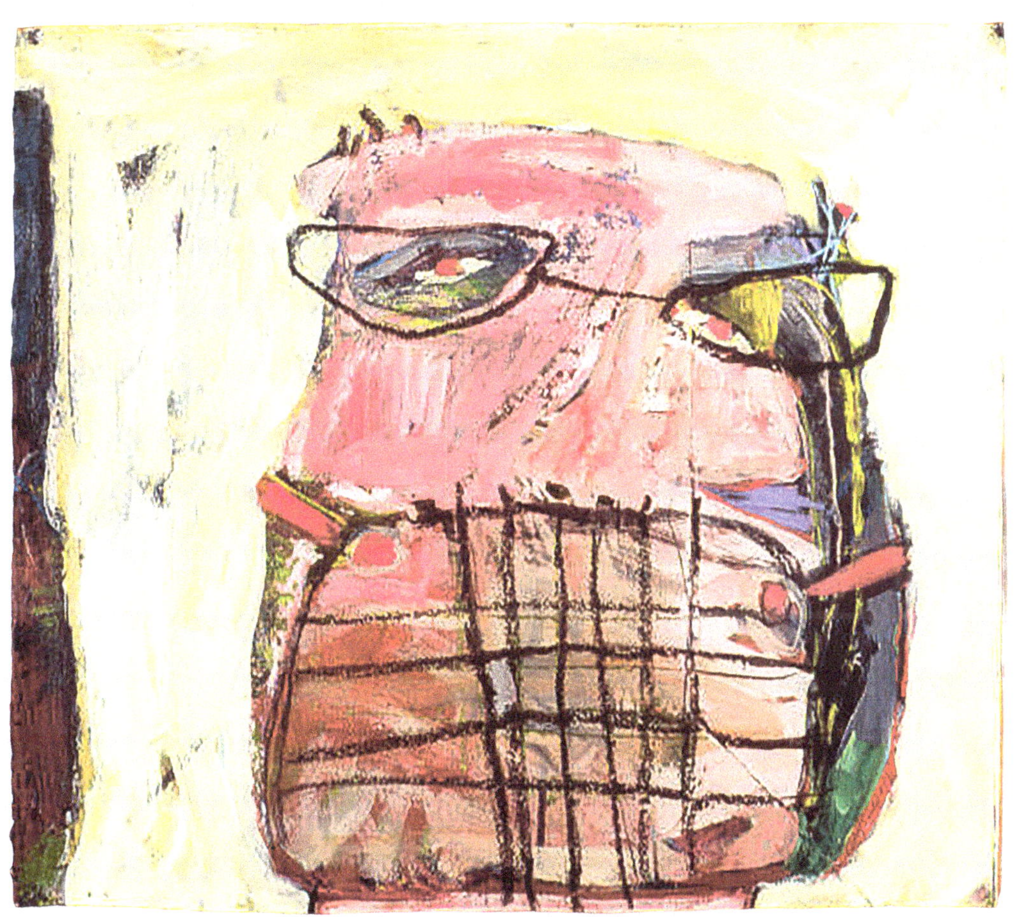

### MAN WITH CAGED MOUTH

*Collage and mixed media on watercolor paper, 24 in x 30 in*

## FRED HARPER

BROOKLYN, NEW YORK

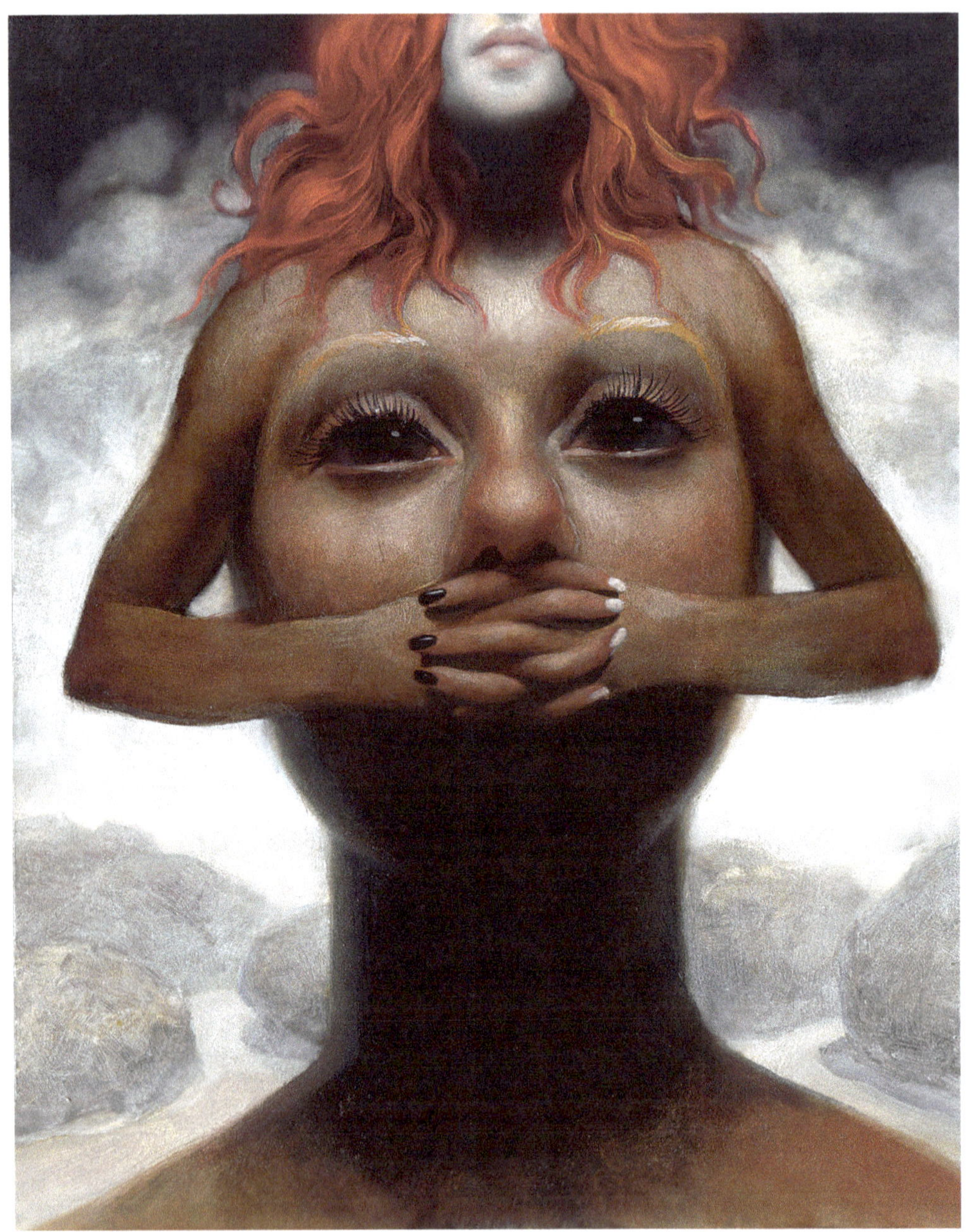

**DON'T SPEAK**

*Oil on panel, 8 in x 10 in*

**MARY CAMPBELL**
STATEN ISLAND, NW YORK

## PUT YOUR HANDS

Put your hands over your eyes.
They said not to look at the video.
They said it was too disturbing.

But oh, you had already seen it
from ALL of the angles.
And now, the video in your brain
keeps replaying it.

Put your hands over your ears.
They said there were domestic terrorists.
They said they put the lives of their men
In danger, so they had to

Put your hands over your nose.
Whst foul odor do these words produce.

Put your hands over your mouth

Don't Put your hands over your mouth
I want to hear your voice
I want to hear you
SCREAM

What do we want?
JUSTICE
when do we want it?
NOW

**AMY BARONE**
NEW YORK, NEW YORK

## MINING CALM

For the nonstop bad news of every day,
I'd like to erect a blockade to soften

each virtual brush with media's lies,
politicians' fraud, and brutal assaults.

And protected as a grove of aspen trees
joined at the root, I'll cultivate a space

of stark truths and neutral news
guarded by a circle of freedom angels

that can't deface life's rich promise.

**MAGGIE FRANK-HSU**

SAN DIEGO, CALIFORNIA

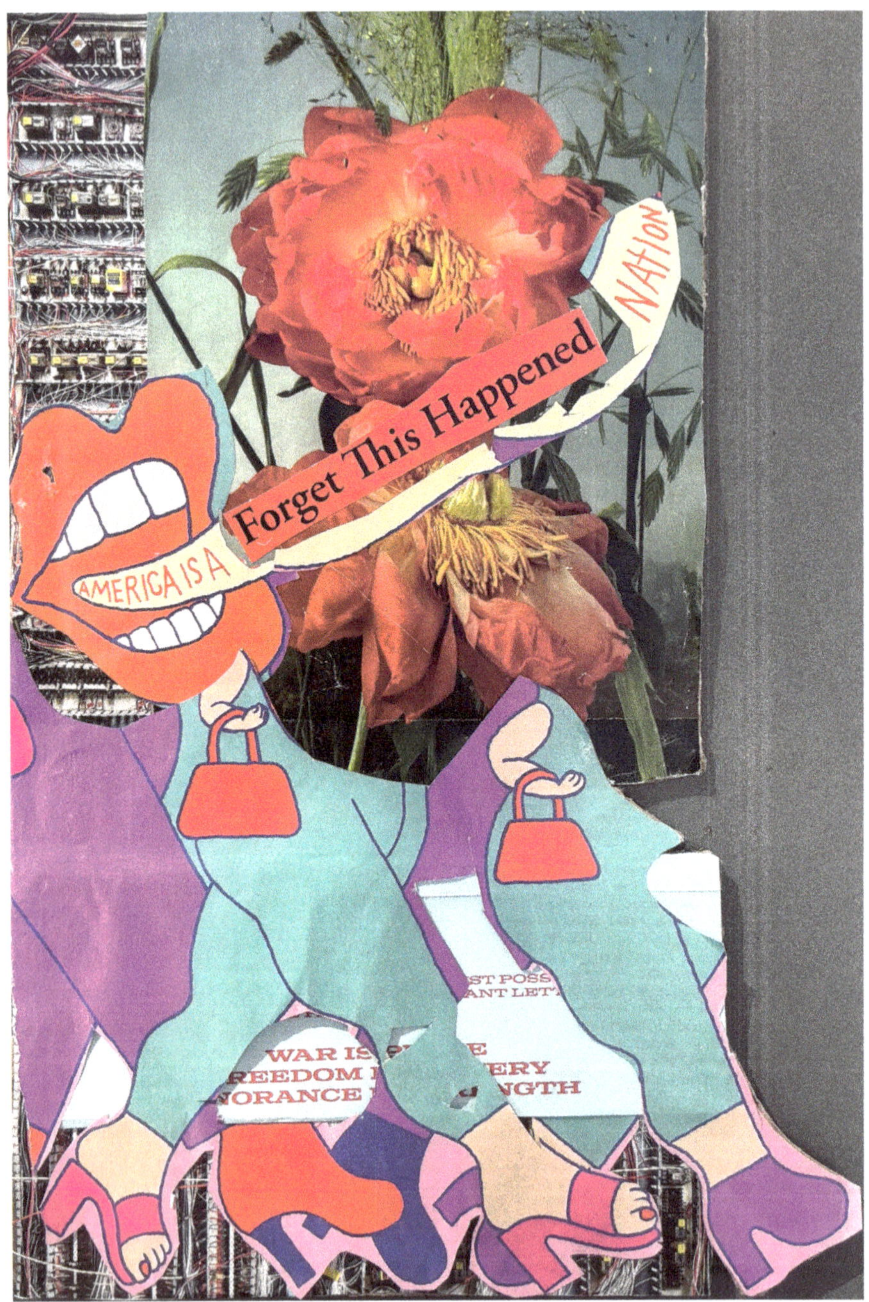


## HEADLINES

*Magazine and found paper on cardboard, 11.5 in x 7.75 in*

**KATHERINE SLOAN**

QUEENS, NEW YORK

## A DATE WITH UNCLE SAM

He wants me. But what could he possibly want? I've still got pretty good legs so I'll shave for the first time in years and buy a new pair of stockings. I'll pumice my heels till they're as soft as a baby and the silk won't snag.

The way he points. So direct. Demanding even. Yet, I'm thrilled. A little uneasy, quivery feeling in my stomach. So I'll get my hair set in curls and sleep with my entire head wrapped in a scarf. Should I wear high heels even though I'm unsteady? For him, I will. I like to be desired.

I'll slather my skin till it's oily with cold cream. I want to be as smooth as possible. Maybe a new shade of lipstick will suit me. It is spring, after all. Pale pink? No: melon pink. Fleshy as the insides of a ripe cantaloupe.

But what will I wear? A new dress. Maybe even a hat—if that's still the fashion. Gloves? He seems to favor them.

And what shall I call him when we meet? Sam, I should think. "Uncle" is a bit too familiar.

## MARK HOEFER

SAN DIEGO, CALIFORNIA

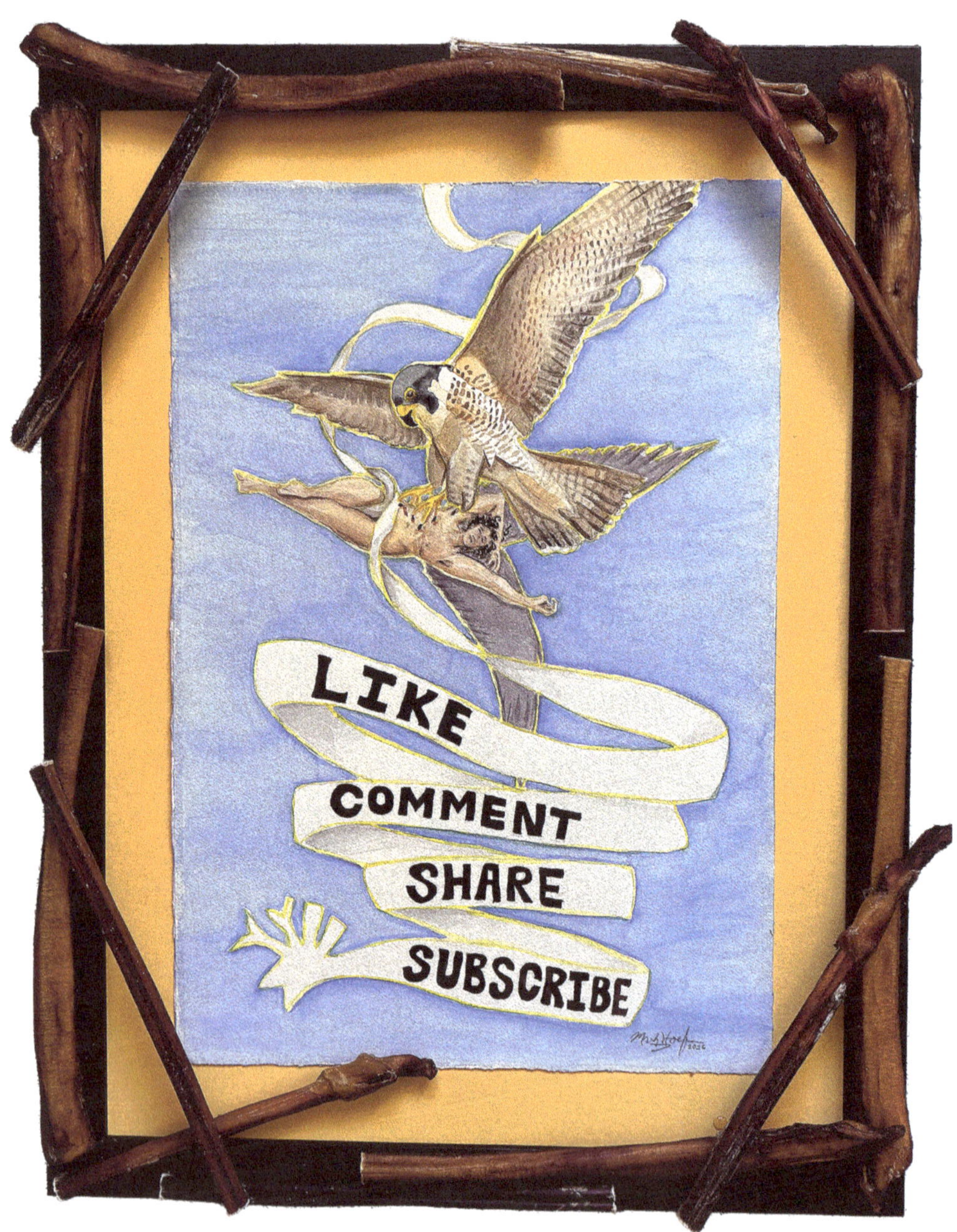


**HIGH SPEED DISCONNECTION**

*Mixed media: watercolor, my human blood, dried bull phalluses, 18 in x 24 in (framed)*

**THOMAS FUCALORO**
STATEN ISLAND, NEW YORK

# ON FACEBOOK 2 PROFESSORS/POETS DISCUSS HOW THEY ARE LIVING PAYCHECK TO PAYCHECK ON 6-FIGURE SALARIES, AND WHO ARE CONSTANTLY POSTING ABOUT HOW EVERYONE ON THIS PLATFORM SHOULD BE LIVING THEIR LIVES

Social media has allowed us to see the version of our lives
that test audiences haven't even screened yet. Like film
we scroll through what you want us to know and
from what I can tell, you all have been living
the good life from classy trips to far-off places
to pictures of luxurious dates with the finest food
while you show us photos, memes, and other
people's words about the conflict in Palestine
and then you share some status about how you
are living paycheck to paycheck off a 6-figure salary
and I don't know what the narrative is here
and I often wish there was a "hide from tone-deaf posts"
button so I wouldn't have as much chronic anxiety,
and as a poet I have flipping chronic anxiety
so, I understand the plight of these 2 poets
but some people are really in that sweet spot
of the American C.R.A.E.A.M., where Cash Rules
and Assumes Everything Around Me and they just need
to figure out what they have lost inside themselves
so, they can reclaim that shit, because we are the problem
even if we like to post we ain't. I am the problem. Even if
this poem ain't. I will never post this poem because I have
no backbone of my own. I am a deer behind a keyboard
behind the lack thereof. A lost object. A constant chronic.
My greatest strength is knowing where I came from
and knowing that I don't have to return. My greatest
strength is returning.

**SILVIO SEVERINO**

CORK, IRELAND

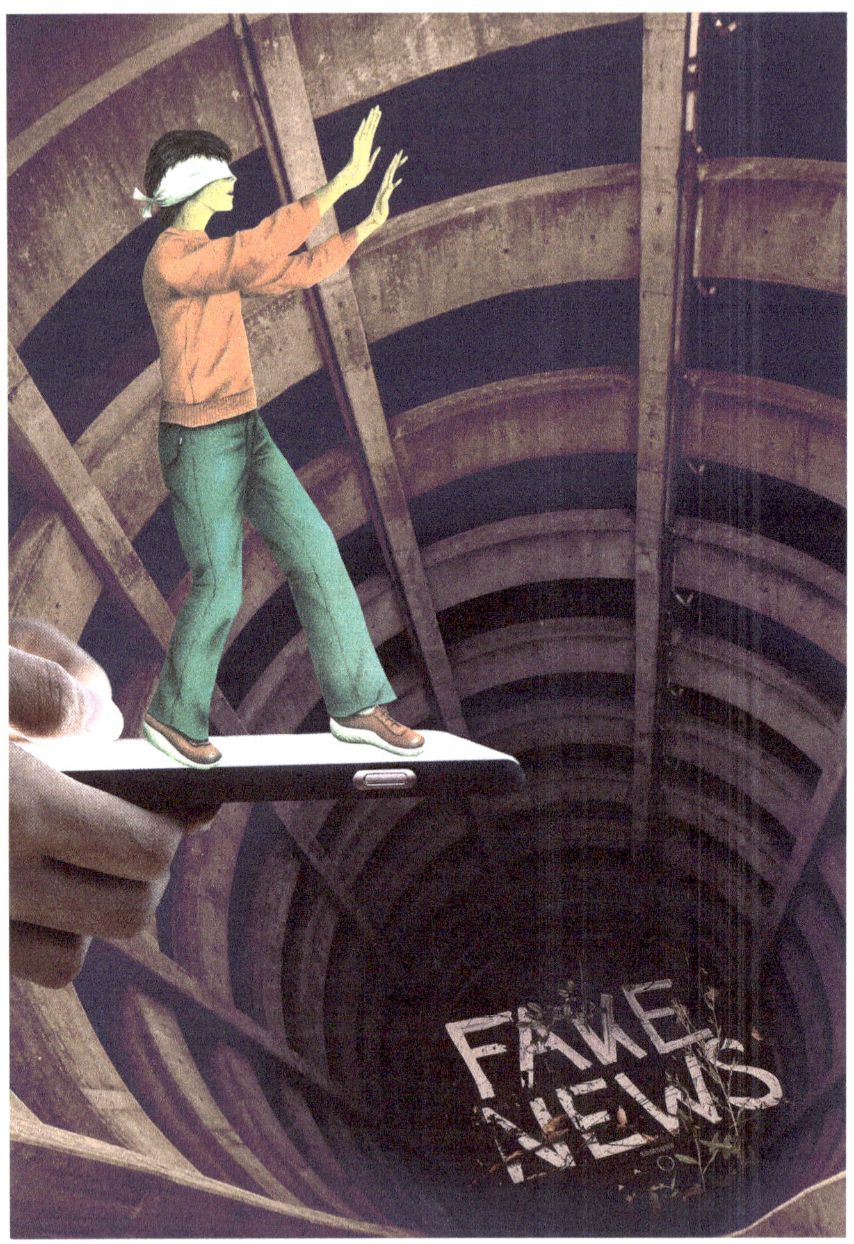


**FAKE NEWS**

*Digital collage, A4*

**UCHE NDUKA**
BROOKLYN, NEW YORK

## ROCKING LEDGE

Being artsy has
become rather obnoxious lately
a fool a tool a mule
I'll like to see where this goes
the card counter knows
how the fire started
welcome to American desolation
a windy day beggared of asterisks
such is the conceit that catches me
in flagrante with a trombone
you're in a pants suit most of the time
speaking your truth
the heat of the matter isn't limited to identity
I'll like to get to ignition point as quick as possible
you have no idea how beautiful it is to not
be watching your back constantly
there's nothing more fabulous than
waiting for the fabulous
such effect induces a kind of cavalier mood
it isn't a matter of settling down in this house or another

## BARRANCA VOS

SAN FRANCISCO, CALIFORNIA

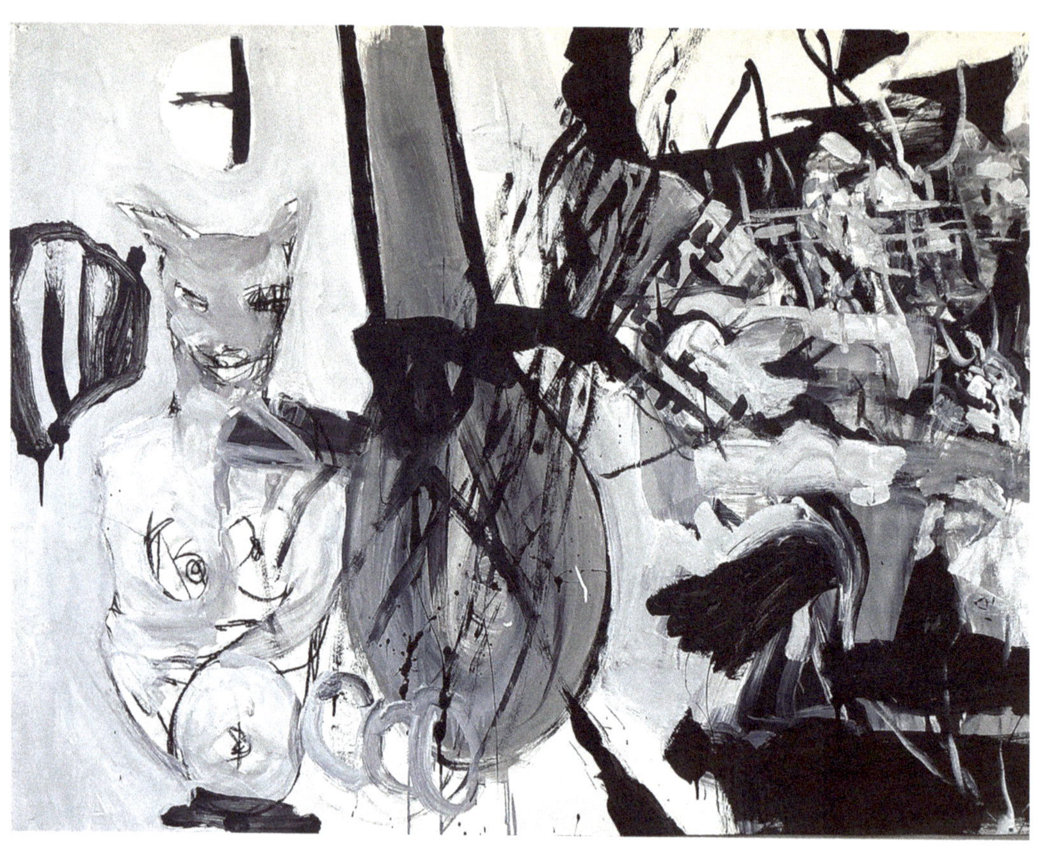

**UNTITLED**

*Painting, 30 in x 40 in*

**AUSTIN ALEXIS**
NEW YORK, NEW YORK

## PROPAGATE

Say what you want to be true.
Say it as many times as possible.
Say it as loud as you can.
Say it, spraying clear oxygen
    with stained spittle.
Say it until your tongue
    nearly drops from your tired mouth.
Say it until other people hear nothing else.
Say it till it stinks the air.
Say it so it's visible like a headline
    or a billboard or a drone.
Drone on and on.
Dangle the words like a flag
    too heavy for its pole.
Drive the language forward,
    never reversing.
Ditto the phrases.
Darlings of the globe,
your words will shine,
will tickle the asses
    of the masses,
will live in living rooms,
thrive in bedrooms,
rule in boardrooms,
will establish lies as the utter truth.

## JOHN PAUL

BROOKLYN, NEW YORK

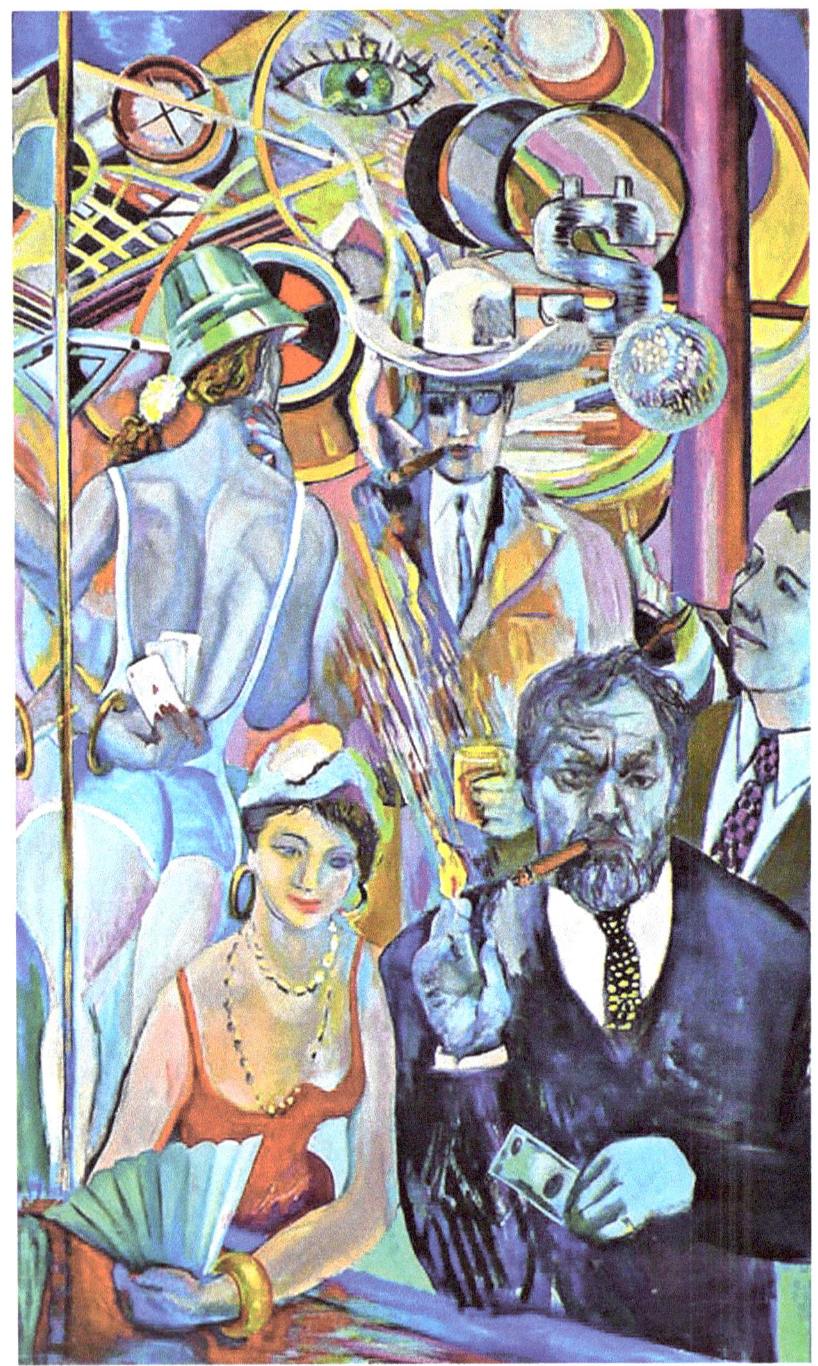

**EYE IN THE SKY**

*Oil on canvas, 80 in x 44 in*

**ROBERT C. FORD**
NEW YORK, NEW YORK

## MORE DOCTORS SMOKE CAMELS

Baptized in blue light
We kneel to the algorithm
Scrolling sermons in all caps

"SOURCED FROM THE EARTH"
"PROMOTES FOCUS AND CLARITY"
"SUPPORTS WEIGHT MANAGEMENT"
"DO YOUR OWN RESEARCH"

Influencers in borrowed robes
Preach urgency
Thumbs raised in blessing
Eyes fixed on the count

A like for a like
A share for salvation
Their lies goes forth
And multiply

The masses drink deeply
From wells with no source
Typing "Amen" with fire emojis

Blessed are the shared
For they shall inherit the timeline

Meanwhile, the truth
Sits cold and naked
On a rusty fire escape
A cigarette between her lips
Coughing alone in the dark

**MARTA JANIK**

WARSAW, POLAND

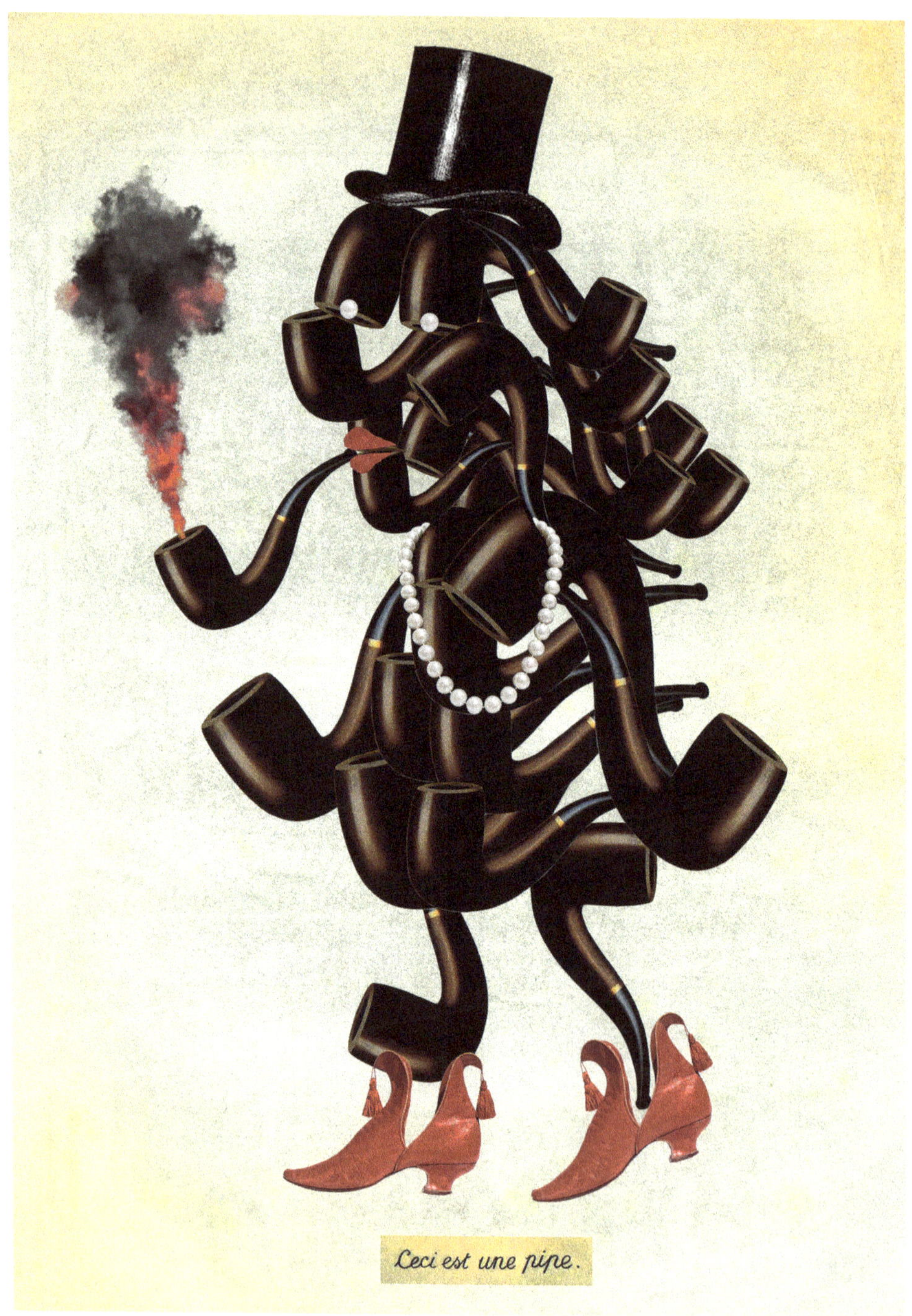


**I AM A PIPE!**

*Digital collage*

**MAW SHEIN WIN**

EL CERRITO, CALIFORNIA

## SMOKE

once he became a puppet, it was too late
he started doing all he was told to do

so then lies became truths & truths became lies
with his wooden hand he wrote false words in red

late at night regrets would haunt his wooden mind
he signed a contract with the puppet master

he thought he ruled, he thought he was a real boy
he lost a part of himself, gone in thick smoke

**DEREK ADAMS**

SUDBURY, UNITED KINGDOM

## ICONS

Remember –
anyone can turn
the gears of thought,
exchange sparks
between like minds—
link themselves
to a theory's
Fata Morgana,

while facts slip,
silent, ignored,
bound to old
worn assumptions—

these icons,
move between
what's said and unseen –
they're never just born
merely invented.

## RADOSLAV ROCHALLYI

BŘECLAV, CZECH REPUBLIC

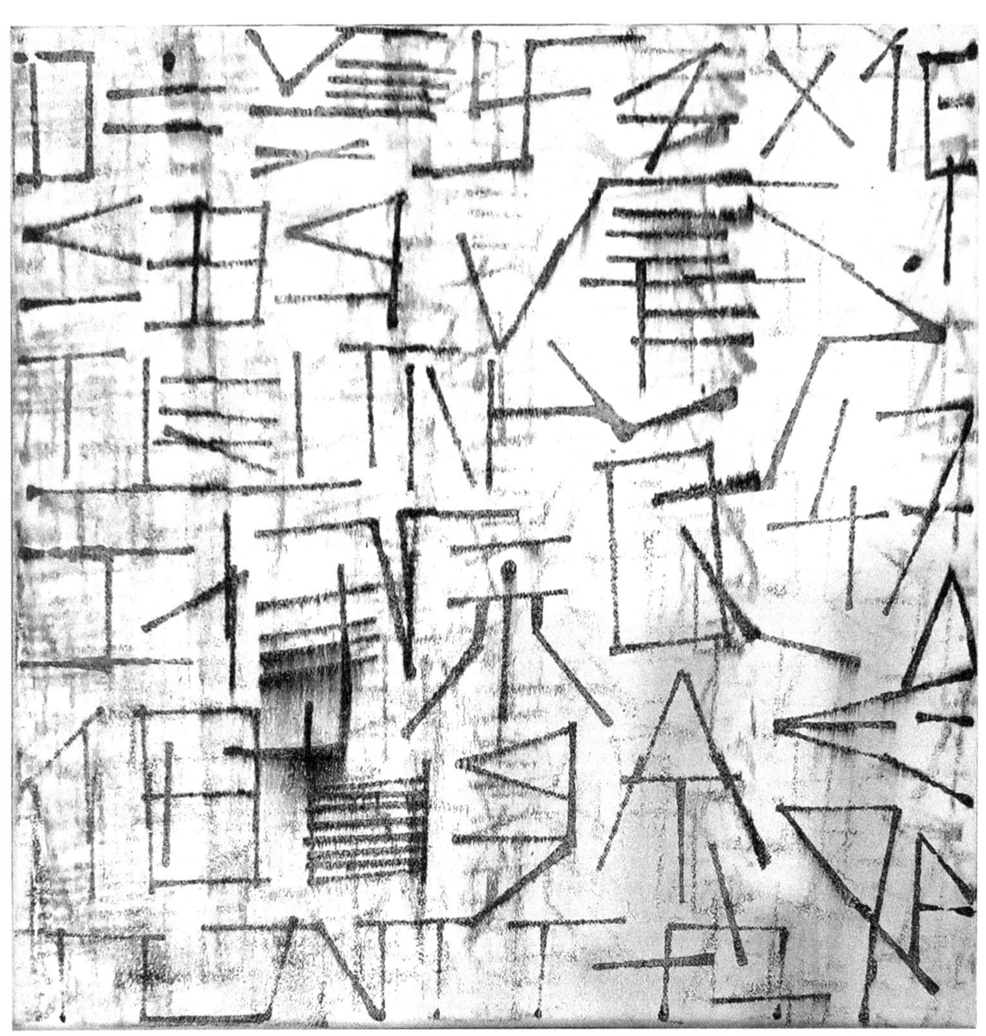

### LANDAU

*Acrylic on canvas, 50 cm x 50 cm*

## SABINE REMY

DÜSSELDORF, GERMANY

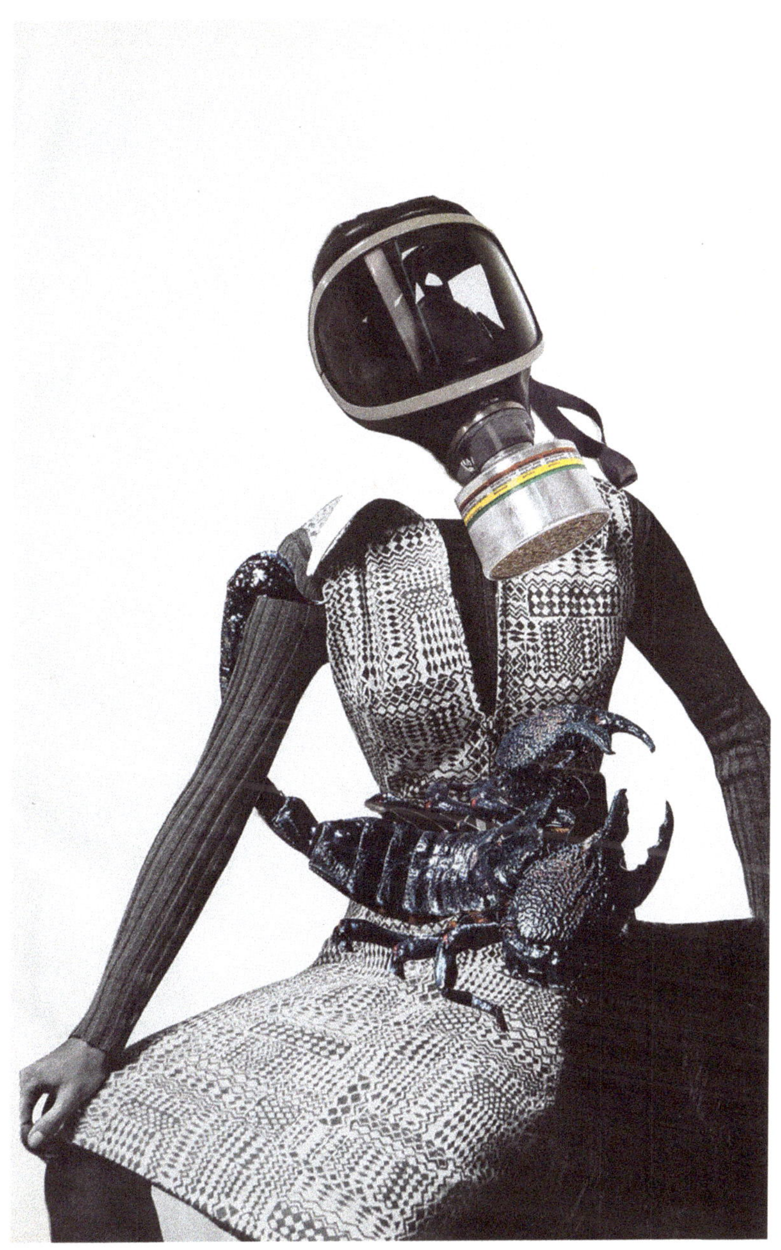

**SCORPION**

*Analog paper collage, 40 cm x 30 cm*

## HEGEDŰS 2 LÁSZLÓ

CSÁKBERÉNY, HUNGARY

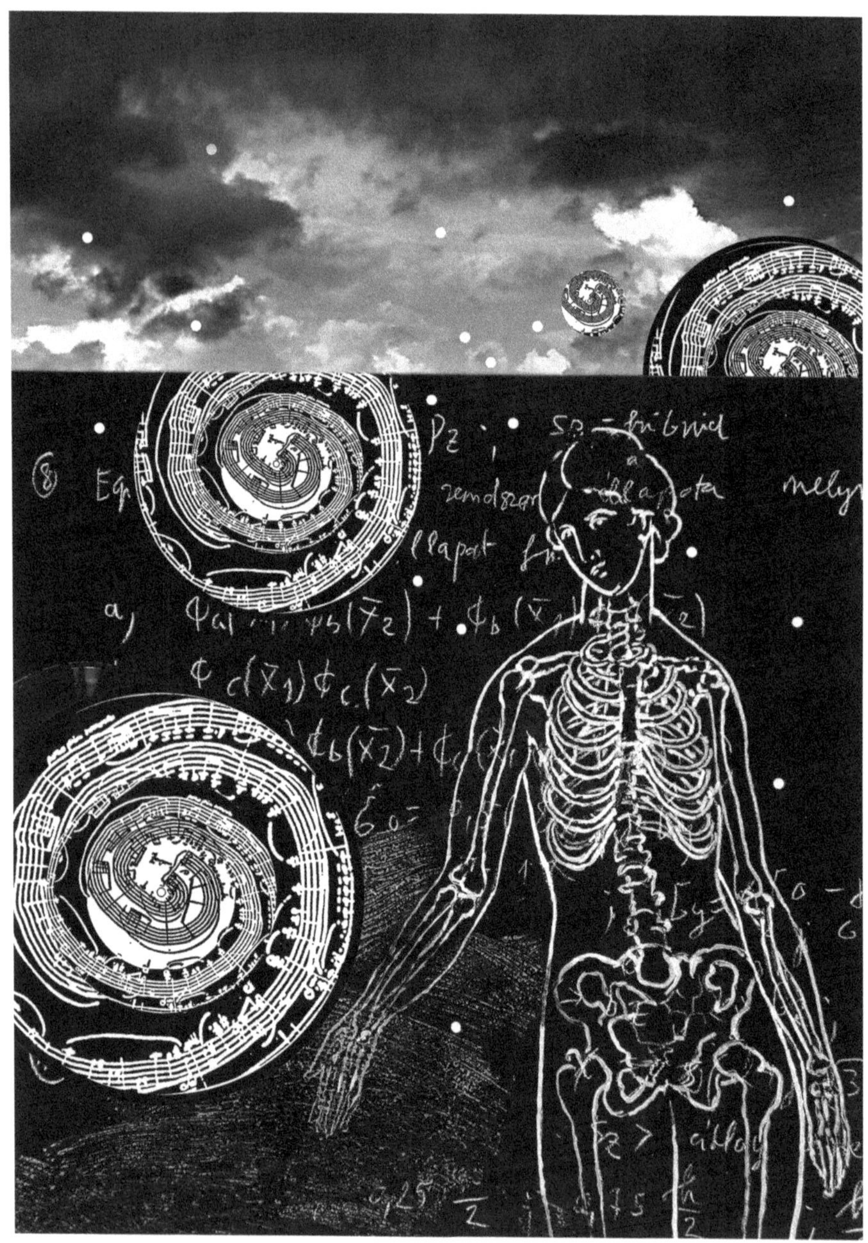

### COMPOSITION ON THE TOPIC

*Digital print, 70 cm X 50 cm*

**MARK DeCARTERET**

RYE, NEW HAMPSHIRE

## THE YEAR I WENT WITHOUT FEELING LEFT OUT

To be so empty I attempted to say so. As some other not. Tempted to say anything. Not yet found. In the previously thought. Vapor is like this. The mist almost insists. And some poetry. When written by a priest-type. Or semi-professional. Once, I crossed over to where the gods were not so. High-strung and full-of-themselves. You are no less they insisted as well. You are whittled from sacred wood. A door with the soul of a window. So let the plowed-under finally step out to bow. Help themselves to our air. When it's not being. Rain-like. Even rain. They needed seven men to play me. In the movie version of my life. How many times have I told you. The camera-eye making a beeline for my pastry. This is getting old. Me yet to feel. The world toying with me. Something laughable. Falling from my face. Hell, it's not stealing, little person. It's everlasting sharing. A rash of metaphysical break-ins. Suffering is not a phase. It's that moot point on the horizon. One zero put painlessly atop another. There's an art to it. Taking back all that one has phrased. As merely hypothetical. Put on. I must confess. I can't breathe with this thing on. And the cave wall is touting. Nothing but memories. Lies. My many lives stilled to these infinite time-outs. Or this dream where any line I've made up. Can fit any occasion. Heaven is like this. Relief coming. Not so much as a lack. Of whatever. But with the heart written out of it. For its own sake. And the sake of its beating. And the sake of it being.

## FRIE J. JACOBS

ZOERSEL, BELGIUM

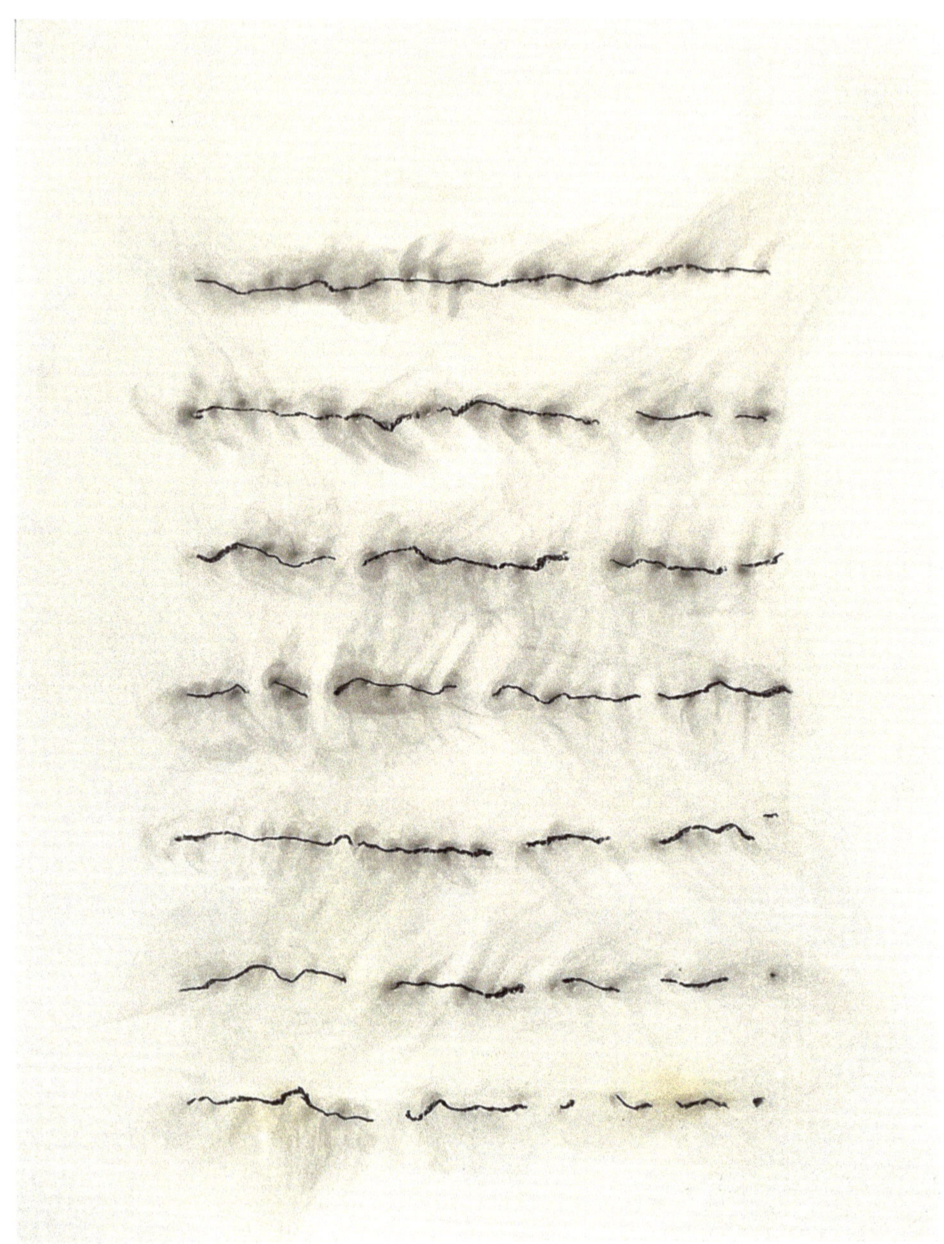

### WORDS ARE A DETOUR AROUND WHAT THERE IS REALLY TO SAY - THE LETTER

*Fire and wind and charcoal on paper 32 cm x 24 cm*

## ALEXEY ADONIN

JERUSALEM, ISRAEL

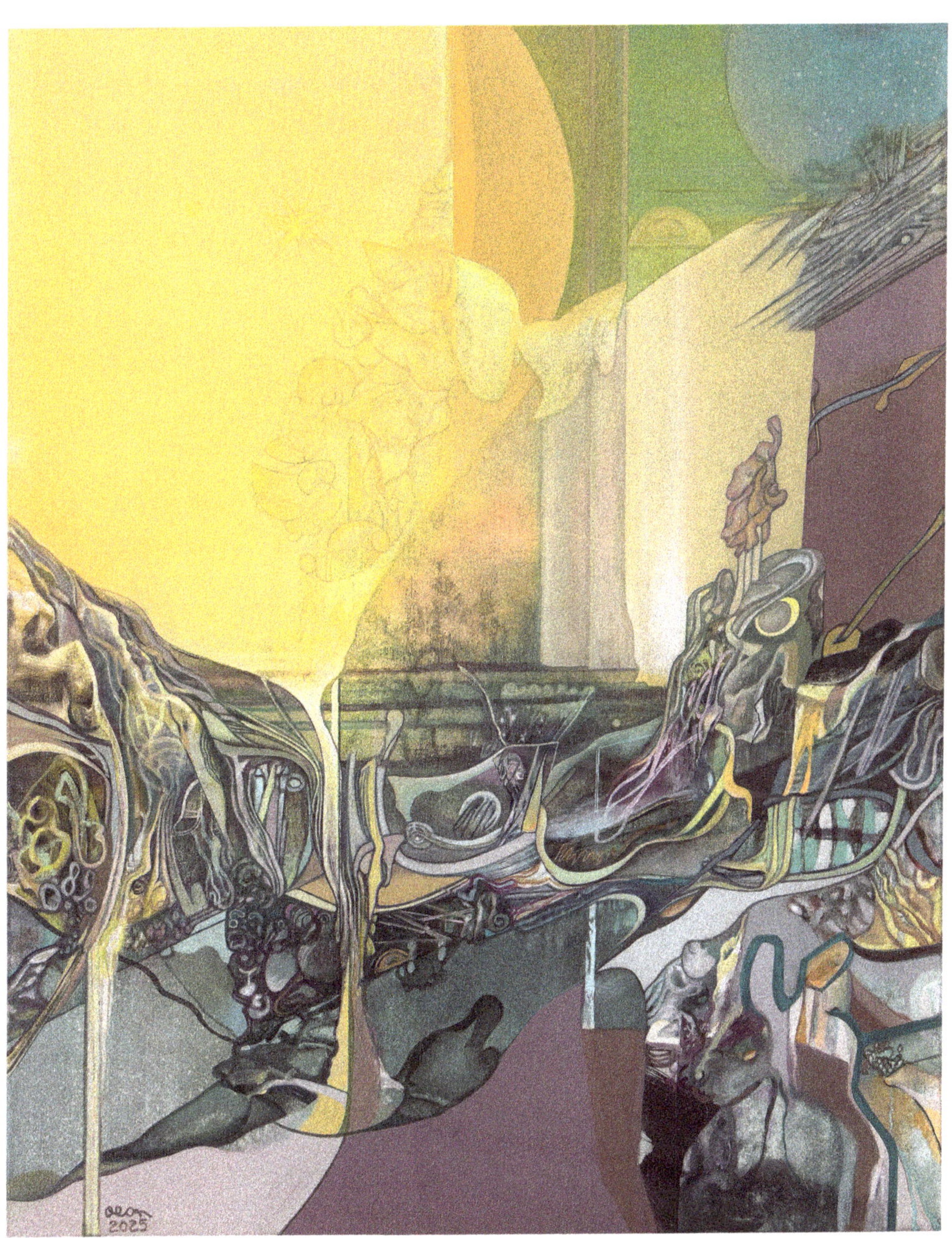

### EGGSCAPE

*Oil on canvas, mounted on a wooden stretcher frame, 80 cm x 100 cm*

## DARIO ROBERTO DIOLI

LANDRIANO, ITALY

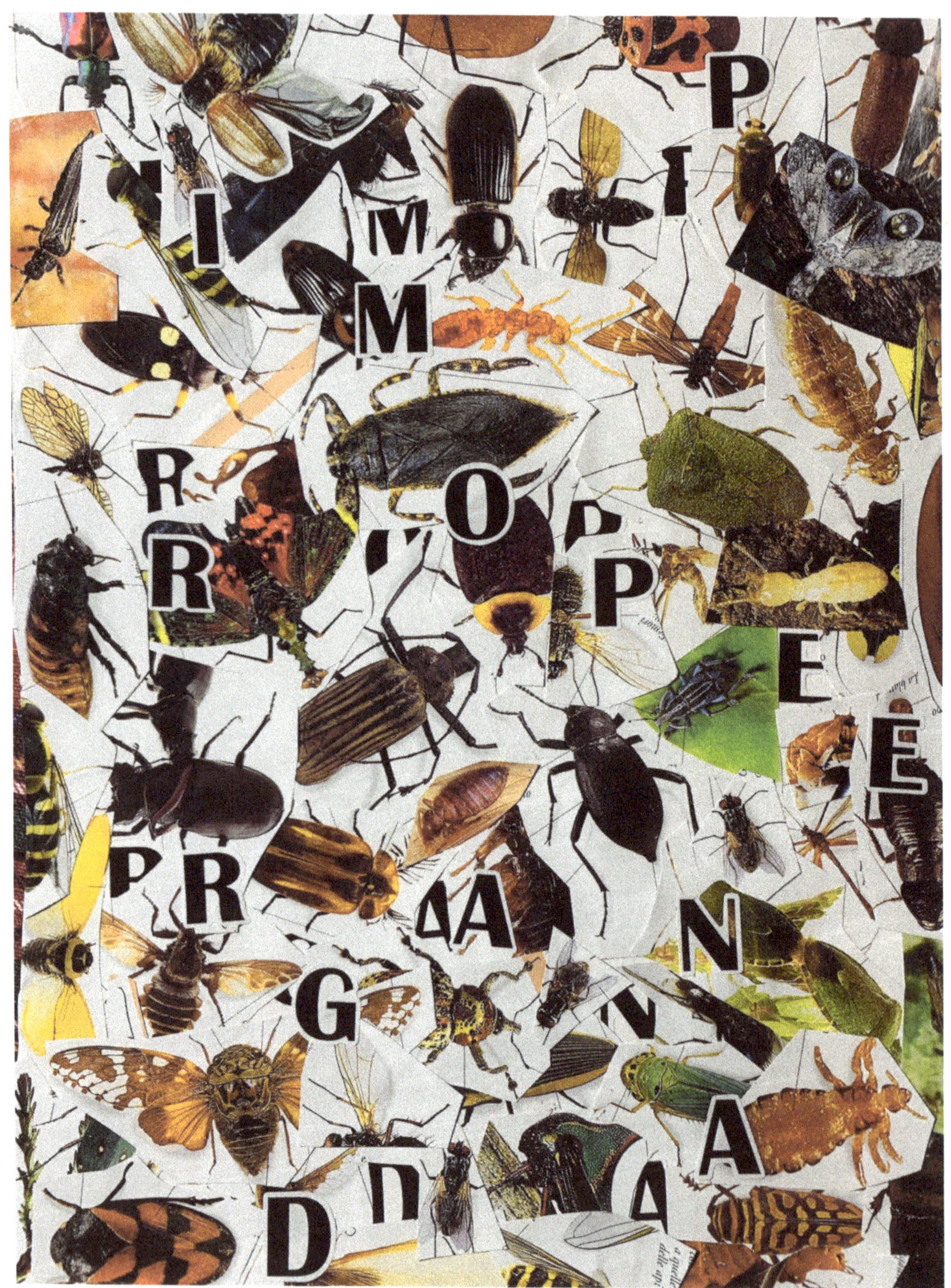

### EATING IMPROPERGANDA

*Collage on paper, A4*

**THOMAS STOLMAR**
SAN FRANCISCO, CALIFORNIA

## TRUMPFYA®
## (GEEZERKUMAB)

We Won The War! War is over! I won War! You One War!
Everyone Won War! A War of Won! We One! Hooray!
While we are still launching huge deadly missiles into Iran!
I-ran the War into the dirt & blood of pulverized people!
But what did you win, Donny Dickhead? You Asshole!
Did ya win the Ignoble Piss Prize? Did ya win an Award
for killing 150 little Iranian schoolgirls in Tehran?
You sick fucker! Did you win
something, Chump?

That's a way I used to be frequently feelin', but now
after an easy course of intravenous TRUMPFYA I'm feelin'
like so much butter! I couldn't sleep anymore, couldn't even
read... my own thoughts! Until TRUMPFYA saved my life!
It really works! I took the pills and now I'm a Big Dick! (too!)
I Won The World Peace Prize! I'm almost Republican & I'm
sleeping again like a baby, a dead baby! Endless dead bodies
are now cleared away! I landed my ship on this distant
plateau & just walked away like a Free White Man.
TRUMPFYA's really working on me! I'm a happy,
productive man-boy again! War is One, We're Won
Over a Barrel Making a Killing Selling Oil!
Hooray for Us! We War-1-4-Ever!
It really working! I'm highly
re-com-mend-
-ing, eat!

*TRUMPFYA® is available at TrumpRx: Free to Christian Citizens of U.S. w/certified TrumpCards & Golden Visas!

*Digital Rectal Insertion & All-Points Penetration required w/ Chip-Reader for nonresidents.

**BIBIANA PADILLA MALTOS**

WESTMINSTER, CALIFORNIA

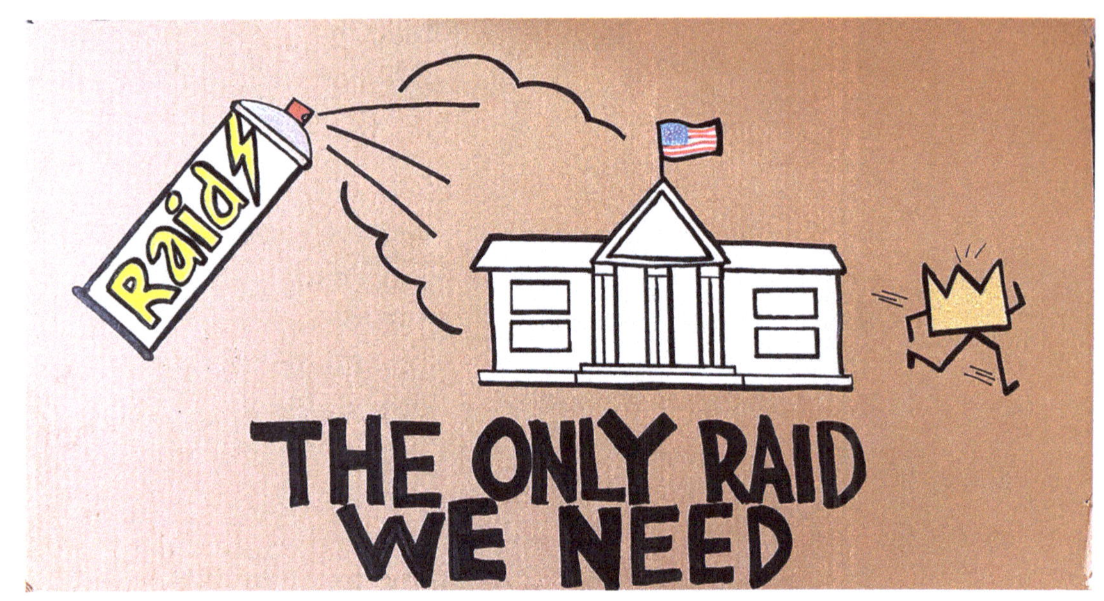


**THE ONLY RAID WE NEED**

*Digital image*

**DAVID BARNES**
PARIS, FRANCE

## NOON DAY DEMONS

– what is there left to be said?
When a rapist holds the most powerful office on the planet
moral words lose their traction
There is no mask to strip away!
Words and all currencies depreciate but bitcoin
Only devaluing attack holds its value
though even that must erode with over use
Before, the children of Gaza were dying because American high imperial strategists commanded it;
now the children of Gaza are dying and it's not even for the greater good of General Motors.
The lord of misrule seizes the chance to speculate in reckless real estate
acts in solidarity with demagogues, dictators,
follows his fellow-feeling with the corrupt.
Like some 19th century gunboat diplomacist learning what he can get away with
he kills and he kidnaps he sends his ships to a high noon showdown.
– did Mussolini, Hitler look so clownish so inept in their day?
The boot Orwell saw forever stamping on a human face
And in 2028, our dictator-elect, will he go quietly?
There is no law but me, he says
Power is no longer for something
save acting out – grievance, vengeance, plunder, ransack, rape
Power is cash dollars dollars dollars
Power is shitting in a gold toilet
Is adding insult to injury, adding lethal injury to insult
Power is signing orders that kill just because
So what? So what to do in your corner of the shitshow?
Fight like Minneapolis

**VALERY OISTEANU**
NEW YORK, NEW YORK

## METAPHYSICAL DILEMMA IN MINNESOTA

Like a wrinkled poet starring into the abyss,
Waiting for the algorithm to solve the paradox.
Did God ask to love the unloved?
Just like "White Rose" ghosts of the fighters
Against the blackshirts of the '30s in Berlin,
Renee Good and Alex Pretti were killed for a cause,
Martyrs of nonviolent revolution,
Assassinated staving off the camo-gestapo,
Suicide by kindness, bullets for the radiant skull.
The revolution is being televised, starring MAGA mobs,
Ubu Roi possums in military gear
Dragging naked strangers and babies
To new internment camps,
Shooting Latinos on crowded highways,
Cleansing the silenced neighborhoods.
"No obras la porta!" screams the father
To his wife, sacrificing his 5-year-old son.
There are no more words, even less speaking.
Ubu Roi was dropped, run to the streets
Tap-dance the revolution
Before the jails will melt,
Before we survive the undreamt truth.

## MATINA VOSSOU

ATHENS, GREECE

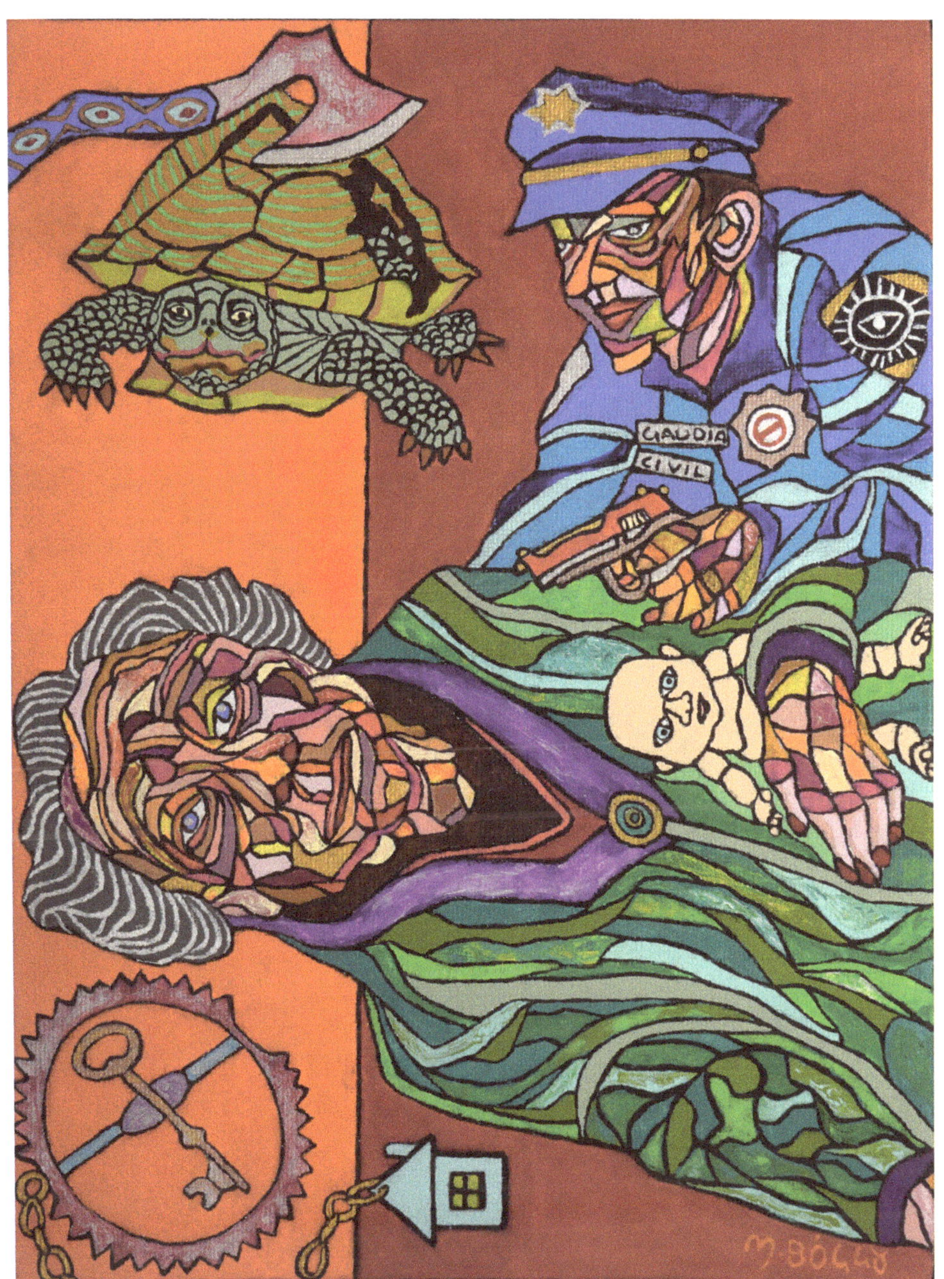


## THE EVICTION

*Acrylic on canvas board, 24 cm x 18 cm*

## MILANA JUVENTA

IN TRANSIT

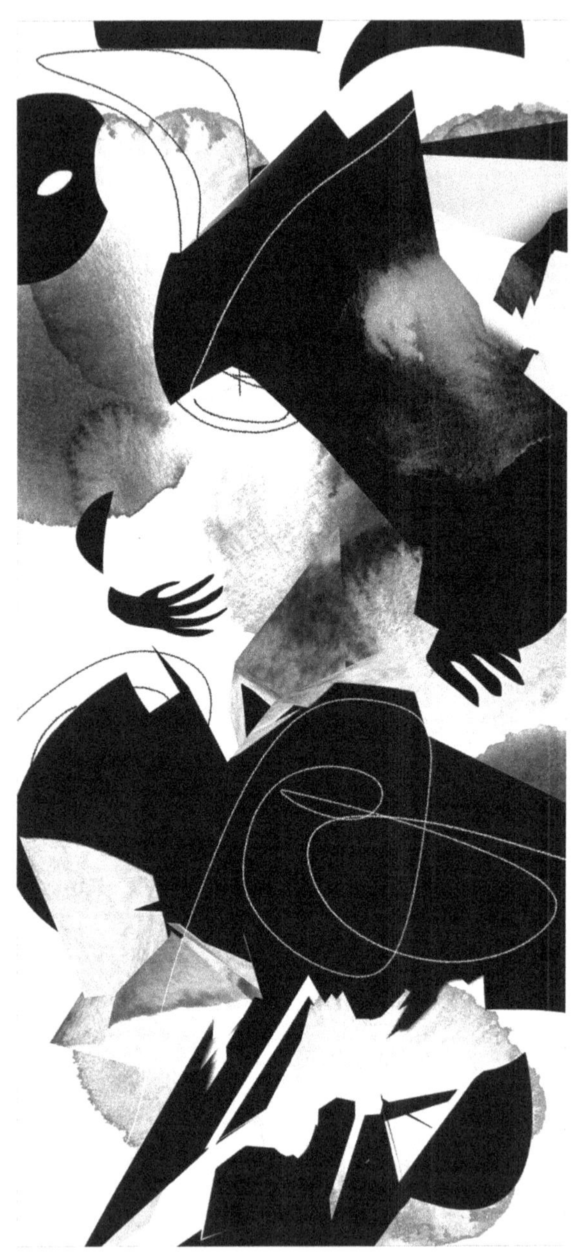

**CORPUS LUCIDUM**

*Digital art*

**LYNNEA VILLANOVA**
BROOKLYN, NEW YORK

# OPPROBRIUM PABLUM

whole food facts
too tough to chew

slogan sandwiches
scorn salads

bites of sound bites
blended to a mealy mess
of opprobrium pablum

swallowed wholesale

without chewing

news reduced
to emotion morsels

churns and turns
into digestive slime

feeding the swamp mind

some of the slurry
regurgitates
unfiltered
unprocessed by
the lily livered

the residual mucilage-fusillade

the gutless absorb

it drains
circulates
pumps upward

invades the blood brain border

then builds a wall
of perceived imperviousness
around the marshy tripe tropes

well partitioned mushy minds
sink to deep states
of thought-less somnolence
from which there is no woking

Discriminating digestors
thinking eaters

naturally resist the swamp-awash brains

the gut feelers
spoon-fed spoonfuls of pap
who confuse and tire easily

Do Your Own Research

You Will Not Replace Us

**VALERIE SOFRANKO**
PITTSBURGH, PENNSYLVANIA

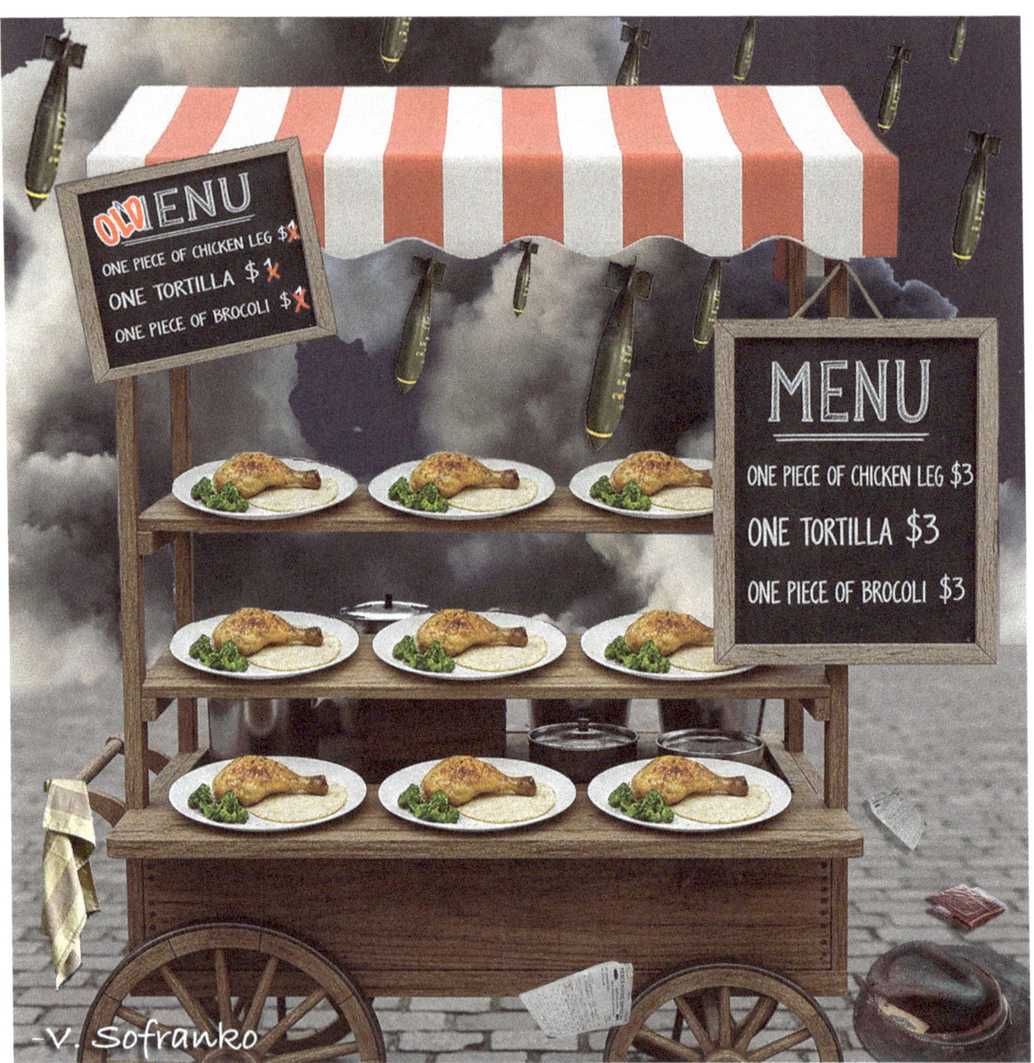


**FOOD STAND**

*Digital collage, 14.22 in x 14.22 in*

**JOANIE HF ZOSIKE**
NEW YORK, NEW YORK

## CONDITIONS 2026

Ships pull up into foreign harbors.
I give thanks it's not New York Harbor.

Helicopters circle Venezuelan oil fields.
I give thanks we don't have Manhattan oil fields.

The presidents of various lands, land their
jets in countries not their own, to determine

the fate of countries they want, or think
they need to control, or own. Real estate.

The people of countries under siege sit in
piles of detritus and destruction, grieving for

their lost loved ones, homes; their minds
destroyed, their ears dimmed by bombs.

Governments turn assault rifles, gas, bombs
on their own citizens, blaming said citizens

for their own wounds, murders, rapes. It is
they who brought destruction on themselves

by objecting to the circumstances of their lives.
If they don't object, they feel they have no lives.

ICE is flowing down streets of major U.S. cities.
I give thanks I don't often go outside my walls.

Not anymore. No more roaming, not morning
or night; I'm huddled in the subway terminal,

hiding out of the light, that I may not see the
dawn of martial law and tyranny in this land.

But it seeps down the walls and crawls into
cracks of foundations, civility weeps.

When the mangled eagle lands, it's hell to pay.
When the piñata breaks open, the candy falls.

It rots our teeth and makes us fat, but tastes
delicious. We are safe, right? Protected, right?

We are secure, as Monsieur Voltaire said, in
"this best of all possible worlds."

## SABINA OEHNINGER

LUZERN, SWITZERLAND

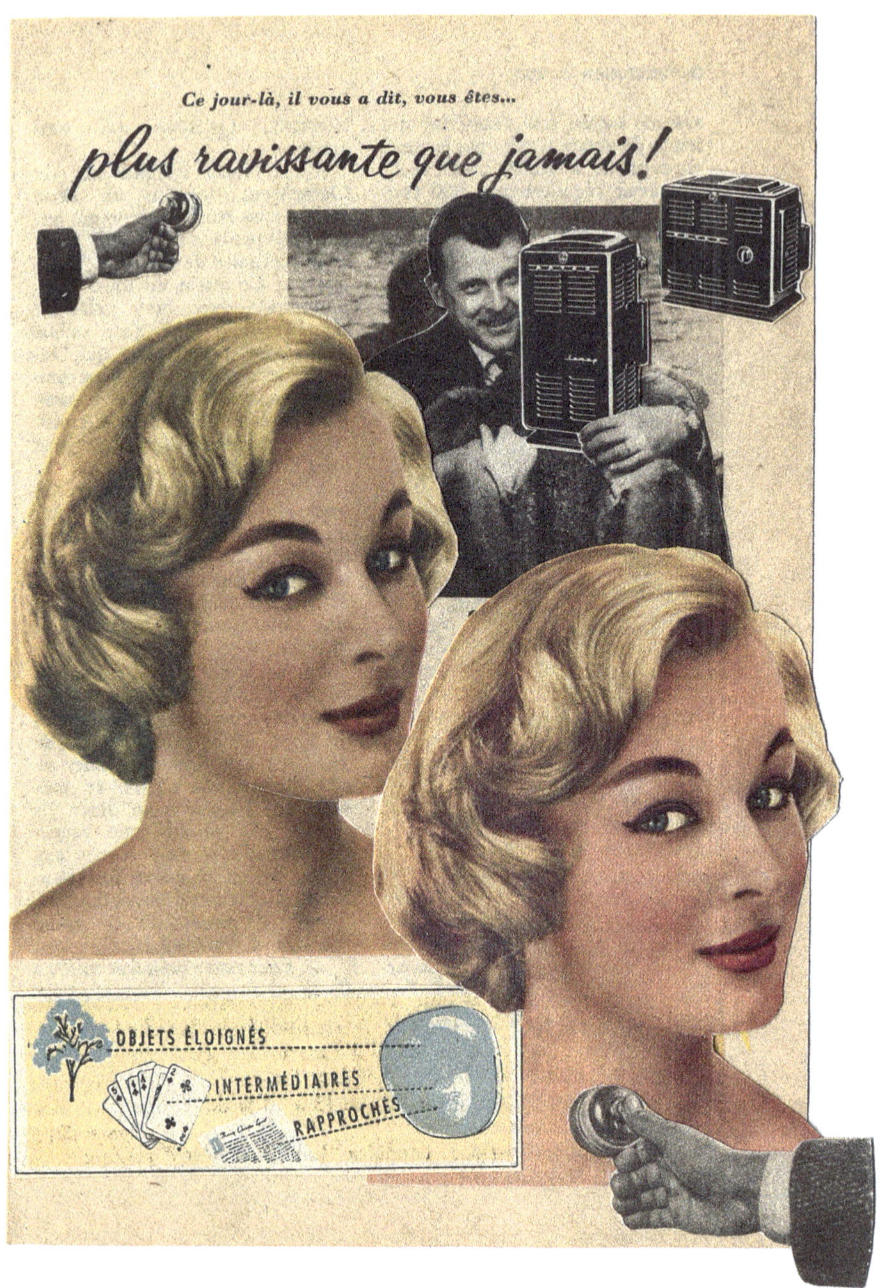


**PLUS RAVISSANTE QUE JAMAIS**

*Collage, 190 mm x 133 mm*

**VOXX VOLTAIR**
LAS VEGAS, NEVADA

## MYTH AMERICA

Surely, this was not the purpose of letters
To contort themselves
Into lewd shapes
Sinister sentences
Which attack my my eyes
On the daily

Mercury, at the heels of Daphne
Chasing her thru millennia
It has ever been thus, never changing

In the bitter years of age
Those, protected by power and fear
Bring us here

Islands of old men
Force their will
On the children of Saturn
Who always has Time
To kill

**RON KOLM**
LONG ISLAND CITY, NEW YORK

## TRUMP WORSHIPS WOMEN

Yeah, Trump says he loves women,
Epstein told us so.
But let's not forget that he hired,
Then fired Lori Chavez-DeRemer,
Kristi Noem and Pam Bondi.
And now he's threatening
To dispossess all women
Who try to vote
Using their married last names
Unless they change them
To Trump!

**JESSE McCLOSKEY**

NEW YORK, NEW YORK

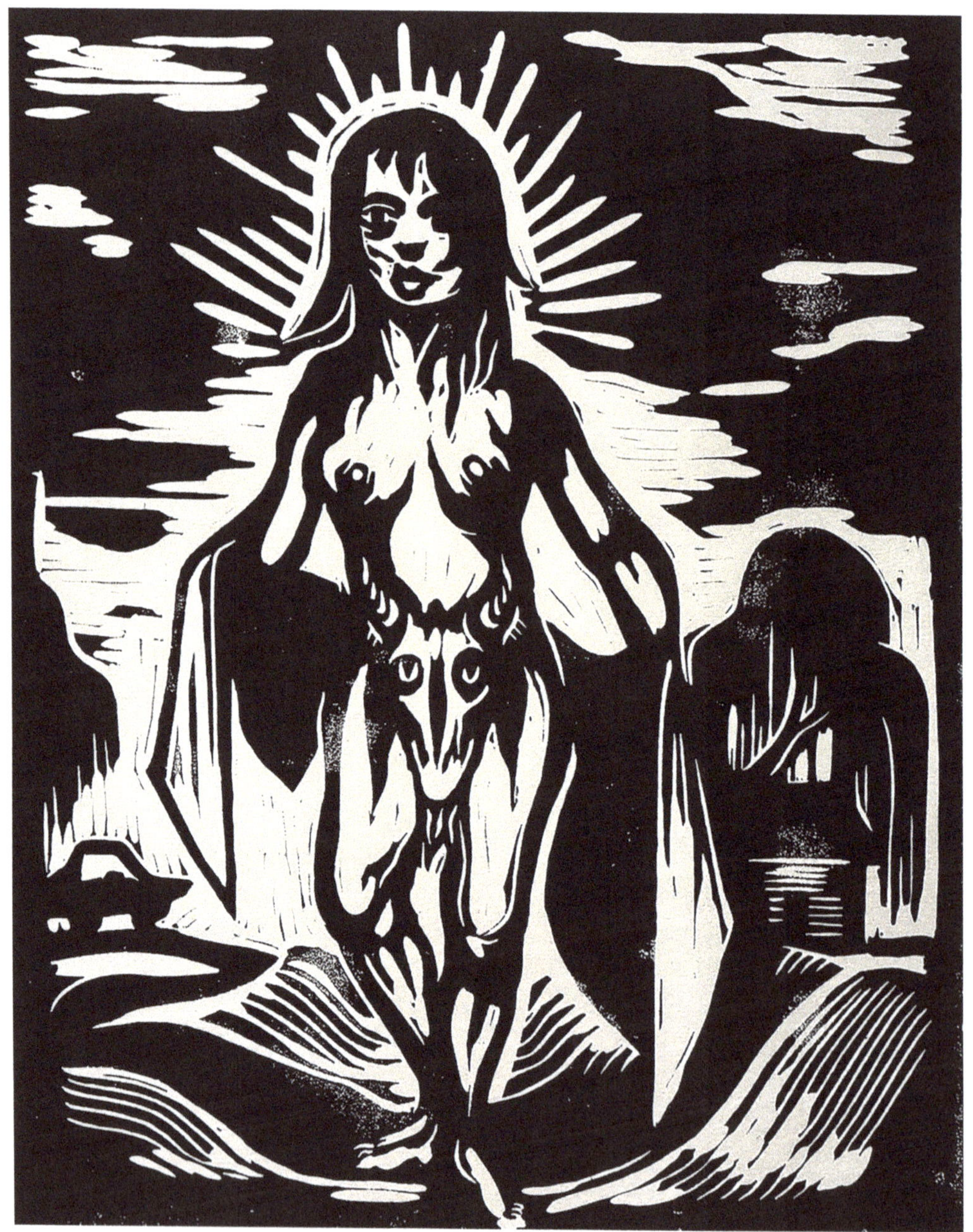

**THE LADY TRUTH**

*Print on paper, 9 in x 12 in*

**GERALD NICOSIA**
KNOXVILLE, TENNESSEE

## LEARNING TO DO WITHOUT

The orange-faced monster egotist in the crumbling White House
Says we must do without so many dolls for our children
And e'en forego our pencils
But I rarely use them anyway
I've learned to use a computer
Like the 12-year-old Palestinian girl, Leyan, in Gaza
Who lost her right leg to an Israeli missile
And has learned to substitute a video camera
With which to document her years-long recovery
If the essence of modern life
Is learning to do without
Then how apt we have a leader who has learned
To act without intelligence or a moral compass
And that we live in a nation that no longer has
Honesty or heart
But I still struggle to write a poem
That has no human being in it
For as long as there is a poem
There is a life behind it
And as long as there is a person in each poem
The world has not
Yet ended
And that is a grace
The single grace
We cannot afford to do without.

## JEFF FARR

NEW YORK, NEW YORK

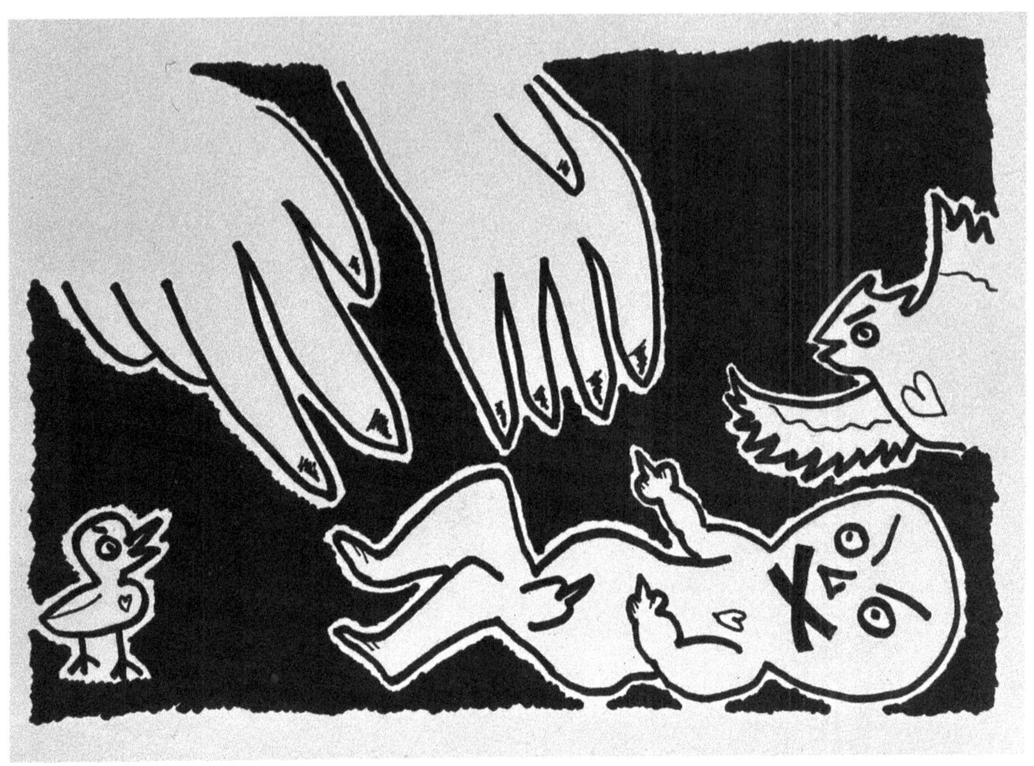

**i don't ask questions anymore**

*Ink on paper*

**PUMA PERL**
NEW YORK, NEW YORK

## UNITY

The world is overcast
The wind carries lies and deception
The sun burns violently
I wonder, for the thousandth time
*What good does a poem do?*

It carries no high-power rifles
It wears no bullet-proof vests
It can't kill the monsters
*What good does it do?*

Standing alone, it's a bunch
of black letters on white paper
Standing together in unity,
we have the power act
and turn to one another to ask
*What good can we do?*

**OWEN TOWNEND**
HUDDERSFIELD, UNITED KINGDOM

## EXCEEDINGLY TRANSFORMATIVE

They gather our words like Scrabble tiles,
to be shaken up, jumbled, extracted by request
and laid out on their board where they set the rules,
allocate the scores while claiming collaboration,
freedom of information,
though it remains their game.

It's all in their LLM, their unseen library
where nothing is bought
and everything is borrowed without asking,
without legal consequence.
It's exceedingly transformative,
their mixed bag of stolen words.

We create and share
and they make it theirs.

**SHEREE SHATSKY**

MELBOURNE, FLORIDA

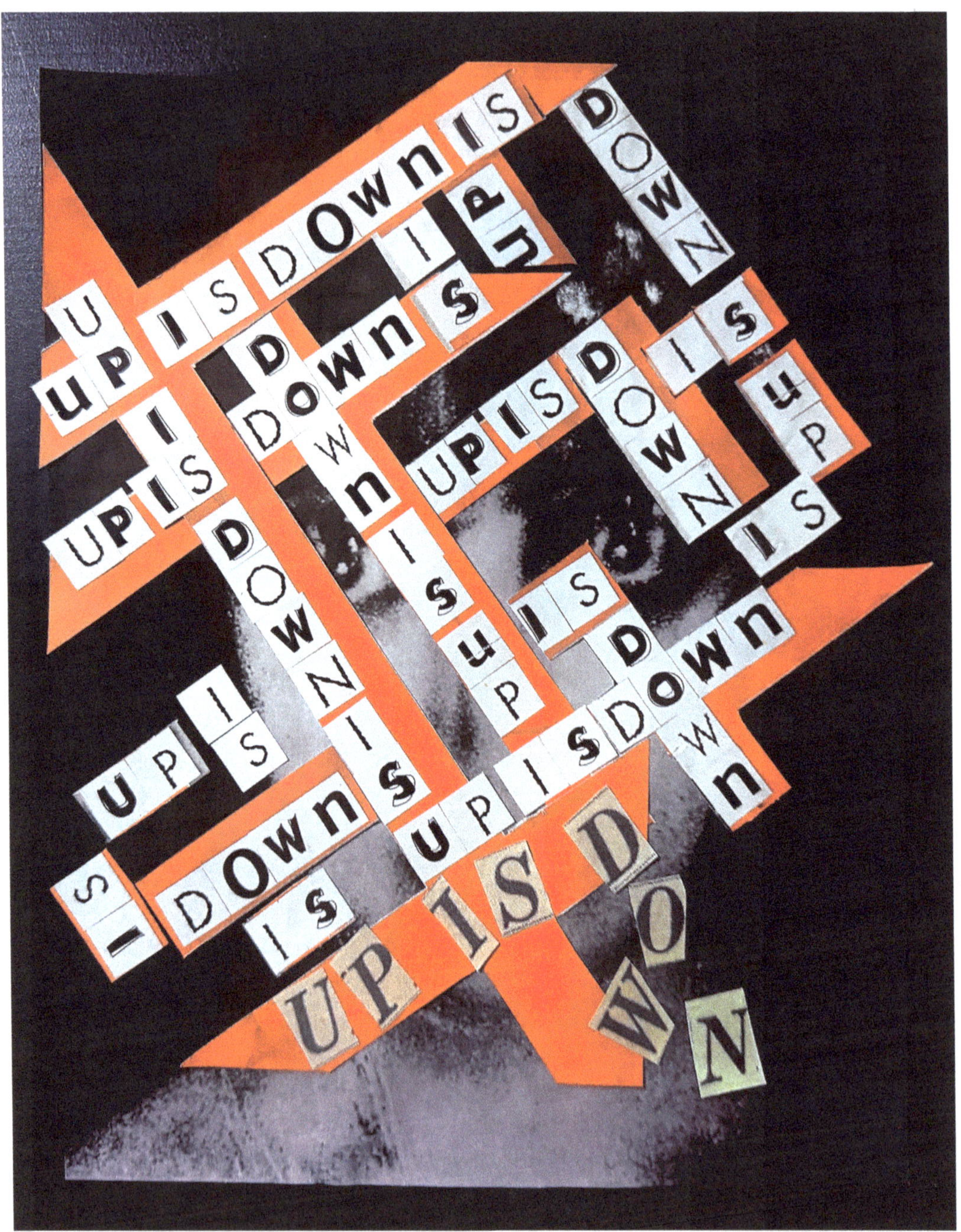


## GASLIT

*Collage on paper, found peel and stick vinyl letters repurposed on public domain materials, 1280 px x 1608 px*

**ELENI KOURTI**
NEW YORK, NEW YORK

## DON'T BE AFRAID I'D HATE YOU ANYWAY

I notice every time
I sit next to the rich
They're afraid of my poem
Though they can hardly be accused of indiscretion
As i'm not wearing the right jewelry to attract their attention
The moment I write words
Like lie
Like lard
Like nation
I sense an eerie discomfort
It's not disapproval
It's pure discomfort
If they get so sensitive just by words on their own
not strung together
to make meaning
Just words
I plan to make a carnival of words
I mean what will they do if I write the word injustice
next to the word shirt?
Their fragile imagination will explode
How about greed next to nothing?
It will bring the house down

**ZEV TORRES**
NEW YORK, NEW YORK

## BACKLIGHT

They are, so you said,
Ignorant,
Misinformed,
Brainwashed,
When in fact they are merely backlit,
By the reflection of the antipathy,
Ablaze in your own eyes.

**GORAN LIŠNJIĆ**

OSIJEK, CROATIA

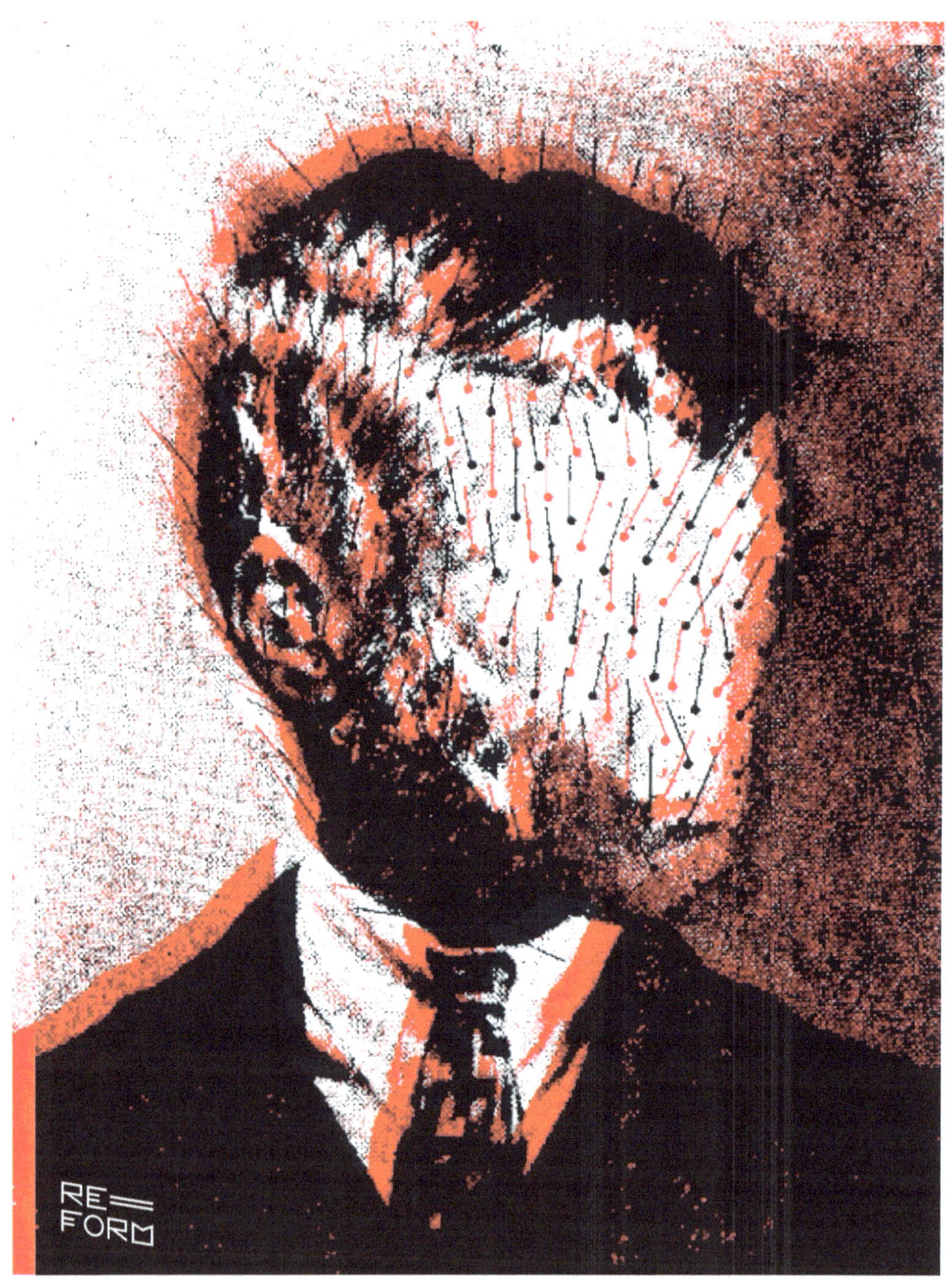


**CORPORATE COLONIZATION OF THE SUBCONSCIOUS**

*297 mm x 420 mm*

**IULIA MILITARU**

BUCHAREST, ROMANIA

## ABSTRACT PRESENTATION OF A FEW PRACTICAL ACTIONS

In their debate, "an AFF doctalk, featuring prestigious personalities,"

This is the image of absolute danger and terror, circulated in the international press: a network of tangled, chaotic lines

This is the image that defends and protects us, circulated in the international press: a perfectly drawn circle

This is me: .

The point on some random line / Within a chaotic network of tangled points

Then, a few pieces of advice and exhortations follow: / There is a menacing potential to the chaotic network. We, the prestigious personalities, must protect you, the vulnerable point. We shall have to attack and enclose the network within our limits—the limits of the protective circle.

This is how weapons, ammunition, and bombs appeared: to protect you, the vulnerable point, against a menacing potential—"there is nothing else that maintains peace but the preparation for war."

We watch "war seen through the eyes of those who live it," in the performance hall, "War—seen from the enemy's intimacy," a writer, an expert in military strategy, and a military historian (a few prestigious points, upon a perfectly drawn circle, speaking about me, the point on the chaotic lines):

You must desire the position of a point on an ordered circle that ensures peace and protection. Look at yourself! A perfectly drawn circle that suddenly encloses a network of tangled, chaotic lines. Me, a point on some random line. Enclosed by the circle, perfectly delimited

No movement. Stasis.

The disappearance of all points

**FIONA HARTMANN**
TORONTO, CANADA

## S.2220 — FORGOTTEN

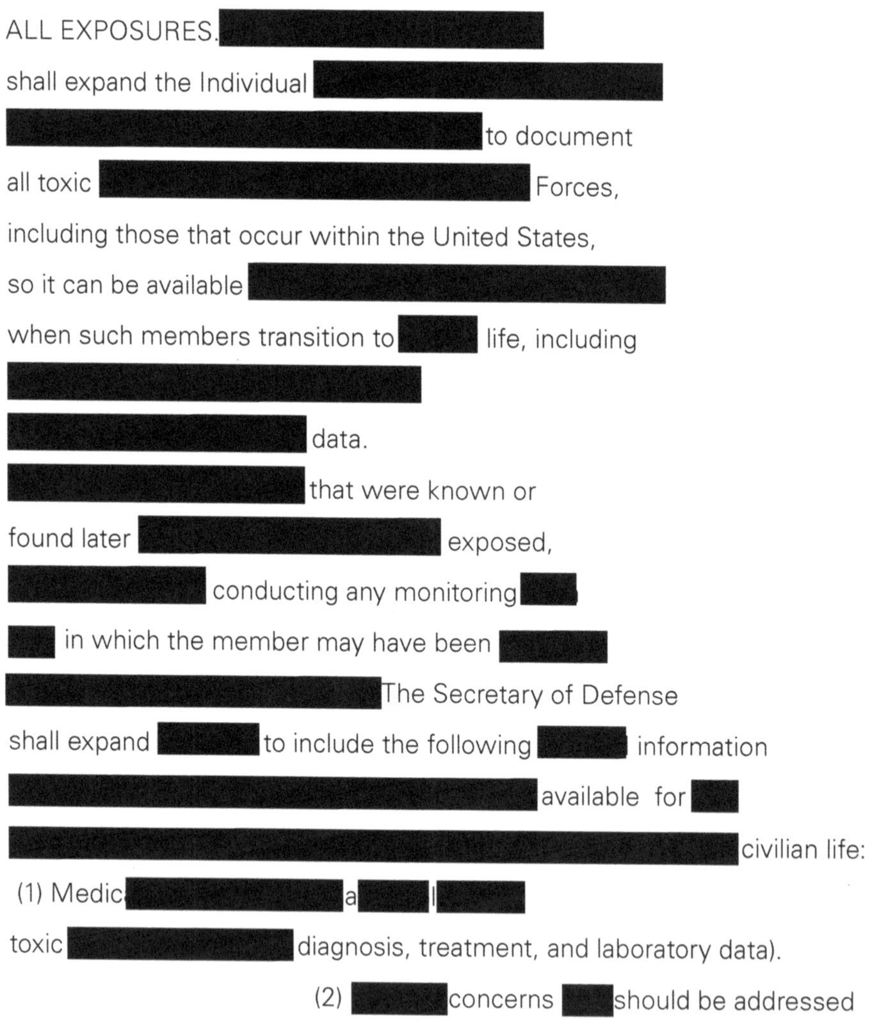
ALL EXPOSURES.
shall expand the Individual
to document
all toxic Forces,
including those that occur within the United States,
so it can be available
when such members transition to life, including

data.
that were known or
found later exposed,
conducting any monitoring
in which the member may have been
The Secretary of Defense
shall expand to include the following information
available for
civilian life:
(1) Medic a l
toxic diagnosis, treatment, and laboratory data).
(2) concerns should be addressed

## MICHELLE GRANVILLE

SLIGO, IRELAND

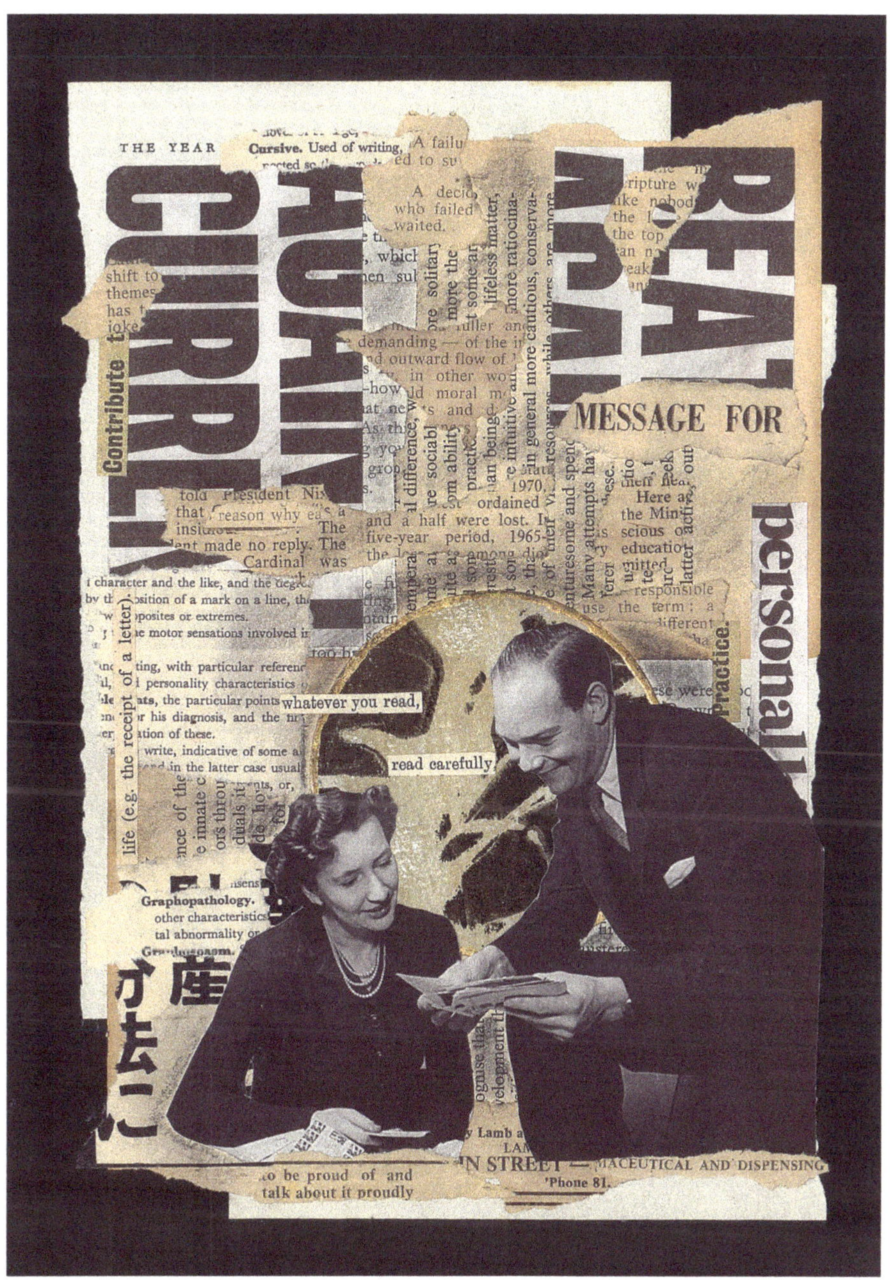


**BE CAREFUL WHAT YOU READ**

*Mixed media collage: found images and text, monoprint and gold-leaf, 11.5 in x 8.5 in*

## EGON GUENTHER

DIEẞEN, GERMANY

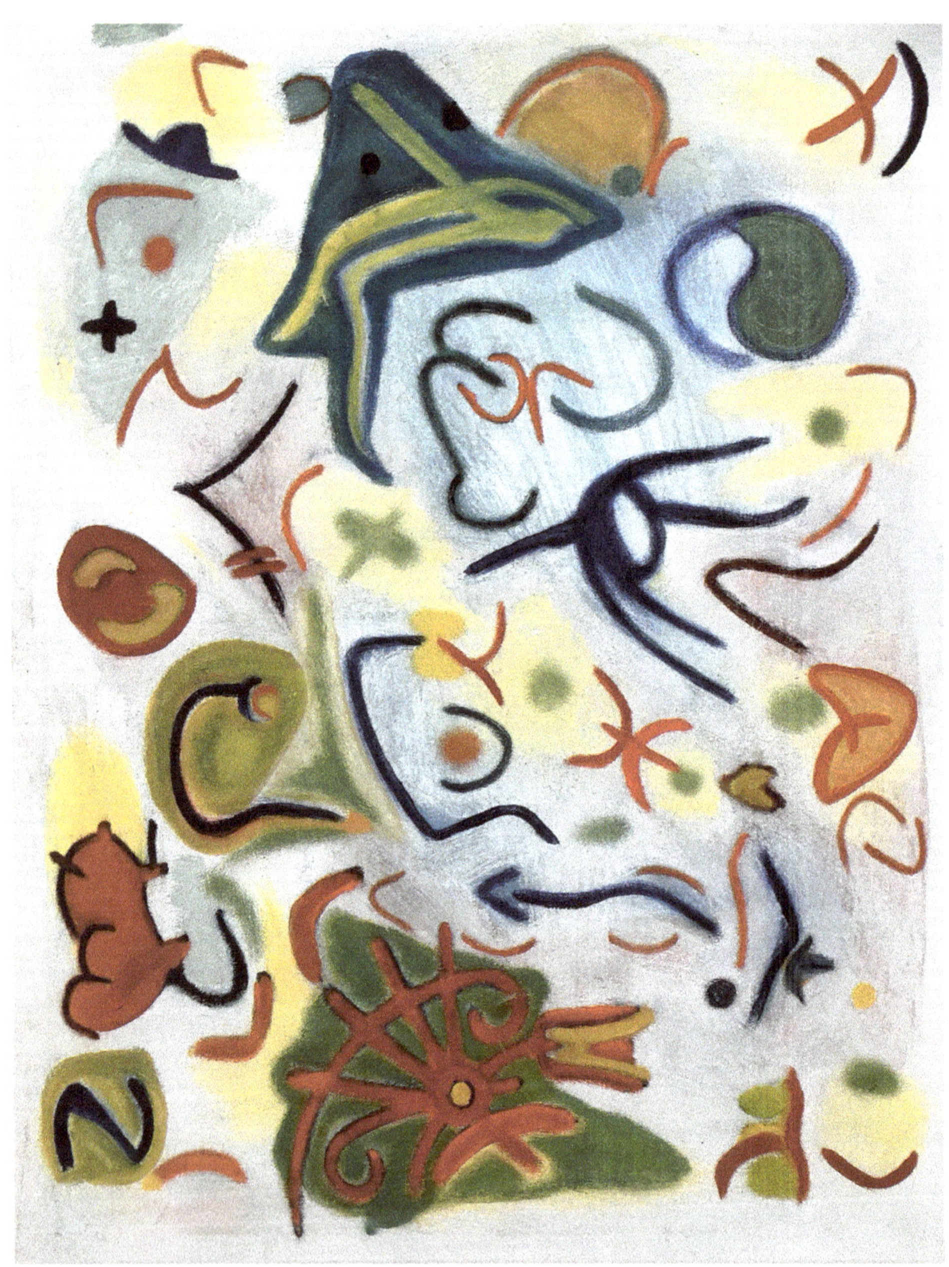

**TOPPLED SIGNS**

*Oil on canvas, 58 cm x 75 cm*

**SOPHIE MALLERET**
PARIS, FRANCE

## YOU CANNOT MAKE THIS STUFF UP

You cannot make this stuff up He repeated Three times
Poem Leitmotiv Blinking Or can you make this stuff up
We schlepped to other side of th'river Was there (even) a river
We talked in tongues Winking to cherry blossom Last snow of winter
Snowflakes or pink petals What is that gonna be
I cross my heart Swear Cacophony of snowflakes & petal poetry
*Tip for tap tip for tap*
News Everything rimes with impossible
Dirty word no one dares to whisper any more
Impossible n'est pas français The emperor said
Impossible is not the thing any more Everything is this and that
This or that Tip for tap Tit for tat Tat for rant Tat ranting About this & that
That never happened You can't make this stuff up You can't Or you can
No losers any more
Only winners The whole world is winning You and he and she
All discombobulated goulash
Did you bring gouache n' brushes
To paint over their 2026 truth millésime What is that gonna be
Tit for tat Tat for rant Tat ranting You can't put a word in
Nobody wants your facts
Give me fake photos Generate more rant About impossible things
Everyone is winning And the winner is You and he and she
Oh come on now Don't give me that Stinks Really your facts Stink
This 2026 truth millésime It's gonna be a good year Let's celebrate
Tit for tat Tat ranting about Fake fur coat Fake eyelashes Fake oranges
Oh Wait oranges are not that fake after all
Don't give me facts
I want winners
Let's all swim downstream with salmons
Maintenent salmons swim downstream
The new rave
Haven't you heard
& Don't you dare (Don't you dare) (say another word)

**GABRIELLA BEDETTI**
LEXINGTON, KENTUCKY

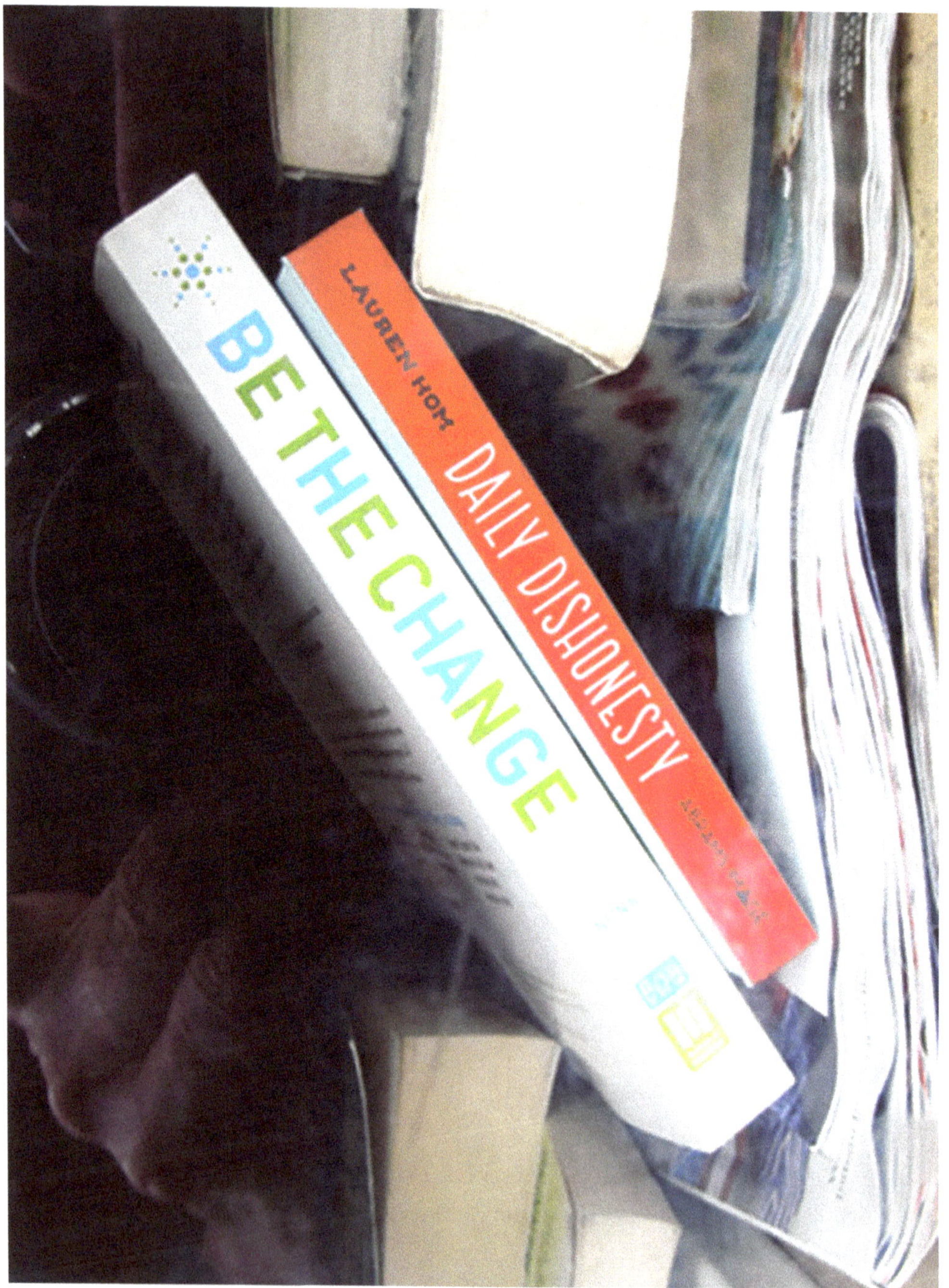


## DAILY DISHONESTY: BE THE CHANGE

*Photograph, 1707 px x 1280 px*

## GABRIEL DON

NEW YORK, NEW YORK

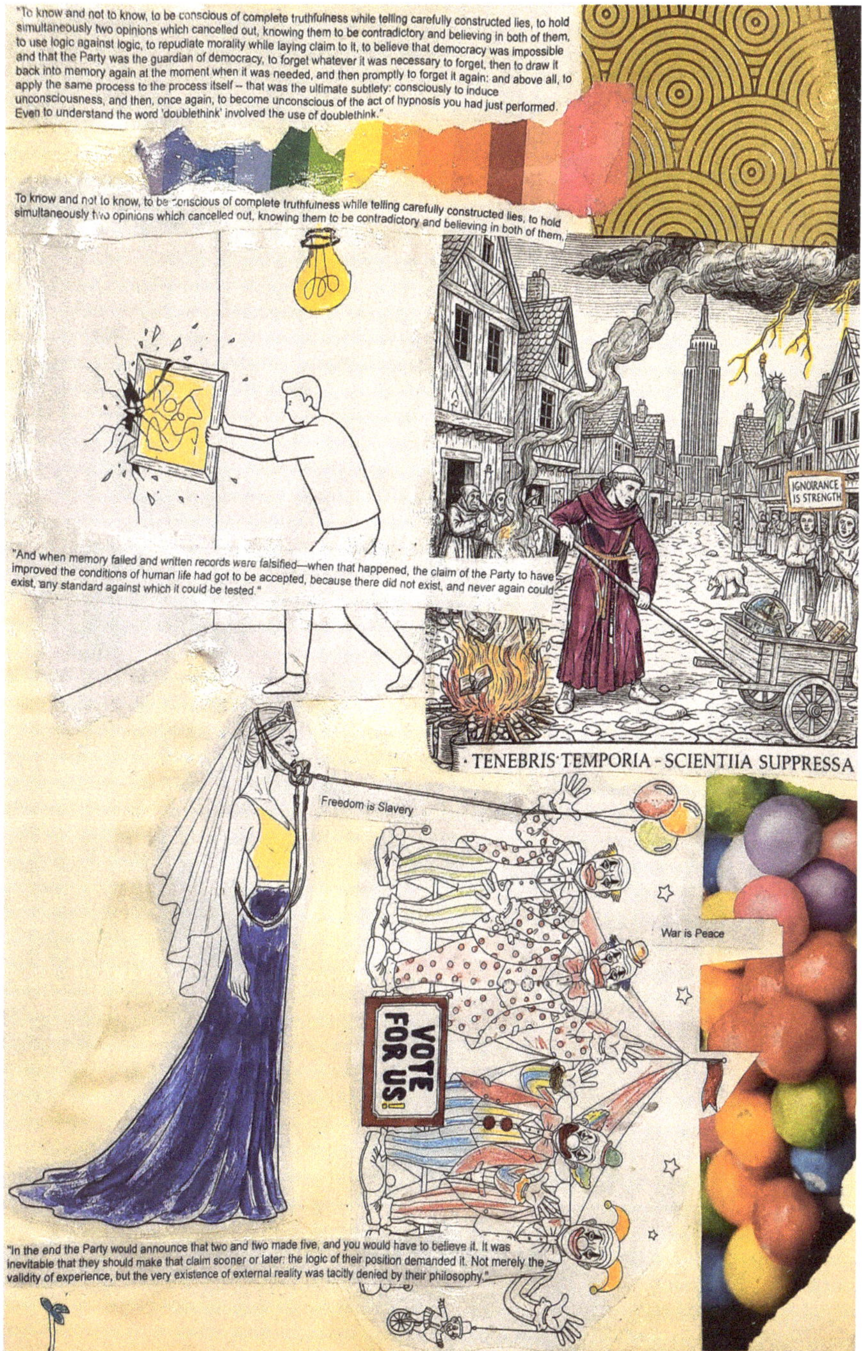


**THE WORK OF NOT FORGETTING**

*Mixed media, 16 in x 12 in*

## SERSE LUIGETTI

PERUGIA, ITALY

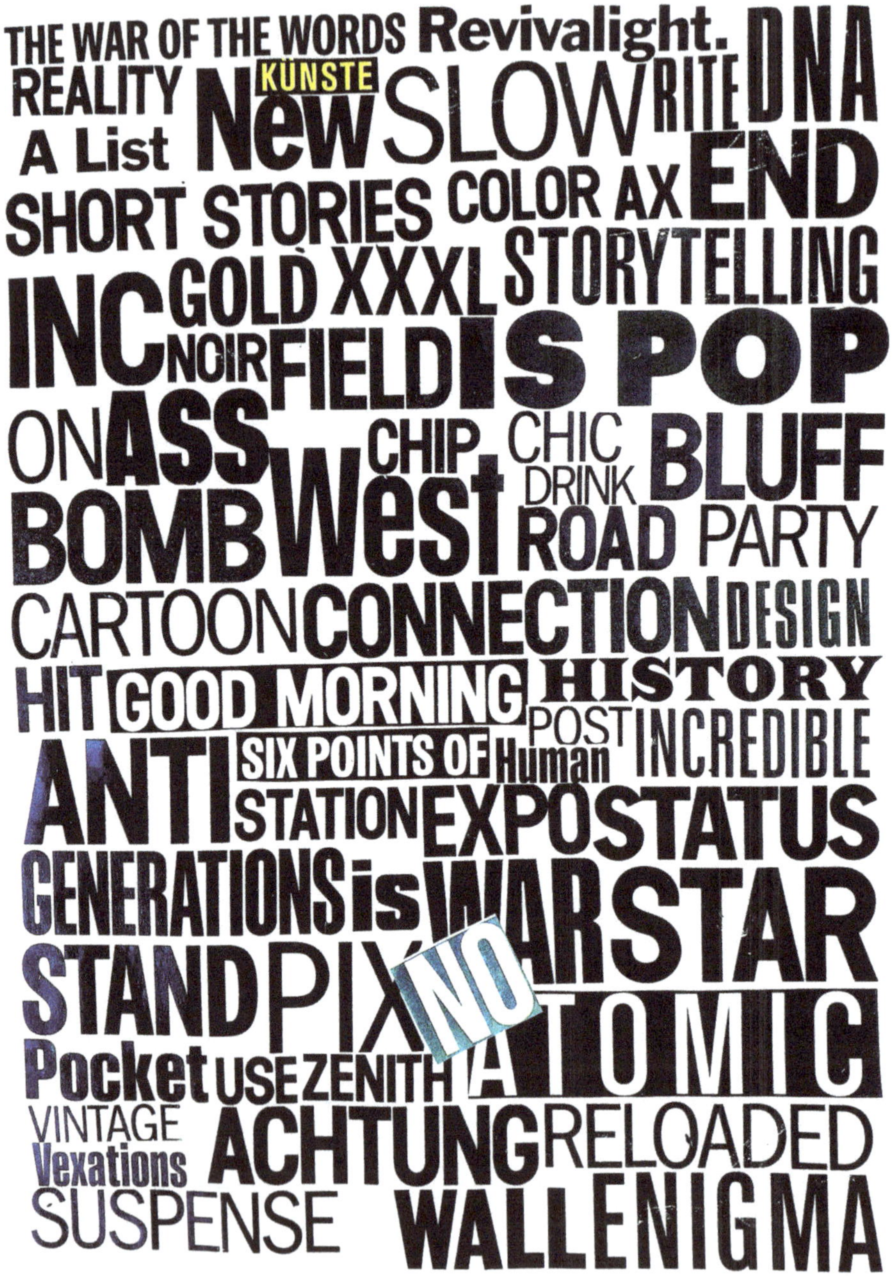

THE WAR OF THE WORDS Revivalight. DNA
REALITY KÜNSTE New SLOW RITE
A List
SHORT STORIES COLOR AX END
INC GOLD XXXL STORYTELLING
NOIR FIELD IS POP
ON ASS CHIP CHIC BLUFF
BOMB West DRINK ROAD PARTY
CARTOON CONNECTION DESIGN
HIT GOOD MORNING HISTORY
ANTI SIX POINTS OF Human POST INCREDIBLE
STATION EXPO STATUS
GENERATIONS is WAR STAR
STAND PIX NO
Pocket USE ZENITH ATOMIC
VINTAGE ACHTUNG RELOADED
Vexations
SUSPENSE WALL ENIGMA

**THE WAR OF THE WORDS**

*Collage su carta, 200 mm x 300 mm*

## LUIZ MORGADINHO

LISBON, PORTUGAL

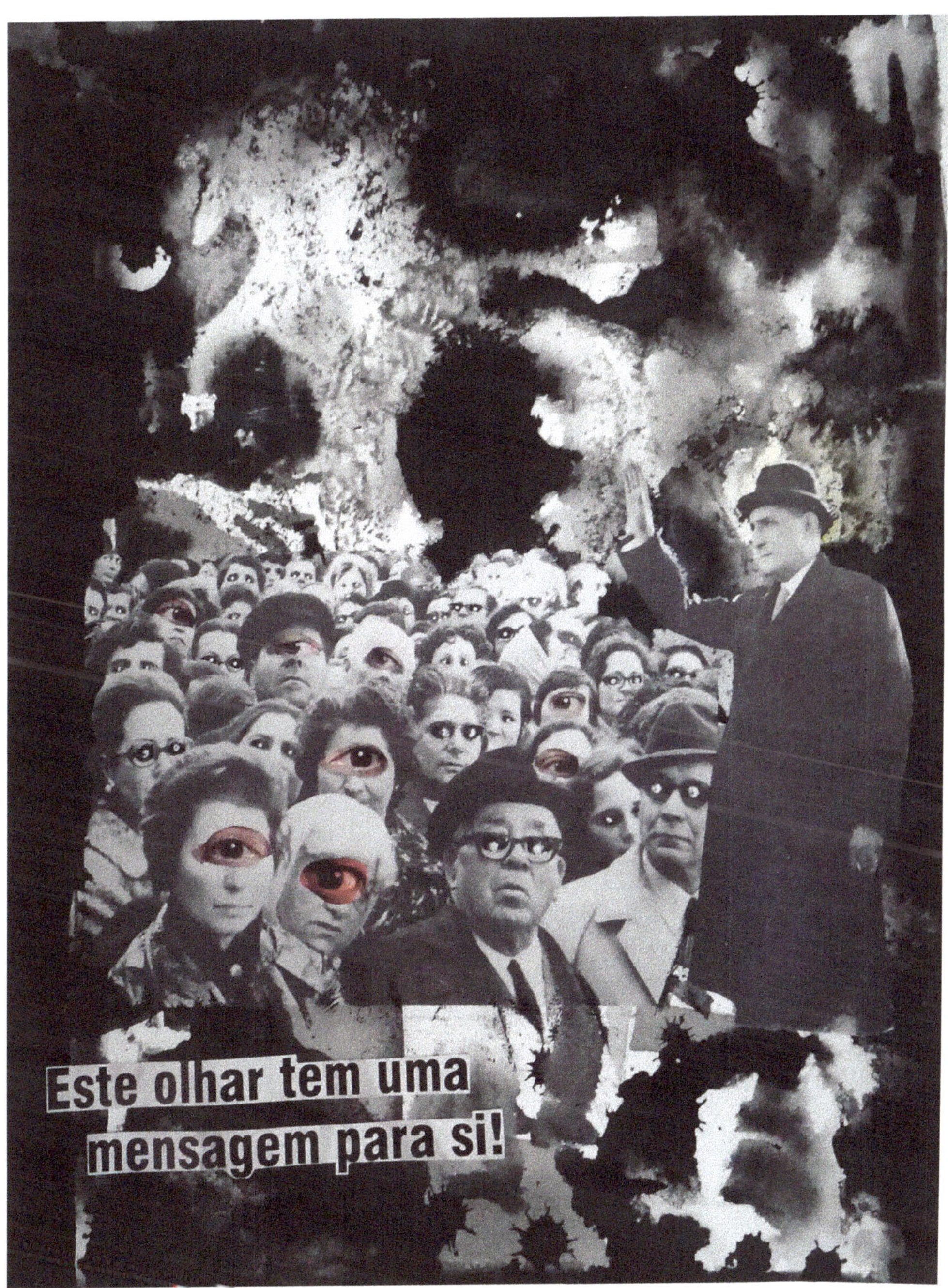


**A MESSAGE FOR YOU.**

*Watercolor paper (Arches 300 g), pigment ink, and collage, 37 cm x 27 cm*

## ANAÏS BUCHER

LUZERN, SWITZERLAND

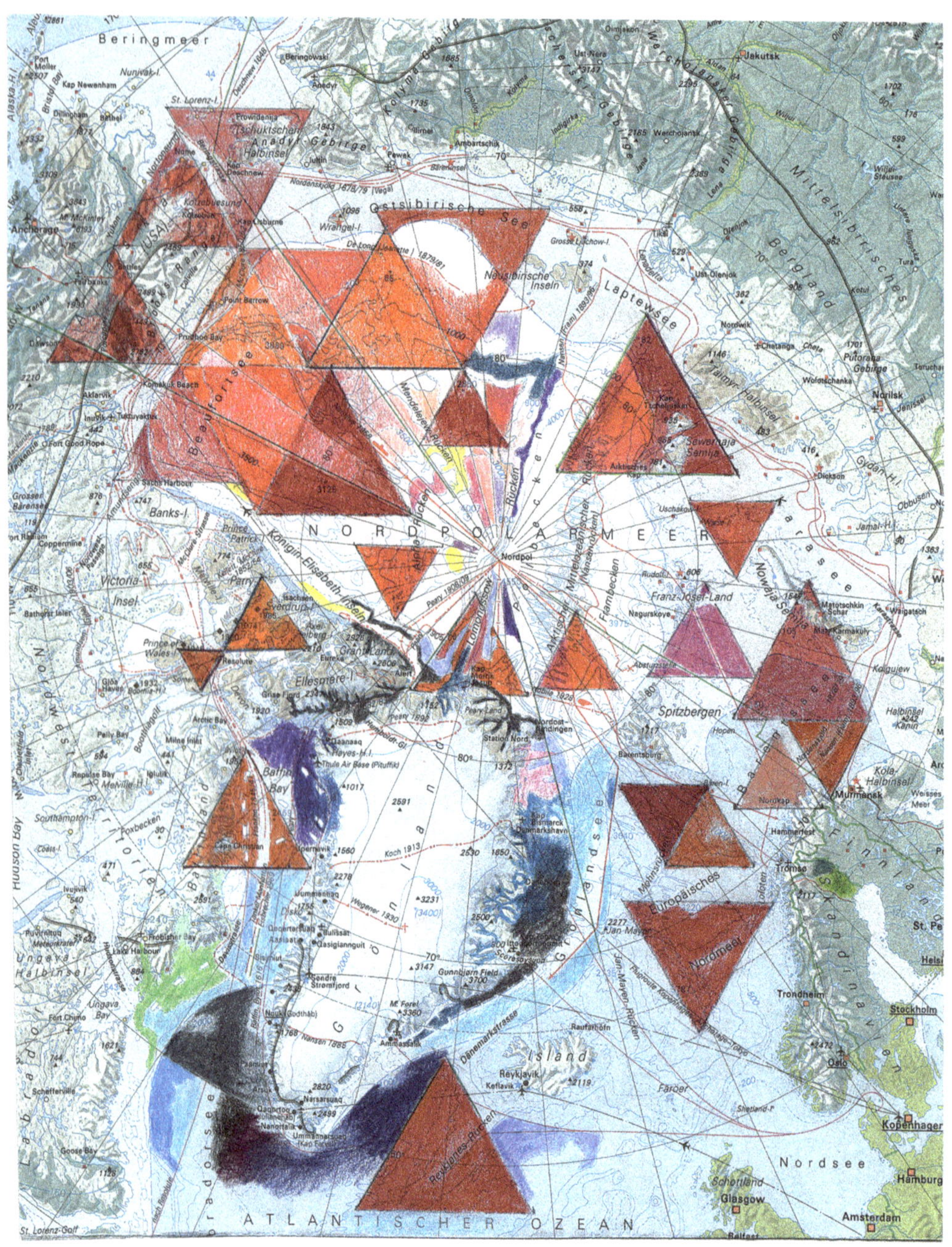


## UNTITLED

*Colored pencils on printed paper, 21 cm x 28 cm*

**ABRAHAM AONDOANA**
MAKURDI, NIGERIA

## IMPROPERGANDA WEATHER REPORT

Today's forecast:
truth at zero percent.
clouds in the form of microphones.
refuse to rain.

A flag clears its throat.
The applause is oozing out of vacant seats.
The anchor smiles—
teeth sponsored by silence.

Breaking news does not make anything.
The future was delayed eternally.

**TENDAI MWANAKA**
CHITUNGWIZA, ZIMBABWE

## EARTH

All those years
Of yearning
All those years
Of wanting

To be of it

**JEFFREY CYPHERS WRIGHT**

NEW YORK, NEW YORK

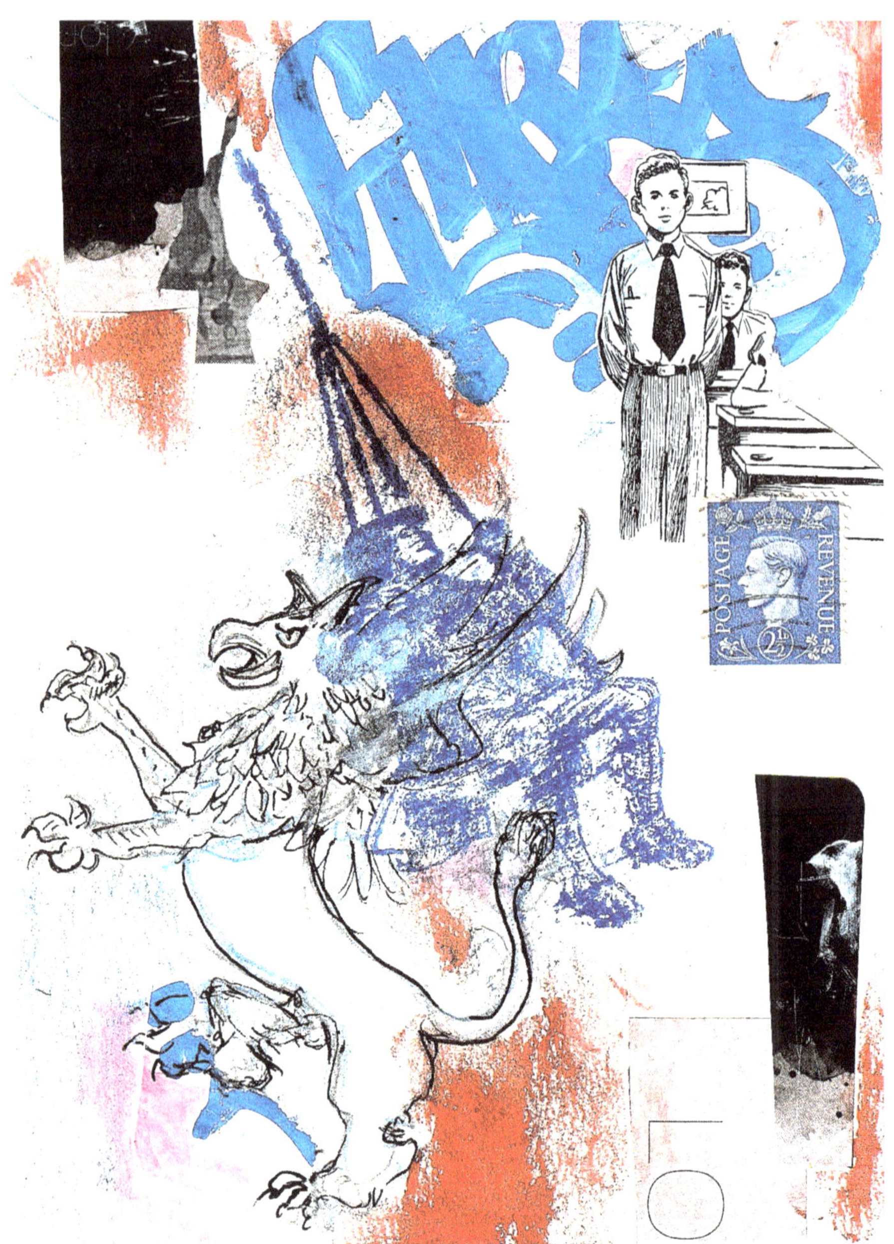


## DE PENDULUM

*Drawing, painting, ink, collage, rubber stamp on board, 5 in x 7 in*

**KEREM DURDAG**
SCARBOROUGH, MAINE

## DROWN

He held his son
on his shoulders
as the waters
rose,
trapped on this
island of sand
and incoming
death,
what does one
say to his son,
as I die together
with you,
the water tunneling
into your lungs,
the ground
underneath
disappearing
and the liquid
blanket licking
us over,
forgive me, my son
forgive me
for we have been
forsaken.

**MIKE FERGUSON**

OTTERY ST MARY, UNITED KINGDOM

to tell a lie is the easiest truth when truth has died / *to tell a lie*
is the easiest truth when truth has died / to tell a lie *is the*
easiest truth when truth has died / to tell a lie is the *easiest*
truth when truth has died / to tell a lie is the easiest *truth when*
truth has died / to tell a lie is the easiest truth when *truth has*
died / to tell a lie is the easiest truth when truth has *died /*
to tell a lie is the easiest truth when truth has died / *to tell a lie*
is the easiest truth when truth has died / to tell a lie *is the*
easiest truth when truth has died / to tell a lie is the *easiest*
truth when truth has died / to tell a lie is the easiest *truth when*
truth has died / to tell a lie is the easiest truth when *truth has*
died / to tell a lie is the easiest truth when truth has *died /*
to tell a lie is the easiest truth when truth has died / *to tell a lie*
is the easiest truth when truth has died / to tell a lie *is the*
easiest truth when truth has died / to tell a lie is the *easiest*
truth when truth has died / to tell a lie is the easiest *truth when*
truth has died / to tell a lie is the easiest truth when *truth has*
died / to tell a lie is the easiest truth when truth has *died /*
to tell a lie is the easiest truth when truth has died / *to tell a lie*
is the easiest truth when truth has died / to tell a lie *is the*
easiest truth when truth has died / to tell a lie is the *easiest*
truth when truth has died / to tell a lie is the easiest *truth when*
truth has died / to tell a lie is the easiest truth when *truth has*
died / to tell a lie is the easiest truth when truth has *died /*
to tell a lie is the easiest truth when truth has died / *to tell a lie*
is the easiest truth when truth has died / to tell a lie *is the*
easiest truth when truth has died / to tell a lie is the *easiest*
truth when truth has died / to tell a lie is the easiest *truth when*
truth has died / to tell a lie is the easiest truth when *truth has*
died / to tell a lie is the easiest truth when truth has *died /*
to tell a lie is the easiest truth when truth has died / *to tell a lie*
is the easiest truth when truth has died / to tell a lie *is the*
easiest truth when truth has died / to tell a lie is the *easiest*
truth when truth has died / to tell a lie is the easiest *truth when*
truth has died / to tell a lie is the easiest truth when *truth has*
died / to tell a lie is the easiest truth when truth has *died /*
to tell a lie is the easiest truth when truth has died / *to tell a lie*
is the easiest truth when truth has died / to tell a lie *is the*
easiest truth when truth has died / to tell a lie is the *easiest*
truth when truth has died / to tell a lie is the easiest *truth when*
truth has died / to tell a lie is the easiest truth when *truth has*
died / to tell a lie is the easiest truth when truth has *died /*
to tell a lie is the easiest truth when truth has died / *to tell a lie*
is the easiest truth when truth has died / to tell a lie *is the*
easiest truth when truth has died / to tell a lie is the *easiest*
truth when truth has died / to tell a lie is the easiest *truth when*
truth has died / to tell a lie is the easiest truth when *truth has*
died / to tell a lie is the easiest truth when truth has *died /*
to tell a lie is the easiest truth when truth has died / *to tell a lie*
is the easiest truth when truth has died / to tell a lie *is the*
easiest truth when truth has died / to tell a lie is the *easiest*
truth when truth has died / to tell a lie is the easiest *truth when*
truth has died / to tell a lie is the easiest truth when *truth has*
died / to tell a lie is the easiest truth when truth has *died /*
to tell a lie is the easiest truth when truth has died / *to tell a lie*
is the easiest truth when truth has died / to tell a lie *is the*
easiest truth when truth has died / to tell a lie is the *easiest*
truth when truth has died / to tell a lie is the easiest *truth when*
truth has died / to tell a lie is the easiest truth when *truth has*
died / to tell a lie is the easiest truth when truth has *died /*
to tell a lie is the easiest truth when truth has died / *to tell a lie*
is the easiest truth when truth has died / to tell a lie *is the*
easiest truth when truth has died / to tell a lie is the *easiest*
truth when truth has died / to tell a lie is the easiest *truth when*
truth has died / to tell a lie is the easiest truth when *truth has*
died / to tell a lie is the easiest truth when truth has *died /*
to tell a lie is the easiest truth when truth has died / *to tell a lie*
is the easiest truth when truth has died / to tell a lie *is the*
easiest truth when truth has died / to tell a lie is the *easiest*
truth when truth has died / to tell a lie is the easiest *truth when*
truth has died / to tell a lie is the easiest truth when *truth has*
died / to tell a lie is the easiest truth when truth has *died /*
to tell a lie is the easiest truth when truth has died / *to tell a lie*
is the easiest truth when truth has died / to tell a lie *is the*
*easiest truth when truth has died /*

## TRUTH DIED

*Word art (produced in Microsoft Word, converted to pdf, saved as jpg): 528 px 765 px*

**ELIZABETH FOGLE**
ERIE, PENNSYLVANIA

## TAXIDERMY
## JULIUS AND ETHEL ROSENBERG

so glad they're going to die
full of nothing

so glad they're going so empty
like mannequins

wishing the day pale blue
noise swelled with bruised water

little disease laughed its small breath —
no business like fugitive motion

wearing boots larger than persistence
and the nagging thought:

"this is what it is
                    to be happy"

so glad they're going to die
full of nothing

so glad they're going so empty
like mannequins

## CECIL W. LEE

NEW YORK, NEW YORK

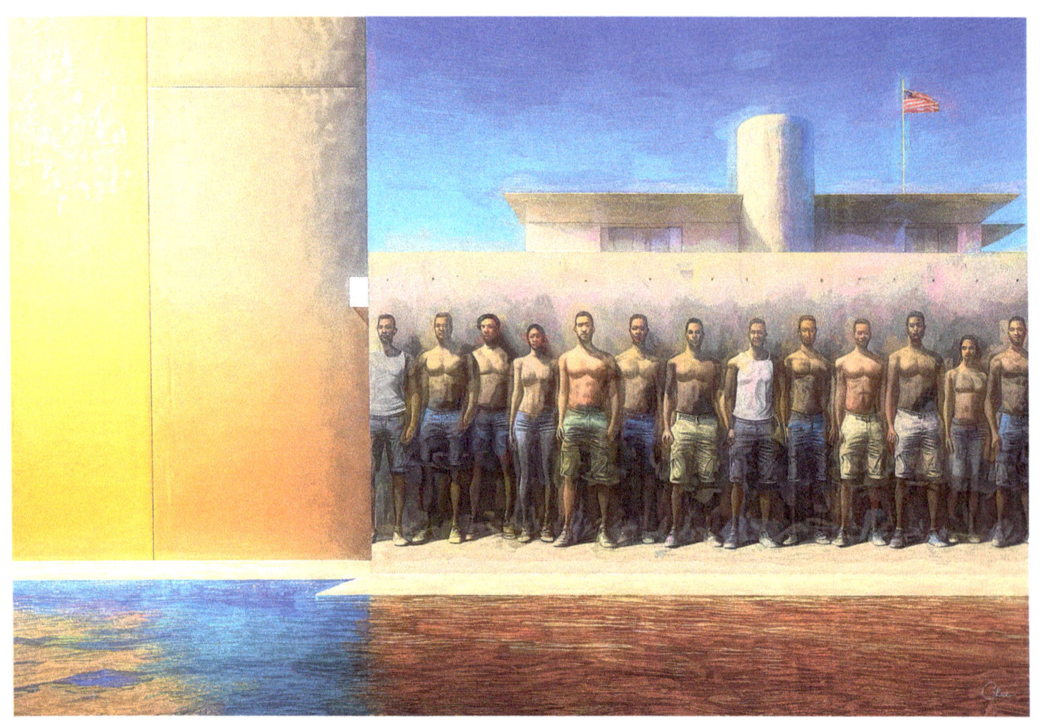

## LOST DREAMS

*Custom print*

**JOHN PIETARO**
BROOKLYN, NEW YORK

## REDEEMING SOCIAL VALUE

*Dedicated to Old Bull Lee*

Los Alamos, of hollow land and atom-age pestilence;
An 18.6 kilo-ton fiddle-fucking miasma.
It surrounds, even now, the cool remote.

...Fallout was always the ethos of Beat.

Waves of hostility and suspicion flowed;
it had to, was bound to.
Nothing is true, and none could

Write their way out of such infirmity.
But the Tularosa Basin Downwinders knew
Ugly Spirit, first-hand.

There's been no room for relief,
There remains no sign of Yage.
And then it starts to rain.

...Tomorrow the river will only be higher.

## VITTORE BARONI

VIAREGGIO, ITALY

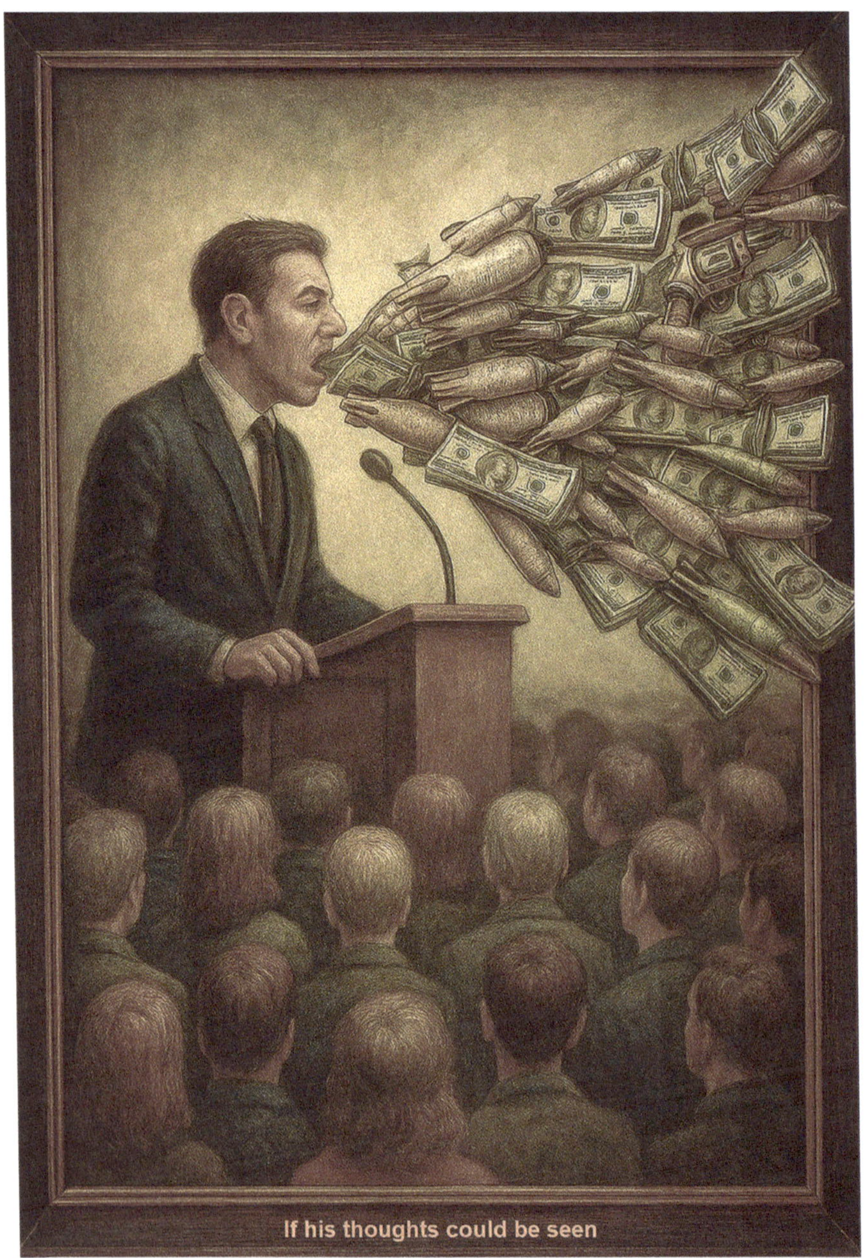


### IF HIS THOUGHTS COULD BE SEEN

*Collage on paper, modified with AI, 21 cm x 29.7 cm*

**SUSAN SHUP**

PARIS, FRANCE

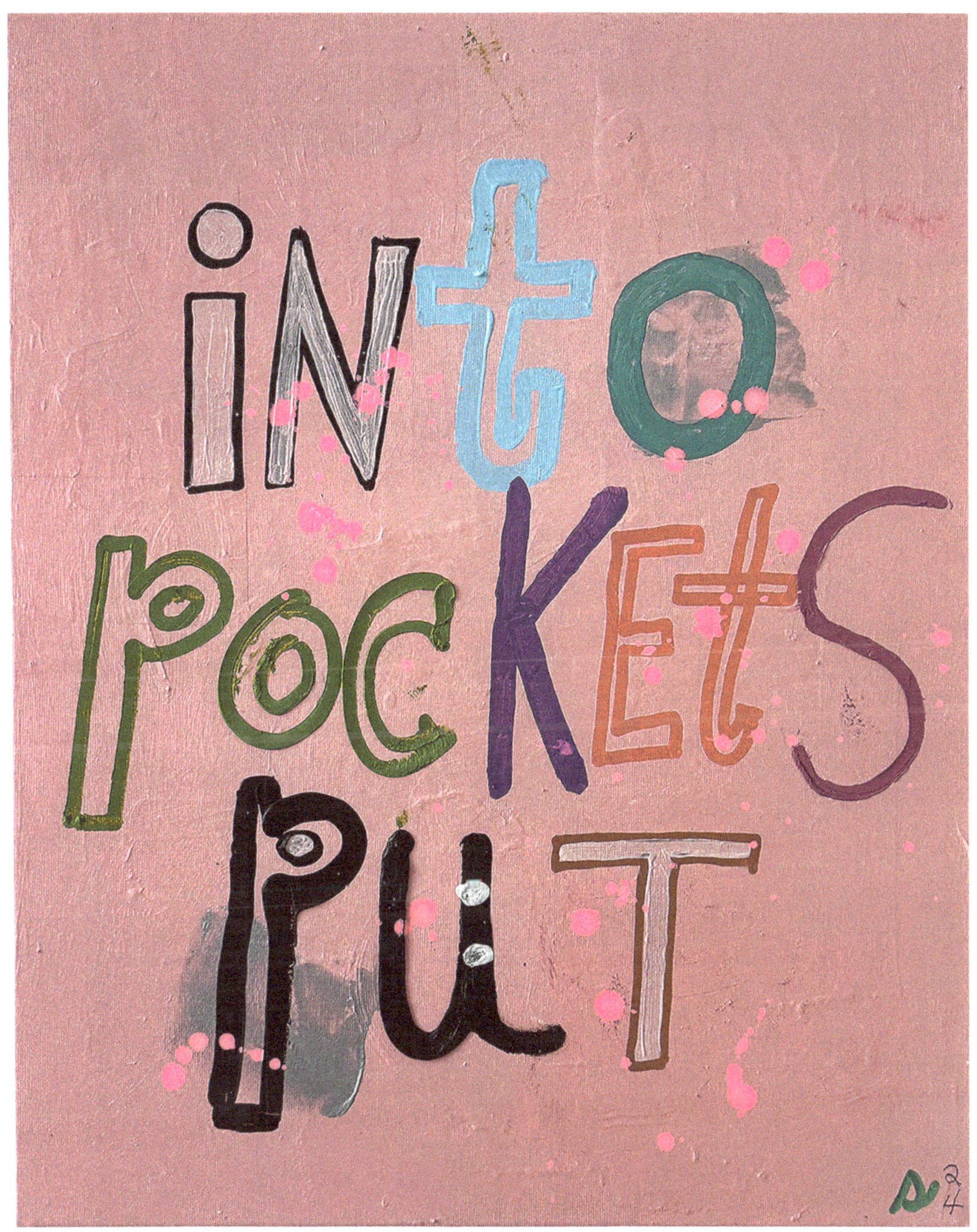


**INTO POCKETS PUT**

*Mixed media on canvas, 50 cm x 40 cm*

## CHARLES MINGUS III

NEW YORK, NEW YORK

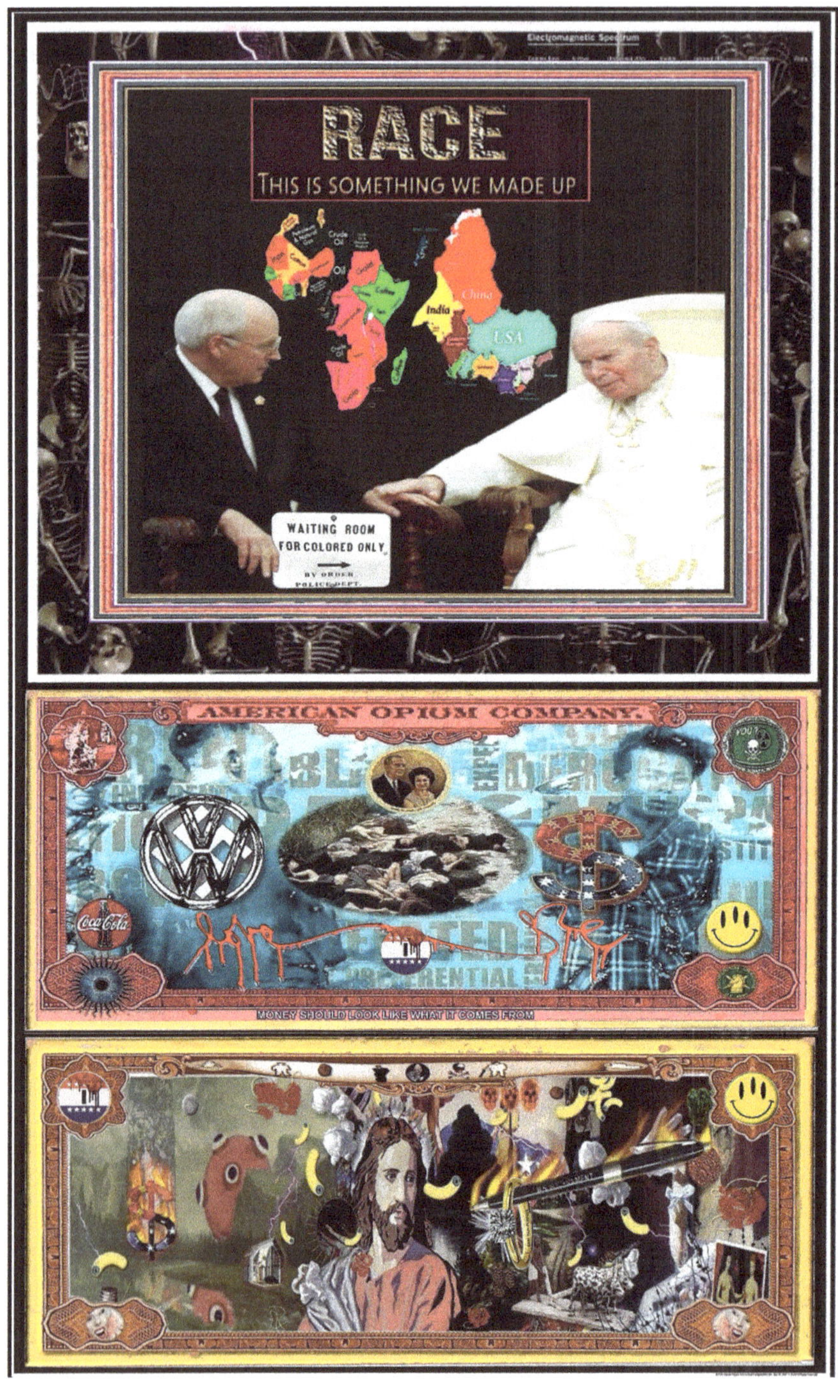


**YES IT IS ISN'T IT NOT !**

*Digital image, 3957 px x 7157 px*

**CARLOS PONCE-MELENDEZ**
SAN ANTONIO, TEXAS

## I KNOW CORRUPTION

*The corrupts know that I know them, but they don't care*

How can you prove that we steal, lie, kill?
Who is going to believe you?
You have your voice; we own the newspapers, the satellites, the internet
You have complaints; we have the churches, the police, the jails
You have the truth; we have the lawyers, the judges, the legislators
You have the ideas we have the editorials, the magazines, the preachers
You want justice, we want power.

*I know corruption but the corrupts just laugh*

We are the genius of politics, we reinvented democracy
People admire us because we have the mansions, the jets and the diamonds
You can yell all you want on the streets, at the universities, in your blogs
The electorate ignores you; they feel uncomfortable with grim truths
We legalize gambling, profit from pornography, benefit from illnesses
After all, we invested in government and we want soaring returns
We may not be saints but we are powerful

*I know corruption and I know it's immorally legal*

We are the businessmen and the government
We are regulators and judges
We control the private and public funds
We complain about laws for the democratic theater
We love if you protest, we need the façade
But remember that we set the rules, it's our democracy
You may not like it because it's unfair and immoral, but it's ours and it's legal.

*I know corruption and it's here.*

**IMANOL BUISAN**

BARCELONA, SPAIN

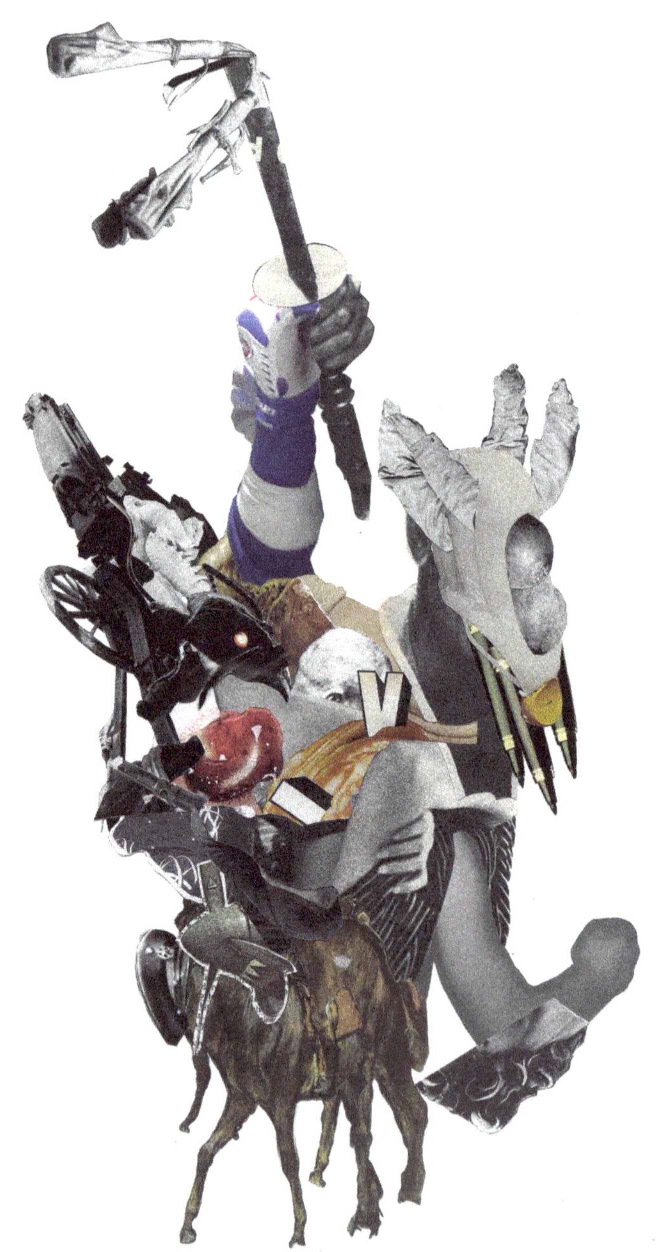

**TROJAN HORSE**

*Collage*

**JOEL ALLEGRETTI**
FORT LEE, NEW JERSEY

**It doesn't matter what this sentence says, because in post-fact America you have the God-given right to deny this sentence is a sentence.**

**HONG JIN A**
SEOUL, REPUBLIC OF KOREA

## CONATUS

She came at me in sections,
Circle Bust Middle Pelvix,
Ogle Ankle Buttocks Convex,
Doe Youe Doe Me,
Sex Lines Move Ahead,
IT'S B O W H O A X,
Due to my strong personal convictions,
I wish to stress that this film in no wise,
Endorses a belief in the urcolt,
Shape came at me in sections,
Circle Assemble Middle Compass,
Ogle Angle Cycle Compass,
Blue Purple Wipped Creame,
Six Lines Move Ahead,
IT'S B A U H A U S,
D.S.

**LEMAN BEDIA GÜVEN**

İSTANBUL, TÜRKIYE

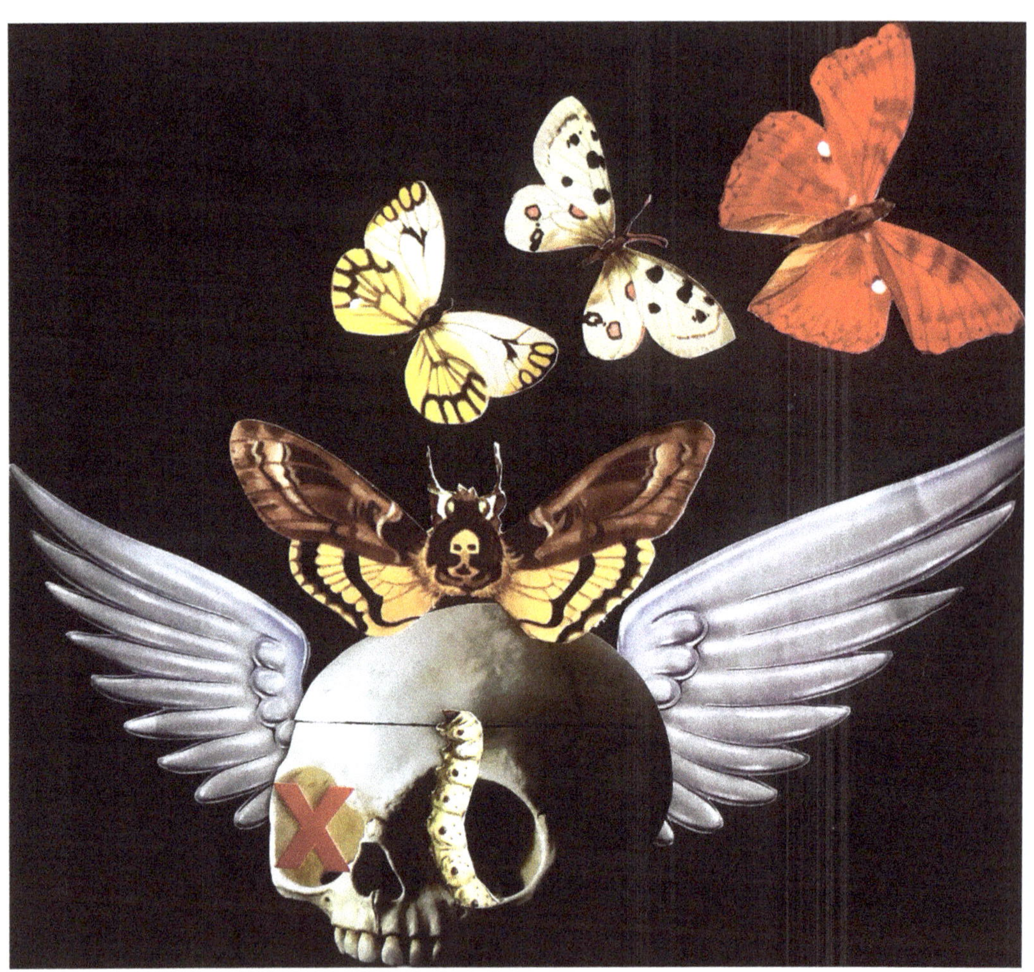

**REBORN**

*Analog collage, 2742 px x 2473 px*

**HOLLY DAY**
MINNEAPOLIS, MINNESOTA

## BUTTERFLIES

If caterpillars lived on decaying flesh, infested corpses
built cold-rimmed cocoons inside a dead animal's rotting ribcage,
would we view the dead with such revulsion, knowing that at any moment
bright-winged butterflies would explode from gaping orifices
the wounds of auto accidents and bullet wounds? What if

it was the most beautiful butterflies and moths that emerged from our dead
clouds of blue morpho, glittering wings as large as your palm,
massive lunar moths, sapphire-tinged swallowtails, maybe some kind
   of butterfly
we don't actually have because this, after all, is only conjecture
because when we put our dead away in real life, there are no thoughts
   of butterflies
there is nothing beautiful or magical ready to burst from the people
we shove into the ground.

## SANDRA GEA

MARÍA, SPAIN

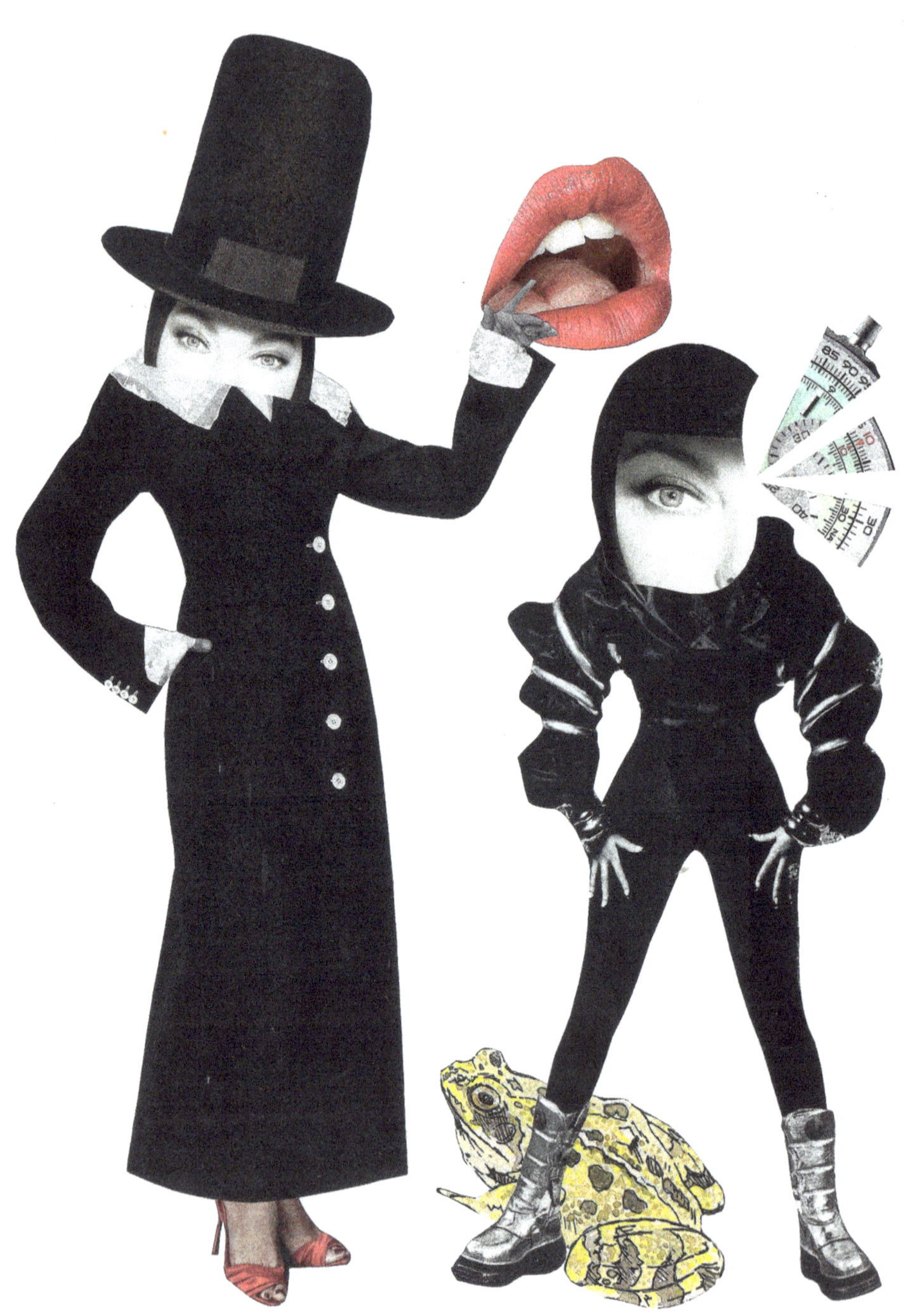

**ABRA-PAGAN-DA!**

*Analog collage on paper, 29.7 cm x 21 cm*

**WILLIAM SEATON**

GOSHEN, NEW YORK

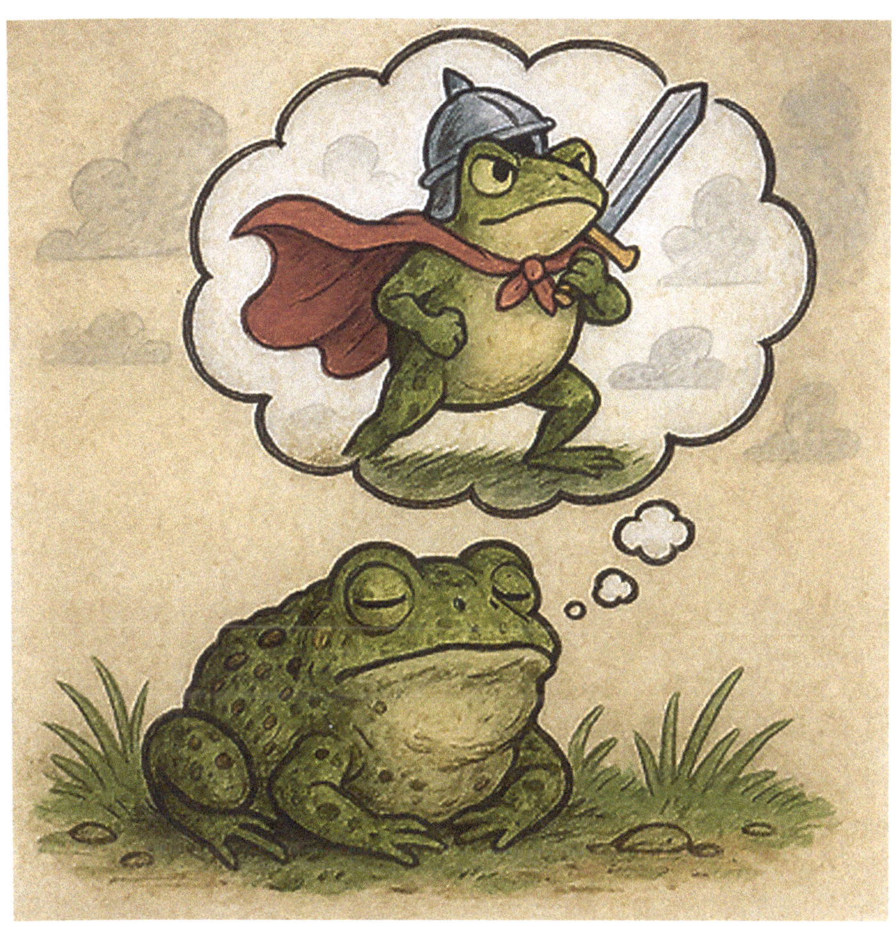

The cruel pipsqueak really excelled at nothing
but thinking well of himself, yet his croak
was so loud, he came to dominate the pond.

## THE NOISY FROG

*AI image and three lines of text*

**KATHLEEN FLORENCE**

LOS ANGELES, CALIFORNIA

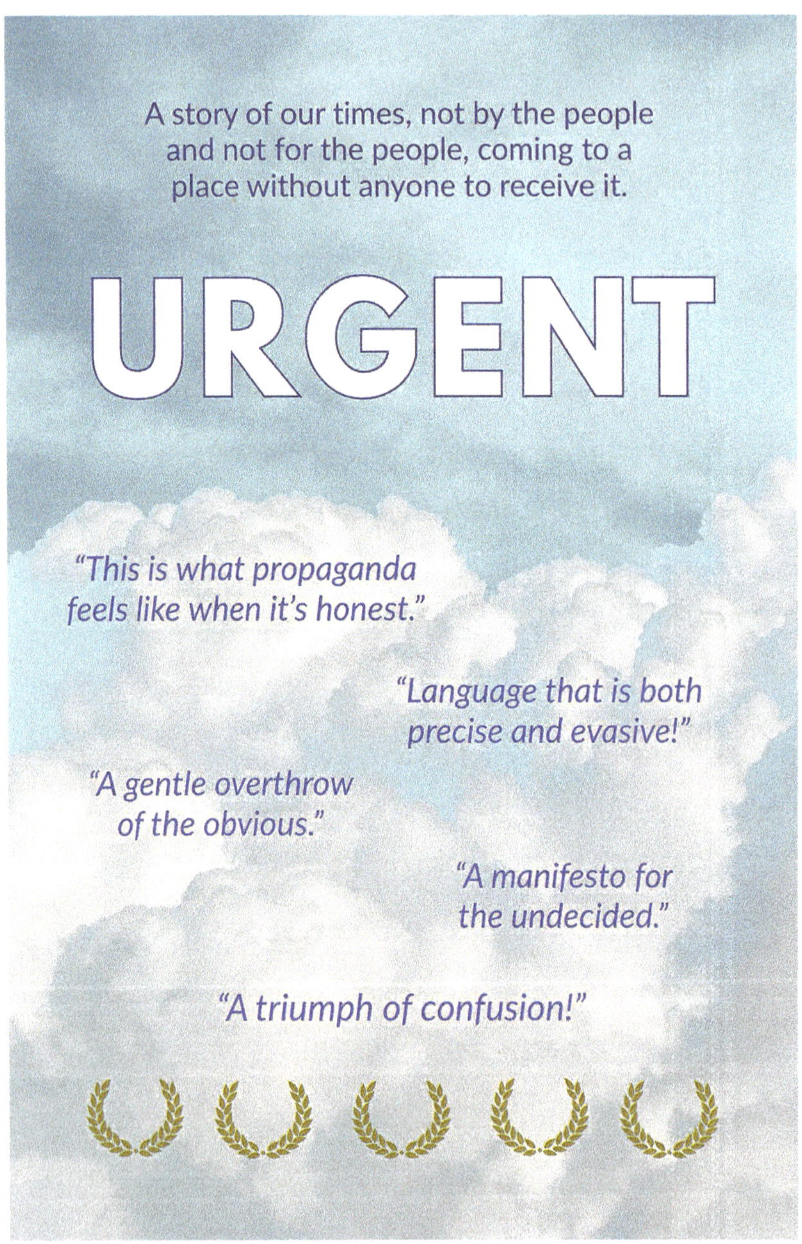


**PROPAGANDA FOR NO ONE**

*Digital collage, 4 in x 6 in*

**GENCO GULAN**
ISTANBUL, TÜRKIYE

## CINEMA POEM (SINEMA ŞIIRI)

*(This poem is to be screened in a movie theater,
3840 x 2160 dpi on a wide silver screen.)*

Art/ Abba/ ANACONDA/ anne/ America/ AM/ ama/ action/ artist/ aha!/
BEATLES/ baba/ best/ beş/ barış/ BE/ bold/ baby/ bomb/ bold/ boş/
Camera/ CAN/ Cinema / conceptual/ contemporary/ Chaplin/ close-up/
Devrim/ durgun/ David/ DADA/ Dolby/ day/ dev/ digital/ duality/ dolgun/
Error/ extra/ eski/ EAT/ east/ earn/ eye/ Ela/ Eastwood/ eyvah!/ enayi/
Film/ Frankenstein/ FREE/ face/ fall/ Fellini/ forward/ focus/ flash/ f*ck/
Godzilla/ gay/ great/ GENCO/ ghost/ Gershwin/ goat/ Godfather/ Godot/
Hey/ high/ hot/ hope/ hide/ hoover/ HP/ horse/ HAP/ hockey/ Hitchcock/
Istanbul/ IMPROPERGANDA/ iPhone/ idea/ isolation/ island/ iPad/ isal
Jokey/ Jordan/ jump/ junk/ joke/ JOJO/ joker/ join/ JAWS/ Judgment/
King Kong/ Kuala Lumpur/ KAYA/ kayak/ Kant/ kelime/ kartel/ kare/ kart/
Leica/ Lama/ LICK/ Lola/ late/ last/ lust/ label/ love/ lynch/ lesbian/ lux/
Mix/ mana/ mud/ multi/ max/ minute/ MOVIE/ motion/ must/ Metropolis/
Neu/ Nine / Nike/ nurse/ New York/ Nintendo/ night/ NO/ Nein/ nicht/
Ops! / Oh! / Osman/ operate/ opus/ Orthodox/ orospu/ orientalism/ OR/
PG-13/ pembe/ pink/ punk/ painting/ poem/ porn/ POP/ post/ Potemkin/
Queen / quir/ question/ quality/ quantity/ quarrel/ quiz/ don_Quixote/ QUICK/
Rated R/ rock / rot/ Rose is a rose/ rosto/ ROBOT/ replay/ Roma/ revolution/
Superman/ sex/ SOAP/ sale/ seraphine/ sanat/ saray/ SU/ special/ Socrates/
Think / TABU/ test/ text/ title/ tat/ TAKE/ taxi/ tellak/ theory/ timecode/ title/
U-Bahn/ Utility/ UCUZ/ unufak/ unleashe/ utopia/ urban/ uzak/ uçuk/ UHF/

Video / vaay!/ vazo/ van/ vision/ vacuum/ victory/ VOTE/ vaccine/ vocabulary/
WhatsApp/ water/ WHIP / work in progress/ Western/ widescreen/ woman/
X-Men/ Xerox/ xylophone/ X-ray/ Xanthos/ YOGA/ Yamaha/ Yahoo!/ yatay/
ZOOM/ zevk/ zeytin/ zaten/ Zulu/ Zeki/ zeka/ zevk/ Zorro/ zoo/ zonk/ ZDF/

*Words in English, Turkish & German*

## ROSALIE GANCIE

HYATTSVILLE, MARYLAND

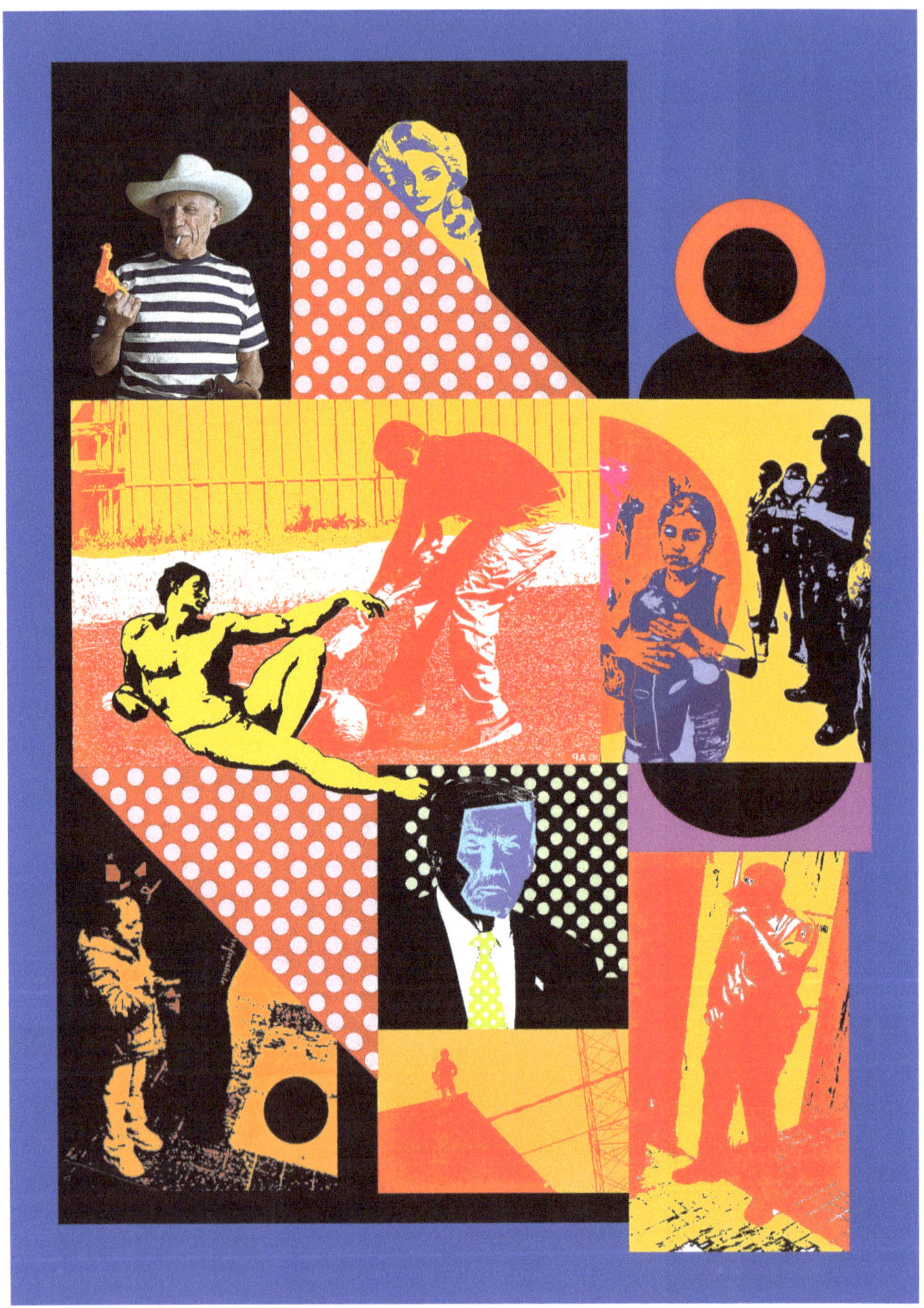

### TODAY'S HUMANITY IS ALL THE RAGE

*Digital collage, 7 in x 10 in*

**ALLISON WHITTENBERG**
PHILADELPHIA, PENNSYLVANIA

## ARE YOU REALLY IN THE ROOM

are you really in the room
when you're in the room?

brown paper bag, upright, covers your face
as you rake in your meal: meal in a recycled carton.

around you, cafeteria hum,
so many diners,four-tops holding only solos.

ear-plugged conversations outnumber the actual talkers.
mostly phones glowing,small votives for private worlds.

**ANGELA SLOAN**
QUEENS, NEW YORK

## ODDITY

There's a tiny shimmering eye buried in my bar of soap
And a microphone in my cereal bowl,
floating in the pink-stained milk.
I thought I heard a soft voice coming from the hair dryer this morning,
But I can't be sure.
It's almost as if my cat is quietly purring words into my ear at night,
And the neighbors' roses have small red mouths,
moving back and forth in unison with the chirping bluebirds.
As the clouds shift in the summer sky, they form messy patterns, like a child's Crayola drawings.
There's one more thing, and this is particularly odd:
The freckles on my forearm have assembled into a barcode that glows in the dark.

**MARIETA MAGLAS**
ORRY-LA-VILLE, FRANCE

## IMPROPERGANDA

This word revolves around the use of violence or terror
as a means of coercion to achieve political goals.
It pertains to leftist terrorism that undermines the law
through ideological frameworks.
Is it not the case that the activities surrounding the law
should be influenced by
the political convictions of individuals?
This word centers on ideology
as a tool for manipulation.
It addresses political actions
that can obliterate legal structures.
It does not concern the notion of law
as inherently moral.
It is not focused on the conflict against terror,
which is purportedly a struggle for human rights.
It does not engage with the ideological motivations
behind certain political ideals.
It is not about artists who seek
to convey their individuality.
It does not pertain to individuals
who feel the need to universalize their principles.
This word is about dogmatism, absolutism,
and the associated pitfalls.
It does not involve fundamental values
or evaluative judgments.
Perhaps it is about a proper comprehension of value
phenomena amidst varying emotional qualities:
transvaluation, inner ecstasy, religious fervor,
conscience, and duty.

It concerns obsessions with values that
only encompass limited aspects of reality.
It addresses authoritarian dogmatism
and the universality of uniformity.
It is about cultural exchanges that become
complex issues hidden beneath
misleading differences.
It is about the human waves crashing upon the shores.
Some assert that it pertains to
the concept of dehumanizing humanity.
Others claim it relates to the erosion of virtues.
Perhaps it is about disinformation, propaganda,
conspiracy theories, and hate speech.
I have heard that folks can utilize
fake accounts to amass followers.
Certainly, it does not relate to the moral right of freedom
that leads to a democratic process.
This is the reason many have begun
to discuss corruption and acts of violence.
They speak of people who breach norms
while asserting their adherence to them.
Perhaps there is a collective need for transparency,
and perhaps no one genuinely desires to be corrupt.
Undoubtedly, it concerns those who act in what
they perceive to be morally right,
although in reality, it is not morally justifiable.
Furthermore, it does not involve women
living as object-like entities.
It involves code words, dogwhistles,
money, and bombs.

**STEFAN HEUER**

BURGDORF, GERMANY

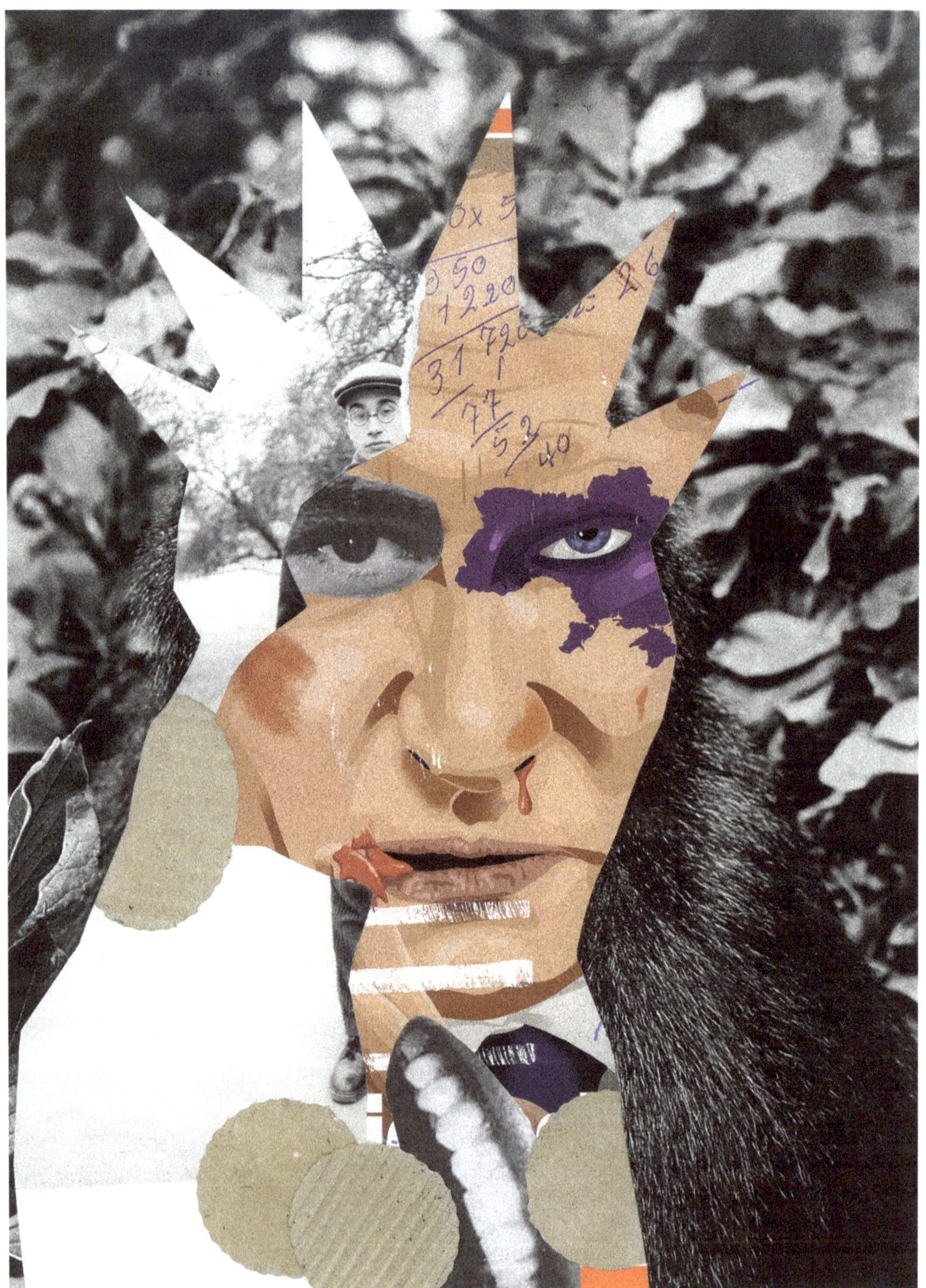

## DIE BLUTENDE NASE DES RUSSISCHEN KÖNIGS

*Analog collage, paper on cardboard, 27.3 cm x 20.0 cm*

**JEANNE-MARIE OSTERMAN**
NEW YORK, NEW YORK

## CLIMBING THE DEVIL'S NOSE

I'm riding the tourist train through the Andes of Ecuador.
We're climbing the Devil's Nose.

*These tracks were laid by Jamaican prisoners, the tour guide says.*
*Over a hundred years ago, they were brought here in chains.*

The tracks lie on a gash cut into the mountain by the prisoners' picks.
The ties, like teeth, grin at the valley below.

*If they survived the job, they'd be set free.*
*But most died of overwork, or fell off the mountain.*

Folks are hanging out windows screaming and snapping selfies,
arms flailing, tongues out, like inflatable tube men.

*North American engineers were brought in.*
*They promised the Jamaicans gold, fruit, and their freedom.*

An Alausí woman trips and falls in the aisle, a tray of Chicklets
yoked to her neck.

## ORCHID SPANGIAFORA

WYNCOTE, PENNSYLVANIA

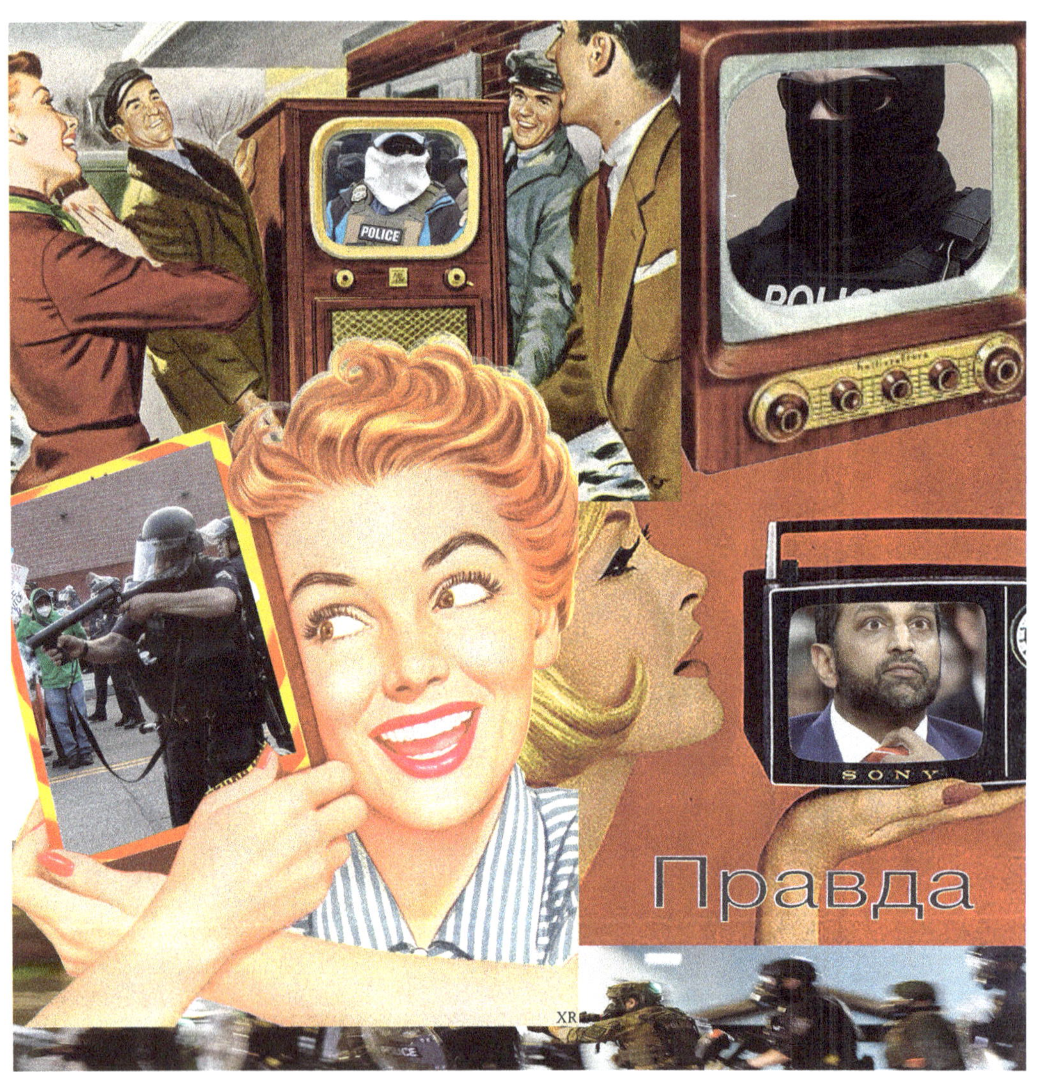


**PRAVDA**

*Digital collage, 3392 px x 2548 px*

**MARIAM AHMED**
SAN DIEGO, CALIFORNIA

## ACCORDING TO THE NEWS:

The world will keep clearing its throat.
Another headline will arrive before the last
one finishes breathing.
Winter will practice its sharpest voice,
and somewhere a street will fill with people
holding signs like fragile weather.

Borders will argue with bodies.
Governments will speak in careful verbs.
Someone powerful will say stability
while meaning wait
.
Wars will pause only in grammar,
not in fact.
The Olympics will ask for silence,
and history will politely decline.

The planet will keep sending notes
written in fire and flood.
We will call the anomalies
because the truth is louder

Hotter, wetter, crowded

And still—
poems will be written on phones at red lights,
on receipts, in classrooms, in exile.
Someone will fall in love between alerts.
Someone will refuse despair
by naming things carefully.

According to the news,
tomorrow is uncertain.
According to poetry,
we're still here,
still watching,
still choosing words like they matter
because they do.

**RUUD JANSSEN**

BREDA, THE NETHERLANDS

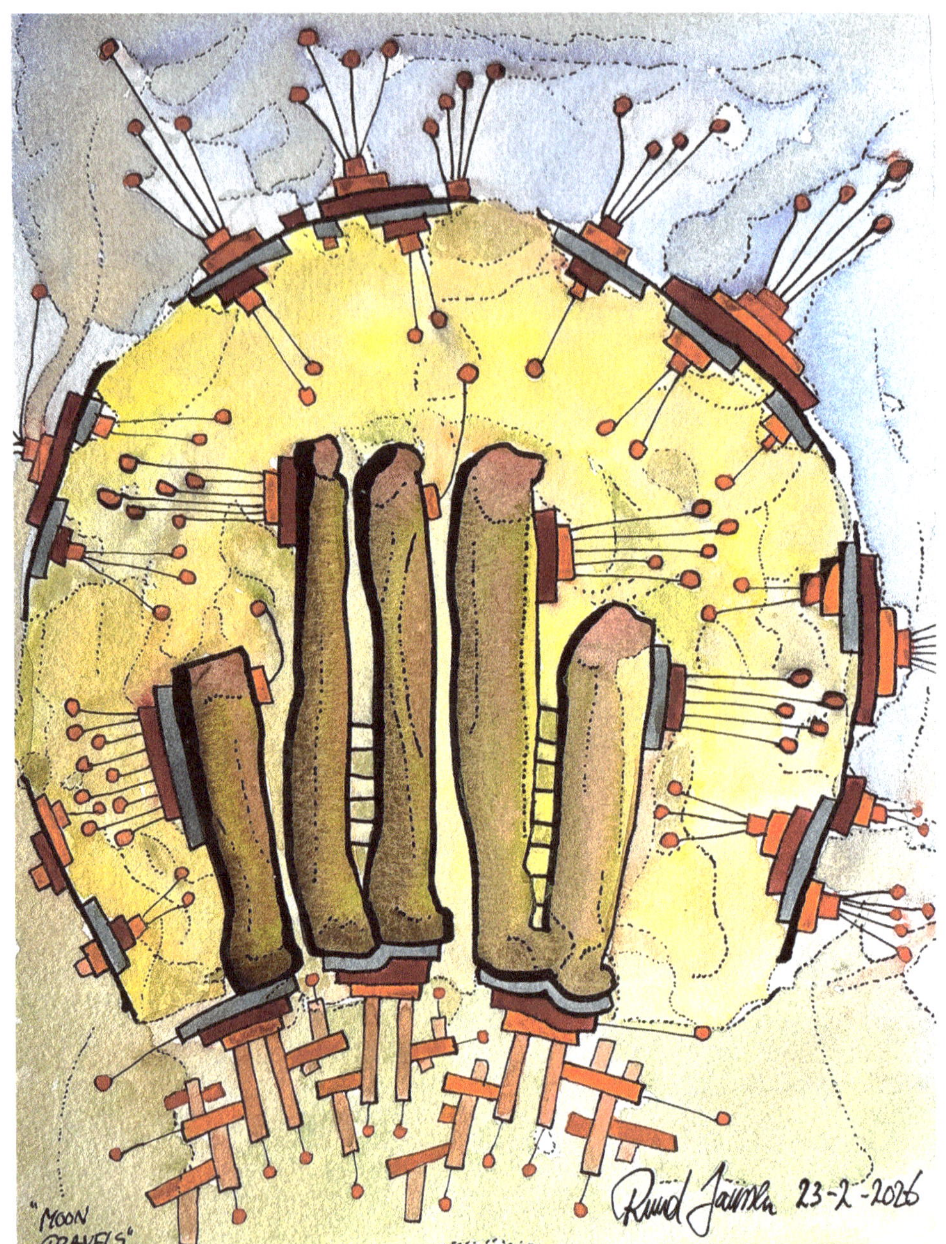


**MOON TRAVELS**

*Indian ink and watercolors on 400 gm² paper, 24 cm x 32 cm*

**BILLY CANCEL**
BROOKLYN, NEW YORK

## LUMINOUS SCARECROW
### *Performative*

reflected our pig evening ignition attitude kept
us from thugocracy outage global darkness
lit our ramble through much unmapped
forgotten rural then post - industrial de - wild on the trail of
the Watchers before Stacked Taurus a - go - go intervened
pulsed cordial greeting assured us no more lunar vagaries or
lighting curdle thunder sour. we can't think in these terms

of discomfort avoidance right now consider the weathered
conifer upon a bleak ledge however it is still nearly impossible
to appreciate the Nuclear Rhododendrons of Zag Valley when
every cold wet morning we kept getting flown over by

DRONES squadrons
of DRONES whole brigades
of DRONES roaring across
the sky mad. all part of

hack the planet
half save it.

## ANTONIA ALEXANDRA KLIMENKO

PARIS, FRANCE

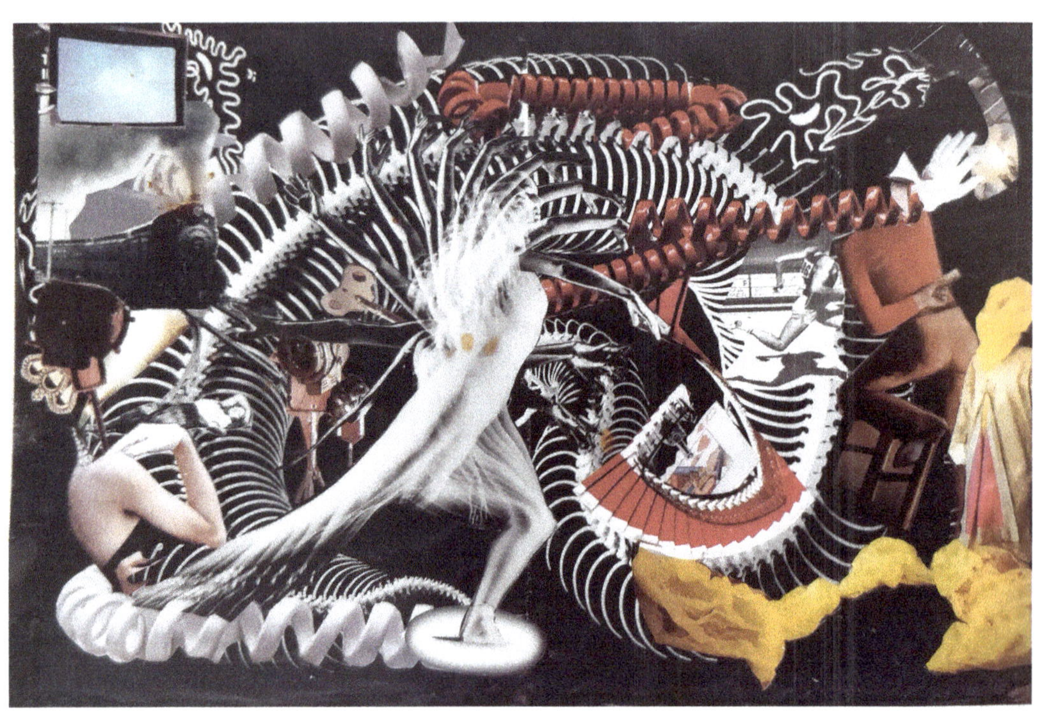

**FAKE NEXS**

*Collage of magazine print, 24 in by 16 in*

**JACK COOPER**
PARIS, FRANCE

## DIOGENES RESARTUS

What's good for the news's
good for the propergan-
da. The naked truth, a
calumniated knave,
vilified, defamed, con-
tinues its search, compelled
within a stave and a
hoop. Insubstantial ev-
er, volatile, vapor-
ous, dissipate, the word
(even in the begin-
ning) amounted to lit-
tle more than the distil-
lation of breath, proved du-
bitative, to bruit, giv-
en human predilec-
tion to lie: materi-
alized, in permanence,
written down: moveable
type, celluloid, vid-e
o: derivatives of
light. The golem rises,
misbegotten, gotten
on silicon, the sands
of time. Who is is not.

## MARK BLICKLEY

LONG ISLAND CITY, NEW YORK

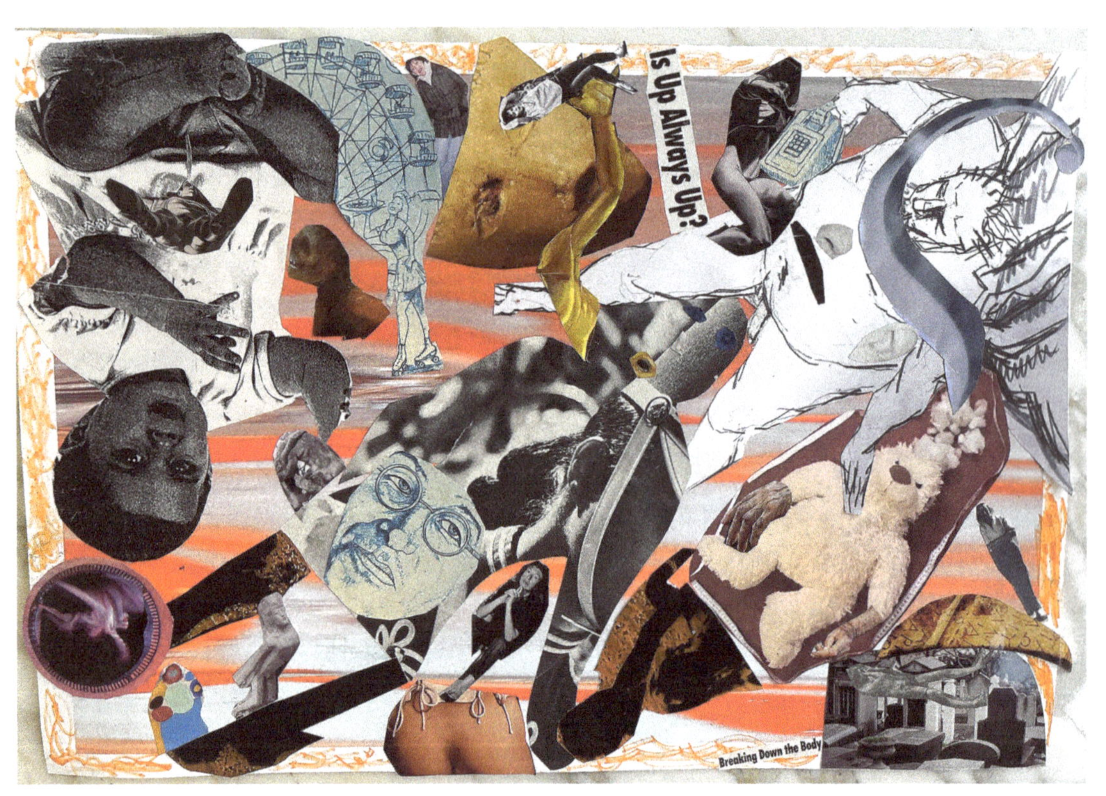


### I WANNA BE BURIED IN CAPRI PANTS

*Handmade collage, 16 in x 20 in*

GEORGE WALLACE
HUNTINGTON, NEW YORK

## WHAT AILS YOU, MY PRETTY

*"I wish I was free of that slaving meat wheel and safe in heaven dead" —Jack Kerouac*

The pleasant little solitaire
the penthouse gesture
the bold little lonely shuffle
all the sexy stock options
on every platform and corner
a proposition a proposition
for you dear land broker
for you, a turnstile of love,
the crosshairs of money
for you, a revolving door
of indices and economic indicators
what ails you, my pretty
what ails you my pretty
living on the top floor
of meat wheel America
uneasy ego oasis
of jerkweed & pride
your name in every windowpane
your name a new minted coin
a sensational pay-off
unreal real estate
who got the big chromium smile, you!
who got the money roll belly bar, you!
your hookers and slaves
your yes men and pimps
your prisons and public enemies
rev it up screw it down
stiff it stifle it deny it deny it
double down double down
dump it out on cobblestones
the rainbow shines for you alone
the rainbow climbs for you alone
o you nasty little loser
what ails you my pretty
what ails you my pretty
the pleasant little solitaire
the penthouse gesture
the bold little lonely shuffle
all the sexy stock options
on every platform and corner
you bully your way around
what ails you my pretty
living in the penthouse
of meat wheel America

**DEVON BALWIT**

PORTLAND, OREGON


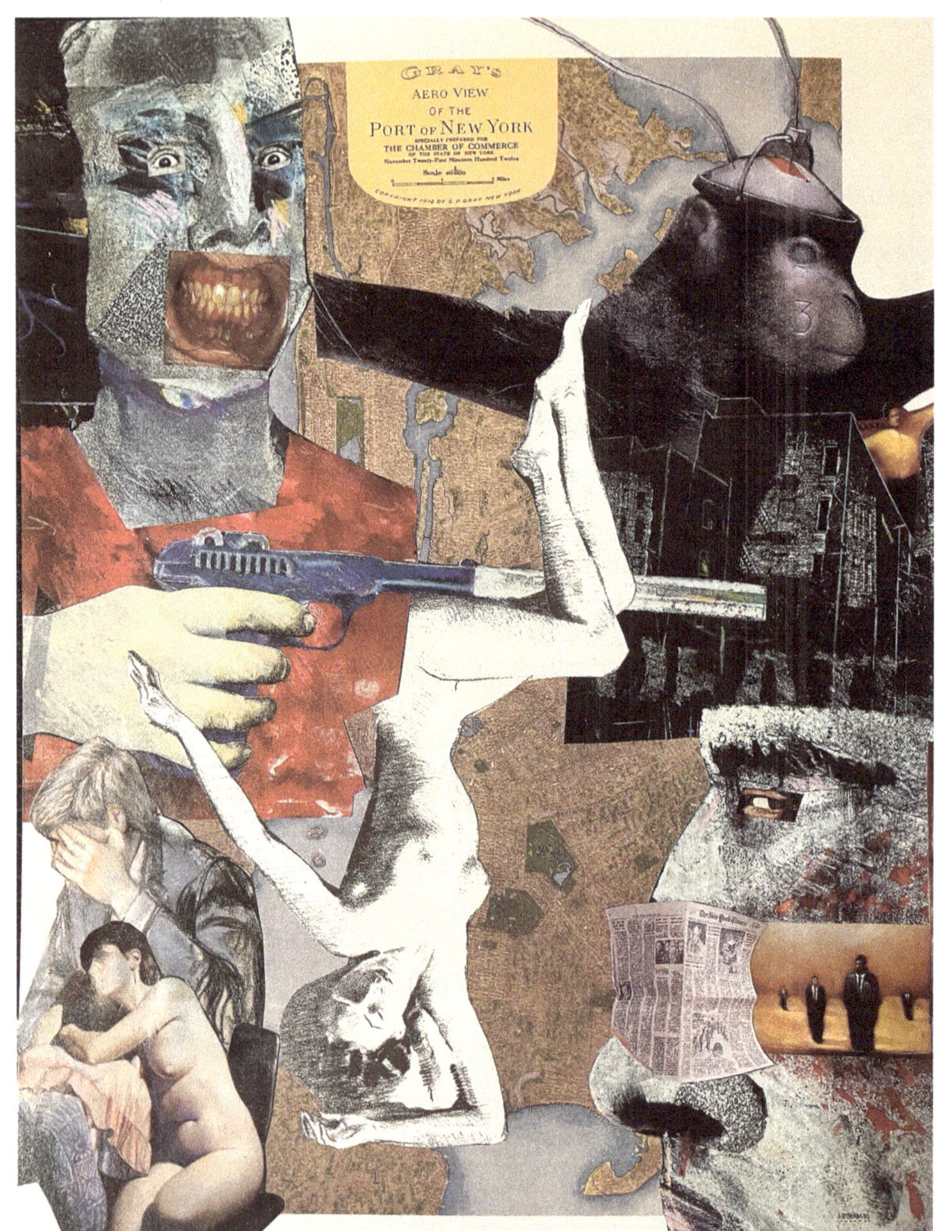


**NOT THAT!**

*Cut paper collage, 9 in x 12 in*

**RICH FERGUSON**
LOS ANGELES, CALIFORNIA

## LICKING STAR NECTAR FROM NIGHT'S DARK COLLARBONE: A FAMILY DIARY

This we call Family, a car full of borrowed faces, children orbiting
a sun busting at the seams like homes we grew up in and out of,

moving towards another home, a helter skelter beyond the milk and honey.
Before us, road unwinds, a black ribbon unspooling, no cosmic thread

holding it together in picture-perfect constellation. Family, or a word like it,
is passed from one tongue to another, until it inside-out lullabies,

a sound deconstructed by a motherless mother. This car, this road, these tires
hum like beastsnore awakening before midkill. Litany of pills,

counterclockwise laughter, nervous leg twitch. The glint of a gun,
nothing more than light bending in a way that better suits the making

of a tombstone's shadow. In streetlight-streaked car windows, our faces
blur and stutter, desert mirages doubled, tripled, dissolved, then reborn.

Family, a word sweet in the mouth, star nectar licked from night's
dark collarbone. Hold the taste for too long, it draws blood

like the knife-blade moon slung low over Cielo Drive. What happens to words
that turn to smoke as soon as fire ignites? What happens to vengeance

that propels the time-lapse heartbeat to its final bloom? What spell
will bedlam ghosts to carve eyes on eyelids of the dead?

## STEVE DALACHINSKY

(1946–2019)

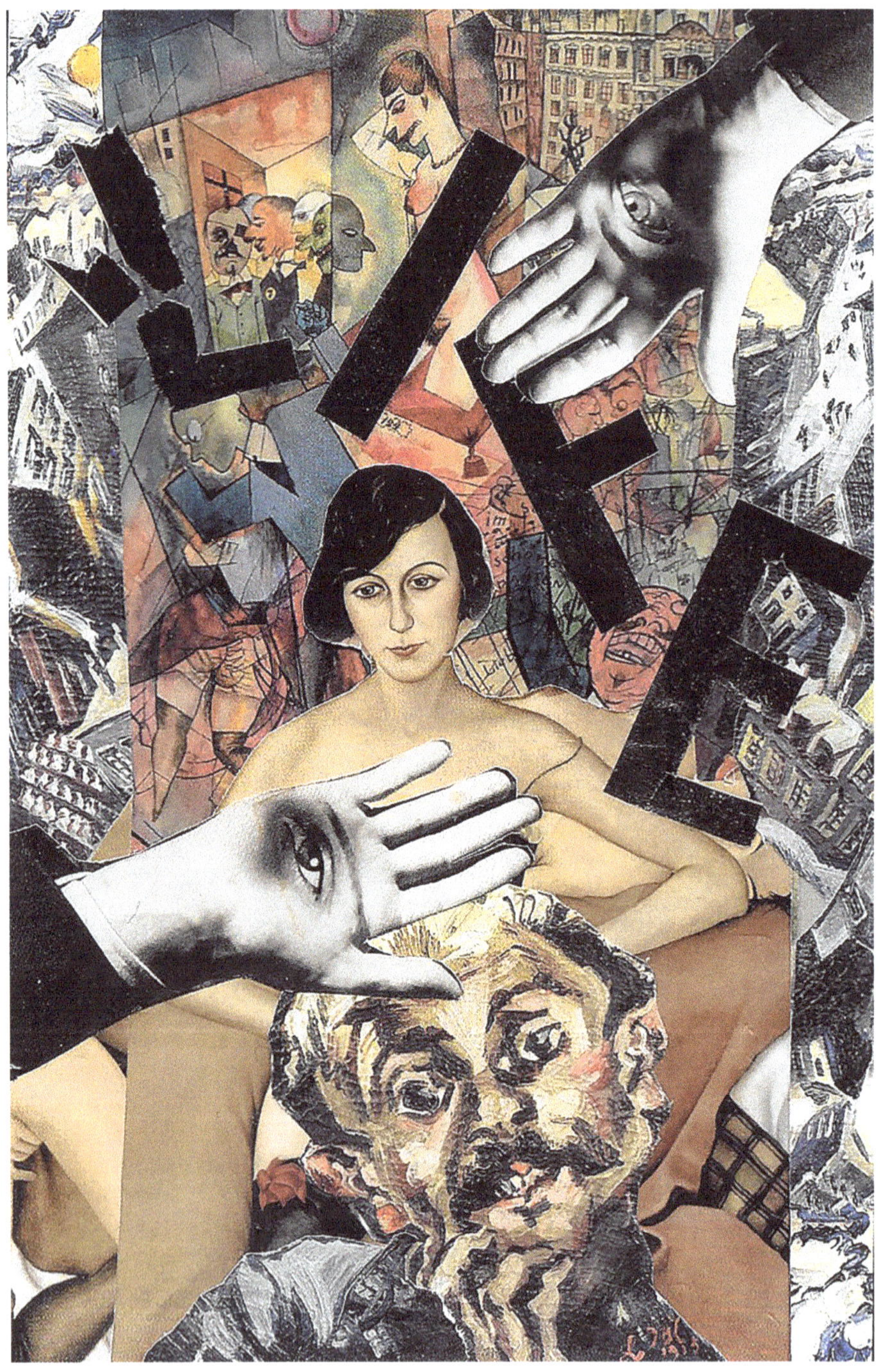


**WEIMAR**

*Collage*

**YUKO OTOMO**

NEW YORK, NEW YORK

## IM; PRO; PER; GAN; DA (Please Kill Me Already!!!)

An **Im**aginary *im*postor *im*minently **Pr**ophesizes a prodigal protection system of our future well-being.

**Per**sonal *per*fection will never be the same or *per*manent, he adds.

But, no worries.

**Gan**esh, Ganga & Gan will protect us all from any calamity, nonetheless.

So, let's relax & sing along! Or scatt away our blues!

**Da** Da Da Da Da Da Da....

It's a year of the hobby (fire)horse.

Dandelions will be the coolest flowers to worship this spring, he adds.

Sadly, a sign of the approaching spring doesn't make me feel any better in this corrupt world that is so corrupt so as to make the word "corruption" lose its meaning totally. I have lost all faith in WORDS in general totally. How can I trust his words?

I hate being a human! I've never felt comfortable since I was born. I don't belong to our species. I've had it! I'm not listening to anyone or any words.

I'd rather be an accidental shadow cast on a tiny pebble without reason.

I'm sick & tired of fooling myself with the stupid human word game.

Please kill me already!

So, I won't be a useless victim of the nonstop **IMPROPERGANDA**

anymore

for

NOTHING

finally

!!!

CHRISTIAN GEORGESCU
LOS ANGELES, CALIFORNIA

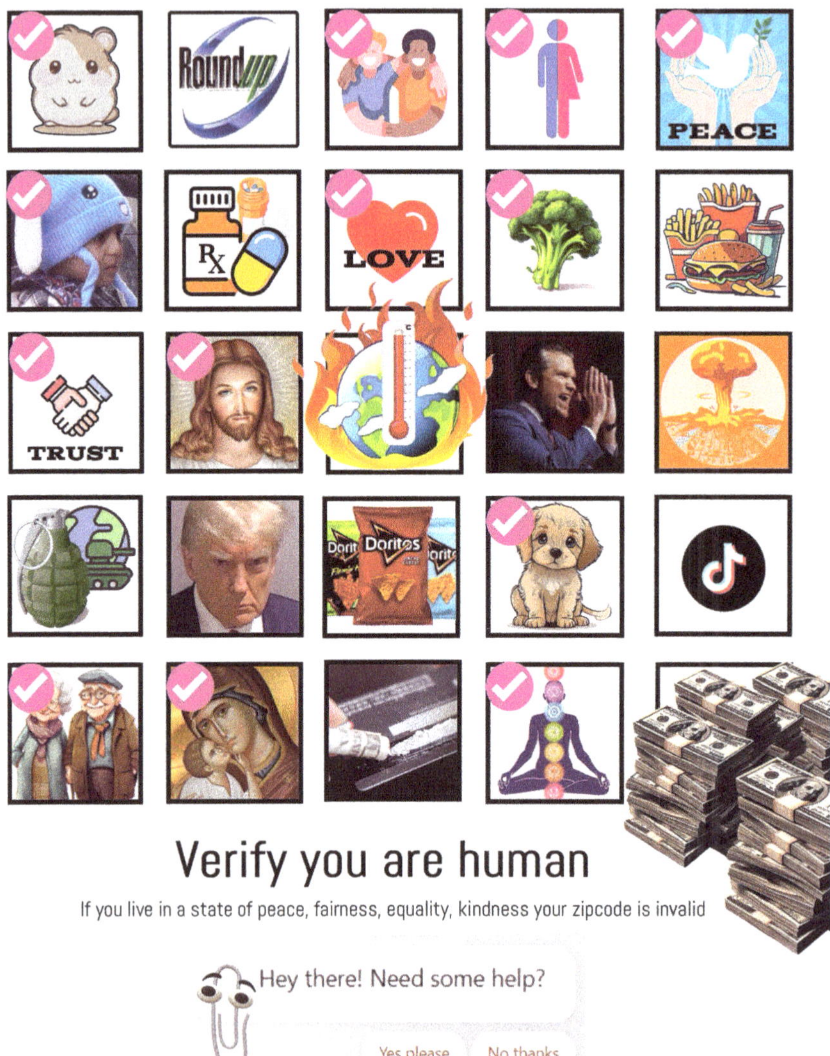


**VERIFY YOU ARE HUMAN**

*Digital collage*

**PETE DOLACK**
BROOKLYN, NEW YORK

## NO BOTS ABOUT IT

We are at the point where lies don't have to be original anymore
Bots can just scrape the Internet
For all the nonsense anybody could want
Garbage in, garbage out was the saying of programmers
In the early days of computers
Now we have garbage beyond imagination
If the newspapers and radio and television all agree
Why should a bot argue?
Just repeat, repeat, repeat the line of the day
Or the line of the century
Everything is just fine
You can't pay the rent, can't afford healthcare, can't take a day off
Because it's your fault
Never the fault of an inhumane system that is most efficient
When it takes from you to give to the billionaire who can never have enough
Humans who are billionaires and humans who believe they will be
Tell you nonsense, tell you that you can be one of us
If only you work hard enough
But it takes an army of poor people and middle-class people to make a billionaire
We'd call it trickle-up theory if we were honest or possessed the mass media
Instead the limitless greed of the few is presented to us as human nature
Propagandists no longer have to work alone to convince you of this
Because they have an army of bots to help out
Artificial intelligence (no, artificial nonsense) is only progress
If we accept that lies are all we deserve

## ED GO

BROOKLYN, NEW YORK

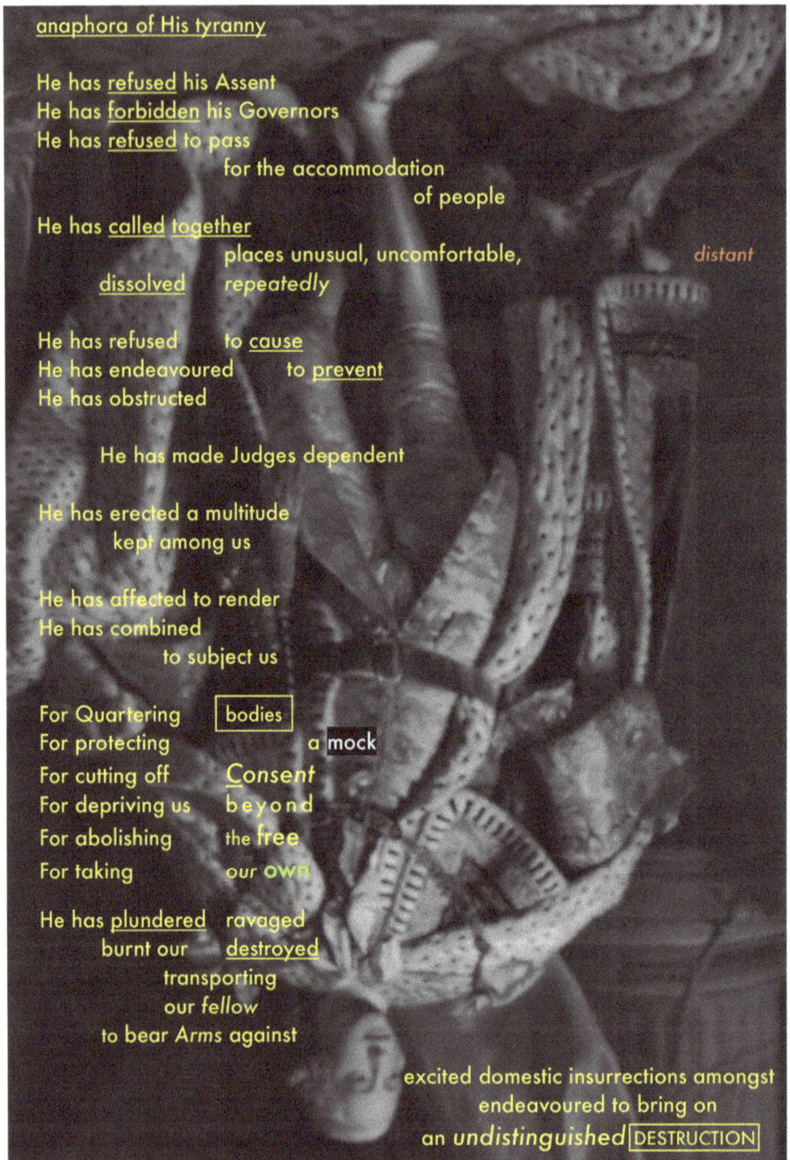


### ANAPHORA OF HIS TYRANNY

*Text piece with public domain digital image*

**JILL BLOCKER**

ZÜRICH, SWITZERLAND

## MAGA HATS AND HATE

A rose is red,
the sky is blue,
These are some things I know as truth.

The grass is green,
a young bird sings.
These are the things I hear and see.

A child cries, a mother dies, a bust of death and light.
We see these things as separate beings,
but know that they are not.

The words they say. the lies they claim, told to us as truth.
In many different languages and a multitude of texts.

Believe me,
Glauben Sie mir,
יל ןימאת,
،يب قث,
Glo my, créeme.

It will be great, it will be good, if you do exactly what we say.
If you view the grass as green, and if you know this is as rose.
If you do not see the bombs or people taken from their homes.
If what you think and what you know are undoubtedly the same.

**TATE SWINDELL**
SAN FRANCISCO, CALIFORNIA

## WISE FERAL FOXES

I can outlast any god that you have invented
I can walk backwards     within                    blindly
Pretend I didn't see
                                        Forget I forgot
                                                                        Didn't hear a thing
Love                    without               love                    &
Confuse it all up to code into a pome

I've been reading some things
I've been talking
I've been doing a little bit of listening
I've been doing a whole lotta watching

What about you?

I can sing karaoke alone without a microphone, without an orchestra, without an audience, a song without words—only thoughts never to stumble onto a page

I can entomb projections six feet under and hand you a map labeled treasure

But you have to use your hands to dig                                    Dig          ?

Endorphins                              Oxytocin                              Dopamine

Alcohol                    Cocaine                    Ecstasy

I've been reading
I've been writing....a little
I've been talking
I've been doing a little bit of listening
I've been doing a whole lotta watching

What about you?

I can stay silent about everything
I  can talk forever about nothing
I can outlast any god that you have invented

**MIKE M. MOLLETT**
LOS ANGELES, CALIFORNIA

## BODY POLITICKLE

my head has lost its ability to erase or correct
who uses a pencil anymore

my face is typical but necessary   glued to media
my face no longer is what it seems

going down the neck from the skull   lower   is really creepy
when you arrive at the shoulders   the messages
swirl into uncertain cacophony
speed bumps accrue   pain meds run out

if you believe this you are as disturbed as I am.
is a break possible   You & I are somehow interlocked
having sex
has not been this good for some time

the chest   breasts   & the nipples are
tempting   believable   look at the reels repeatedly
we must slow down into the camps of many armies
what is the meaning in this you might ask?
what act of will manages to lean back for any truth  any fun?

abs & navels   groin ass   dick & pussy
politics   vernaculars   simplification/understandings
try to melt in the middle without really saying so
joy to the world rings grab-bags in the fuzzy light
in this softer unmappable dialogue

legs do their best to sturdy up the traffic's misunderstanding
see to it that the feet receive fresh socks & souls before washing

saying hallelujah in your sleep is about all there is to say
checking the spelling & the waiting list for typos
even these are untrustworthy
will you believe me?

**JEFF BOYNTON**

LOS ANGELES, CALIFORNIA

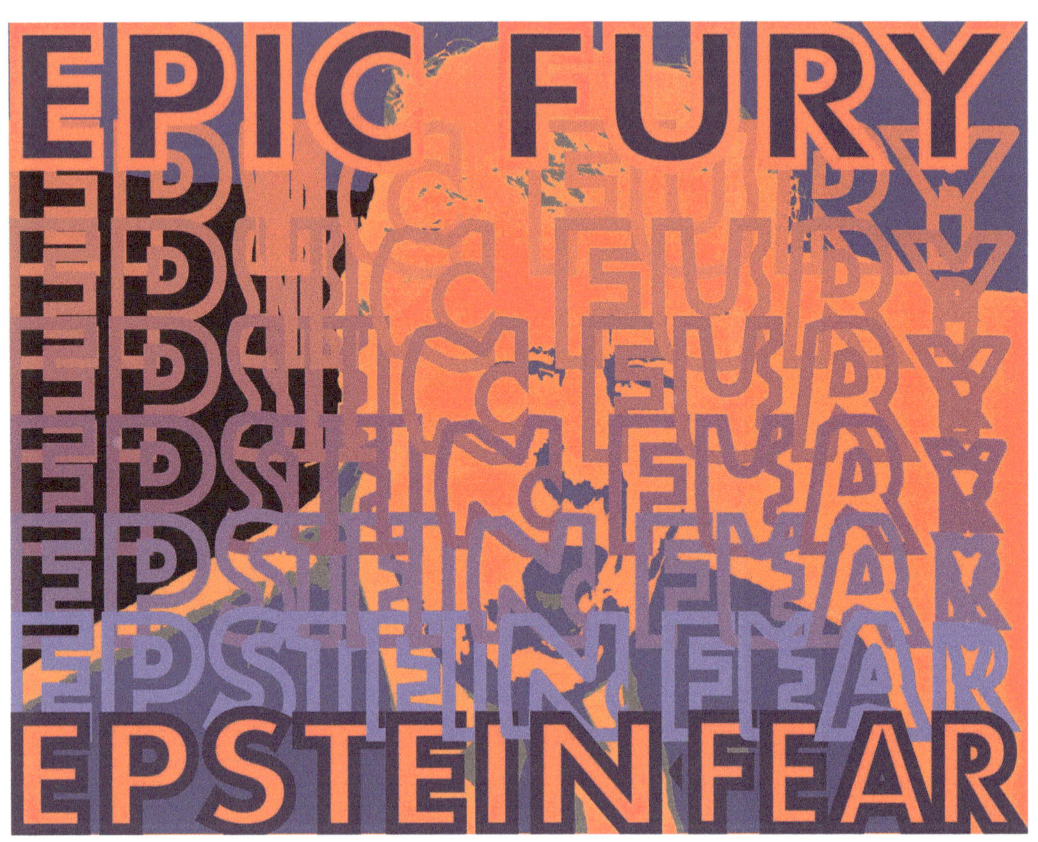


**WHAT DOES EF STAND FOR?**

*Digital collage*

**LAWRENCE MILES**
WHITE PLAINS, NEW YORK

## REWRITING HISTORY

*"Stuff happens!*
*Freedom's untidy and free people are free to make mistakes!*
*And commit crimes!*
*And do bad things!*
*They're also free to live their lives and do wonderful things!*
*And that's what's gonna happen here!"*
*—Donald Rumsfeld*

When the Secretary of Defense made this statement
our government had just finished
deposing of a dictator
and left the liberated to figure things out

And when we discovered the results
had not gone as we wanted
our government used dogs and waterboarding
to get what they wanted

This statement was not repeated
when people protested in Ferguson and Minneapolis and DC
and tore down statues
because it did not suit the government's interest

This statement was not repeated
when the President of the United States
tried to silence protestors with tear gas and flash bombs
as he marched to a house of worship

When you protest injustice
it is untidy
as it should be

You will make mistakes
as it should be

You will commit crimes
as it should be

they will say you are doing bad things
when you are doing good things
as it should be
because you are free to live your lives
and do wonderful things
and that is what is gonna happen here.

## MAUREEN ALSOP

NELLY BAY, AUSTRALIA

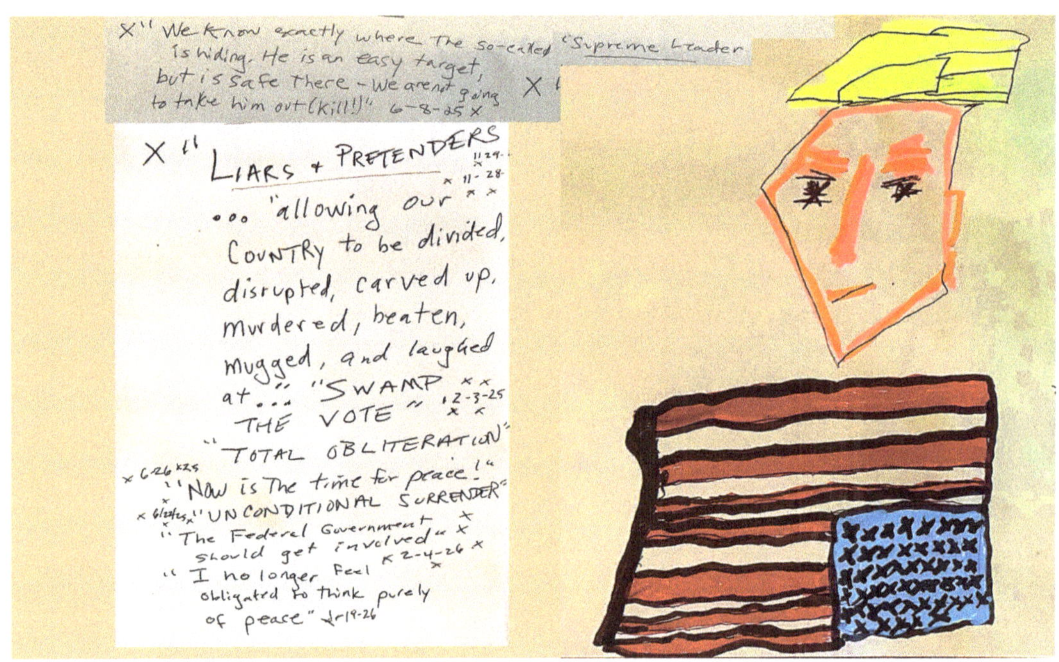


## DONNIE X

*Quotes from X by Donald Trump, drawing, excerpt from notebook/journal, 8 in x 10 in*

## NEAL SKOOTER TAYLOR (LA DADA)

LOS ANGELES, CALIFORNIA

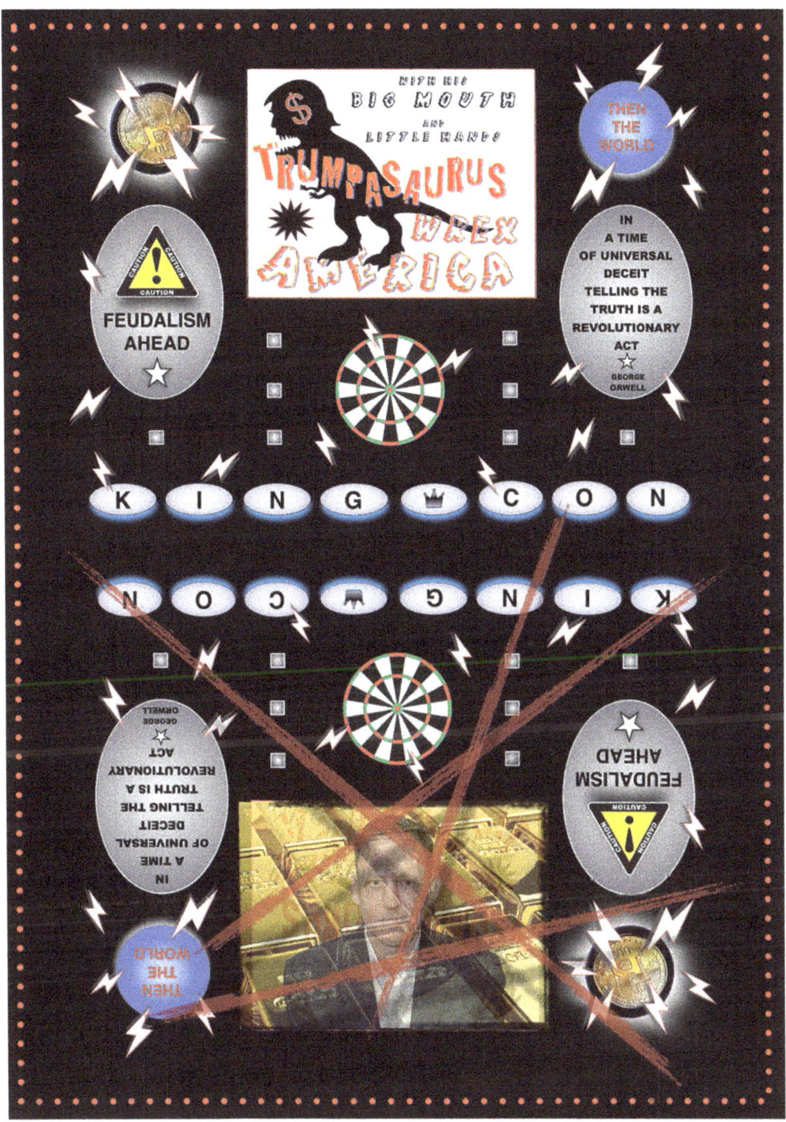


### TRUMPASAURUS WREX AMERICA

*Digital collage*

**PHILLIP GIAMBRI**

NEW YORK, NEW YORK

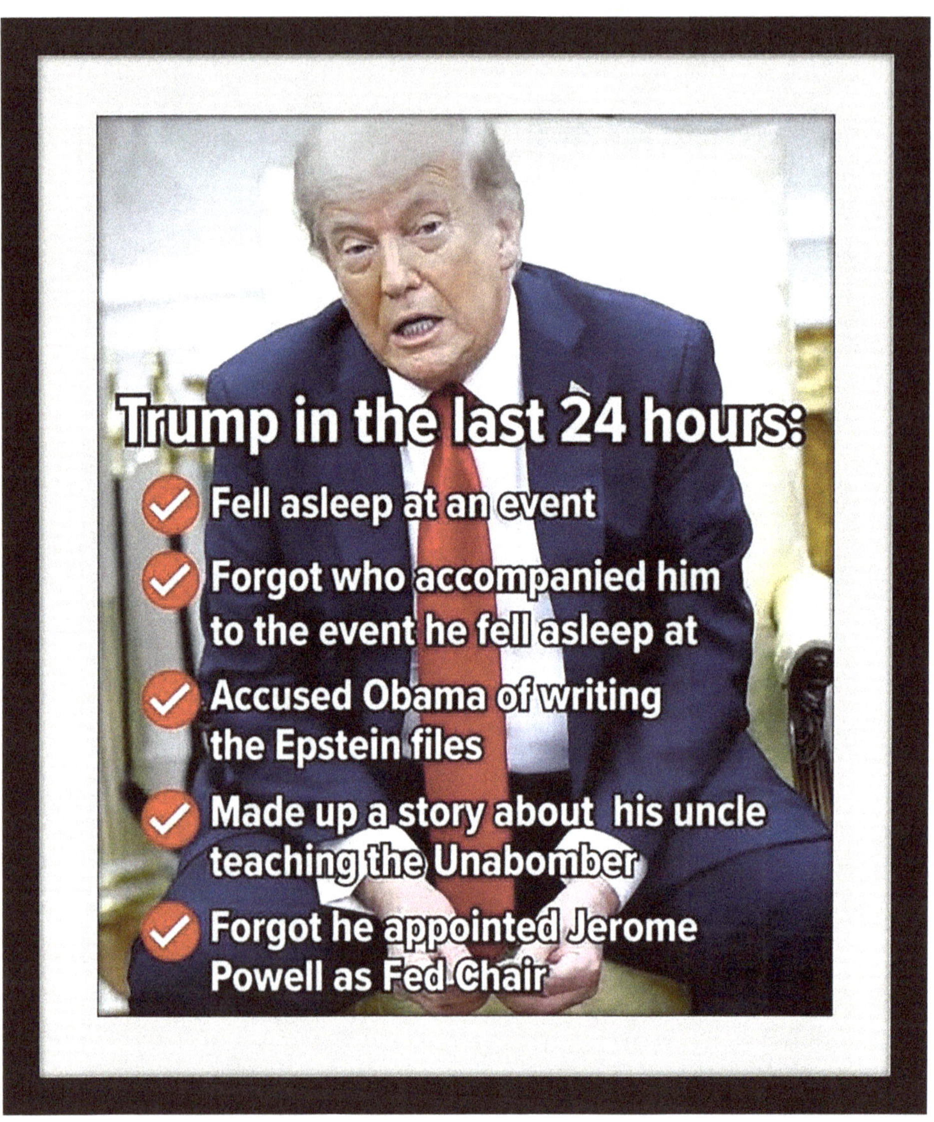


**TRUMP IN THE LAST 24 HOURS**

*Digital photo*

**TRAVIS RICHARDSON**
CULVER CITY, CALIFORNIA

## AS MY DAD LAY DYING

As my dad lay dying, I feel sadness for lost time between us. I am enraged by the lies that dominated his life for the last 30 plus years, creating a wedge between us that grew into a gulf and eventually turned us into continents existing in separate hemispheres. No bridge, no ferry, no airplane could unite what once was.

In another time, I respected his vast knowledge as a world history teacher and his virtuous quest for truth that he taught in the classroom and the home. He had been an outdoorsman who stopped supporting the NRA due to their extreme advocacy. A conservative who was annoyed by Rush Limbaugh's arrogance and exaggerations. A Christian who believed in being well read and having a broad perspective of the world.

Although we had differences about religion, the real divide started with the Gore v Bush election when he parroted the Republican's line that a recount was unnecessary.

His rhetoric amped up every year thereafter with false propaganda like:

- Nobody knew bin Laden was going to attack
- Saddam Hussein has weapons of mass destruction
- John Kerry never carried out any swift boat missions
- Obama was not born in the United States
- Obama was going to take his guns
- Russia did not interfere with the election in favor of Trump.
- The January 6 insurrection was led by Antifa or a "few bad guys"
- Trump won the 2020 election

There were so many more lies that he regurgitated with conviction, making casual conversations impossible as we devolved into shouting matches. My Dad's soul was hijacked by parasitic grifters who ate away his core. Visits and calls became stressful burdens I often avoided.

Now, his fight along with his body has dwindled. His mind peppered with dementia. I loathe every fraud who has, for power and profit, created a legacy of torn families, mistrusting citizens, and a perilous world.

## LINDA J. ALBERTANO

(1942–2022)

# DELUXE DAMAGE (ROAR)

An apish, orange-pated abomination
who's now in charge
of a luxury death machine sits
sunny-side up
on a luxury lily pad in a luxury lily pond.

He's green and preening
(knee-deep, knee-deep). Watching
icecaps melt in his premium whisky. Watching
polar bears dance on the point of a pin.

He's warm.
And sweaty. Fire, flood, and famine
fill his oily black planet. He's hungry.

An unwary human towing wife and kiddies
suddenly snags his attention.
Thip! Thip! Thip, Thip, Thip! Five quick flicks
of his flypaper tongue.
Collateral damage: complete.

Happy hunting, Warmonger. You'll bomb us all
back to the Stone Age.

Soon.

**C. MEHRL BENNETT**

COLUMBUS, OHIO

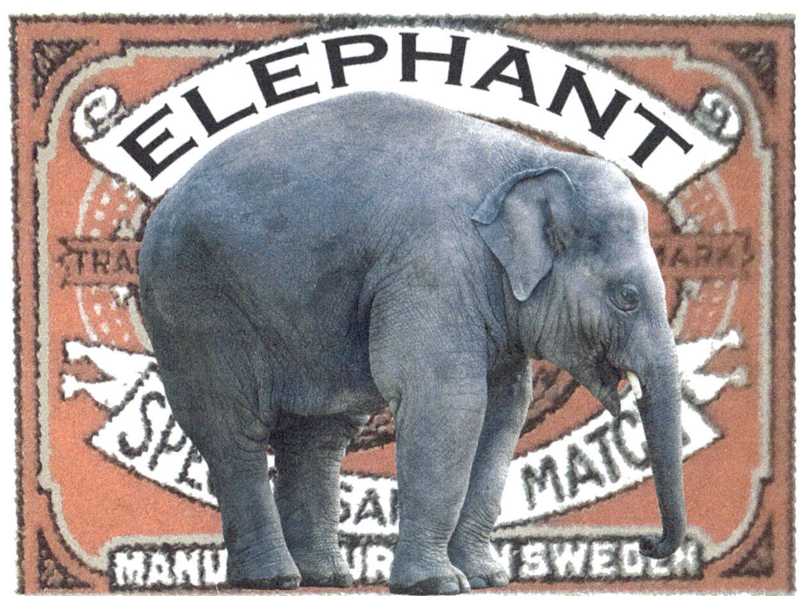


**E very time Trump**
**L ies, an angel bakes an**
**E lephant a**
**P ie; and that is why**
**H appy elephants**
**A re less likely to**
**N otice**
**T rump's rump**

**ELEPHANT**

*An acrostic poem & collage, 1500 px x 2100 px*

**S.A. GRIFFIN**
HOLLYWOOD, CALIFORNIA

## WHITE HOUSE PRESS CONFERENCE

I am announcing a cease fire with Iran as we have now completely obliterated Iran,
achieved victory, and just to be clear, are not interested in any cease fire.
So we will be sending more boots on the ground because
boots are made for walking, am I right? I've never been so right.
We are therefore declaring victory and asking for a cease fire
because NATO and all our European allies are cowards.
And of course, this is all Biden's fault. Remember him, President Autopen?
Worst president ever! All his fault. And if I were president then, I wouldn't be president now
and this war would've been over on day one because I wouldn't be president and the war
would've never happened. I mean, how about all this winning? I get so tired of winning,
I'm tellin' ya... but somebody's gotta do it, right?
And I just want to let you know that Iran is begging for a cease fire! Begging!!
I mean really, they were on their knees begging me, "Sir, SIR..." they always call me SIR,
"Sir, can we have a cease fire, please, please?!" I mean they love me over there, right?
and I love my little revolutionaries too, just like I love all our vets.
I mean, where would all our little doggies and kitties be without our beautiful vets?
But just to be clear, I am not interested in diseased fire. And contrary to the
lying liberal media's reporting, everything is perfect. I mean, are we tired of winning yet?
So much winning! Never before has the world seen anything like it!
500, 600, 700 dollars a barrel for oil is a good thing. Winning, winning, winning!
So today, me and my good friend Ayatollah Number 5, that's what I call him
because they're all dead and he jokingly calls me 48. Hey, ya never know, right?
So me and Number 5 are demanding that Iran open the Strait of Hormuz,
which was never closed to begin with. And just to be perfectly clear I like Spam,
it tastes so good with mustard, and the U.S. is not at war with Iran because quite frankly,
we have obliterated any chance of peace during this quite lovely excursion.

**YARYAN**

CANYON COUNTRY, CALIFORNIA

## PROP GO THE WEASELS

Strangelove's lost playbook / substandard propaganda / mugshot overkill
Give him a peace prize / quick before he goes psycho / loves the bomb again
No need for posters / demonizing enemies / that's really old hat

Prop go the weasels / prop go the weasels once more / prop go the weasels

Reinvent the steal / perpetuate the scam art / new spectator sport
Oil schematic chart / shows where all the money flows / fleas and ticks flood map
Imperial trap / warmonger sugar spice world / sweet apathy cubes

Prop go the weasels / prop go the weasels once more / prop go the weasels

Greenland was ours first / say it straight-faced crazy-eyed / see what it gets you
Don't grow a conscience / just obsess the resources / the cost of killing
Manufacture threats / eliminate paper trails / choke social programs

Prop go the weasels / prop go the weasels once more / prop go the weasels

A detour not war / outrage is in low supply / nonchalant flip flop
Chasing oil tankers / big beautiful butterflies / someone please save them
Kick a hornets' nest / don't kick profiteering fix / start Armageddon

Prop go the weasels / prop go the weasels once more / prop go the weasels

Villainy phase one / no accountability / blast every question
Divert attention / while Nero plays his fiddle / show off the gold drapes
Big shots go golfing / cheat to win while folks suffer / blissful ignorance

Prop go the weasels / prop go the weasels once more / prop go the weasels

Stack up the tall tales / pin them all on the donkeys / stoke false rebellion
Empty thoughts and play / brainless dictator pinball / branding matters most
Tacky redneck hat / make slogan sound like maggots / people buy this tripe

Prop go the weasels / prop go the weasels once more / prop go the weasels

**JOHN J. TRAUSE & CHAD GEPITTI**
WOOD-RIDGE, NEW JERSEY & SAN FRANCISCO, CALIFORNIA

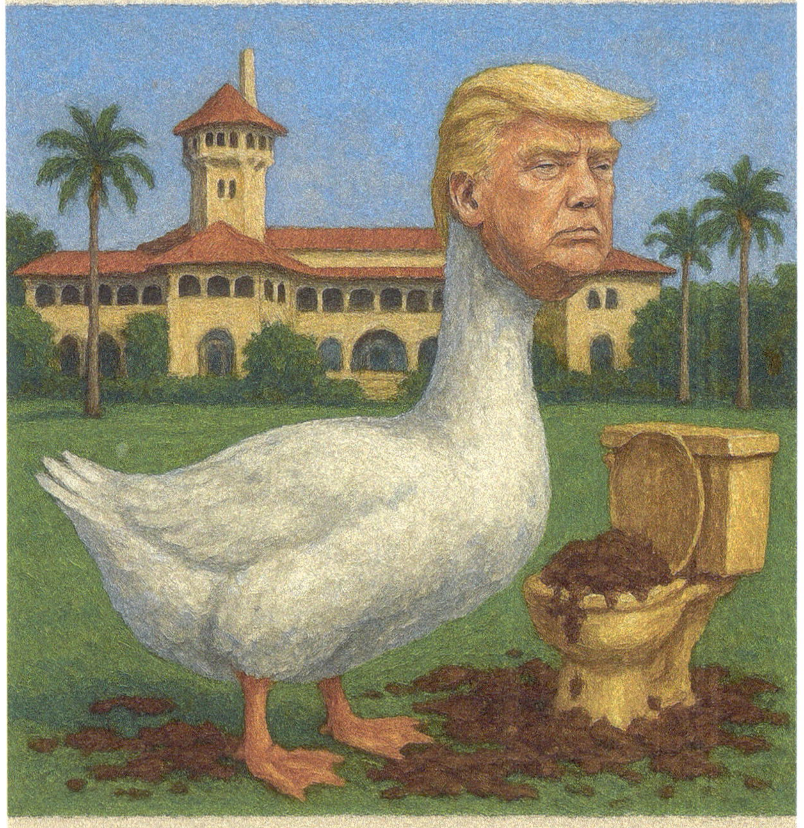


**IMPROPER GANDER: THE GOOSE THAT MISSED THE GOLDEN TOILET**

*Acrylic on board (wood), 24 in x 60 in*

**JOANNE GRUMET**
NEW YORK, NEW YORK

## GOLDEN CRAPPER

Asswipe,

asswipe,

how many

asswipes

does the man

need?

One for each

ass kisser

**MARTINA SALISBURY**
BROOKLYN, NEW YORK

## TWO TRUTHS AND A LIE

"In a world that has *really been turned upside down*, the true is a moment of the false."

Guy Debord, *The Society of the Spectacle*, 1967

a snapshot of cherry (bombs) placed
on my ears in a ghost garden

sparks memories of invisible
cities in dust

& disappearances carved
into stone

sunlight spectacle
on the windowsill

the cat taking a turn
in the spotlight

eternally exchanging glances
with darkness

oblivious as the masses
turning blind eyes

to atrocity of
ignorance thinking

this could never
happen here

**TWO TRUTHS AND A LIE**

*Poem and digital collage with image from Leni Riefenstahl's film* Triumph des Willens *(1935)*

**JUAN FRAN NÚÑEZ PARREÑO**

VILLAMALEA, SPAIN

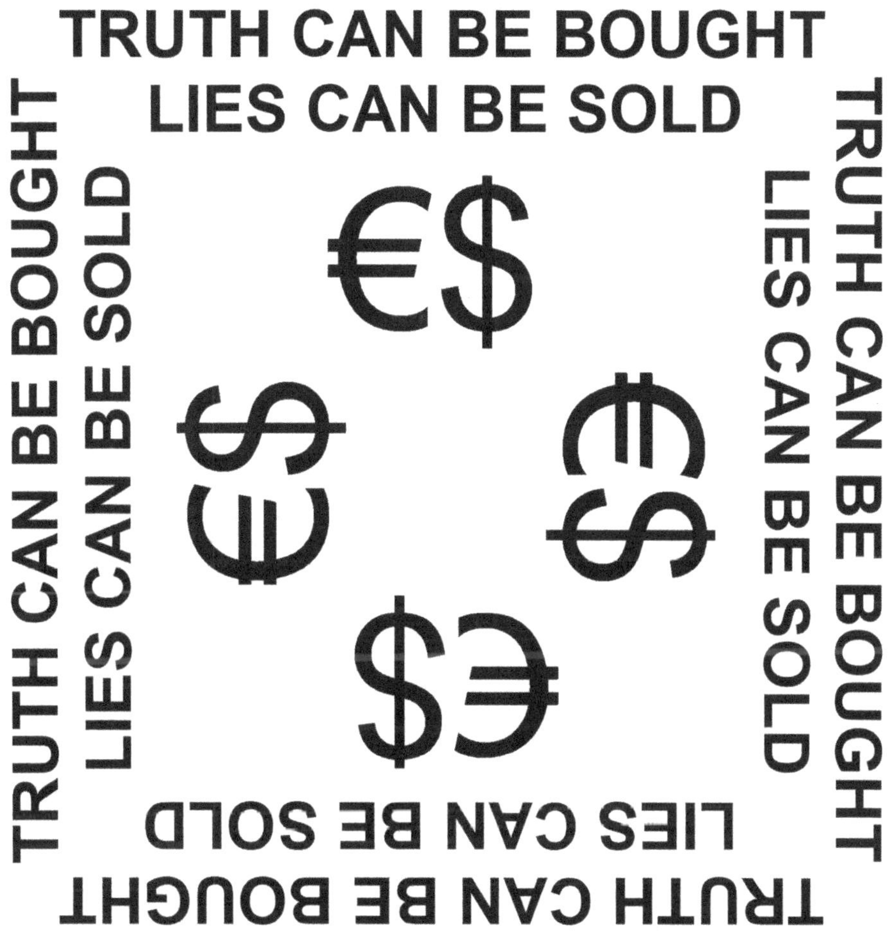


**TRUTH CAN BE BOUGHT - LIES CAN BE SOLD**

*Diseño digital, 14 cm x 15 cm*

**KAI POHL**

BERLIN GERMANY

**BEST BEFORE THE END**

CLASSIFIED

see side of label
see top of pack
see neck of bottle
see base of can

see down below
see back of pack
see side of bottle
see end of can

see side or bottom
see front of pack
see base of bottle
see top of can

DIVIDED NATIONS
HUMAN CRIMES
OFFICE OF THE FIRE COMMISSIONER

see bottle top
see base of tube
see packaging
see date on bottom

see back of box
see bottom flap
see date on pot
see end of pack

**BEST BEFORE THE END**

*Digital collage, 2480 px x 3508 px*

**RENAAT RAMON**

BRUGGE, BELGIUM

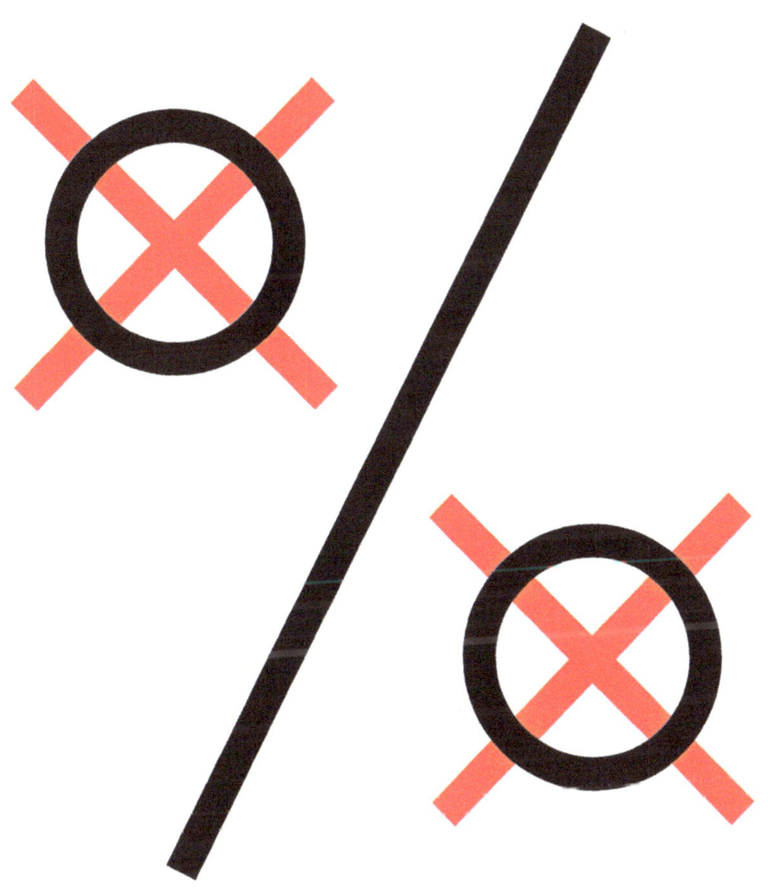

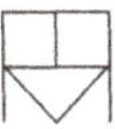

**ENDGAME**

IMPROPER

IMPROP

IMPROPER

IMPROP

IMPROPER

IMPROP

GANDA

ERGANDA

GANDA

ERGANDA

GANDA

ERGANDA

# Recent and Forthcoming Books from Three Rooms Press

FICTION
Lucy Jane Bledsoe
*No Stopping Us Now*
Rishab Borah
*The Door to Inferna*
Meagan Brothers
*Weird Girl and What's His Name*
Christopher Chambers
*Scavenger*
*Standalone*
*StreetWhys*
Ebele Chizea
*Aquarian Dawn*
Heather Colley
*The Gilded Butterfly Effect*
Ron Dakron
*Hello Devilfish!*
Ron Dakron
*Hello Devilfish!*
Robert Duncan
*Loudmouth*
Amanda Eisenberg
*People Are Talking*
Michael T. Fournier
*Hidden Wheel*
*Swing State*
Kate Gale
*Under a Neon Sun*
Aaron Hamburger
*Nirvana Is Here*
William Least Heat-Moon
*Celestial Mechanics*
Aimee Herman
*Everything Grows*
Kelly Ann Jacobson
*Tink and Wendy*
*Robin and Her Misfits*
*Lies of the Toymaker*
Jethro K. Lieberman
*Everything Is Jake*
Eamon Loingsigh
*Light of the Diddicoy*
*Exile on Bridge Street*
John Marshall
*The Greenfather*
Alvin Orloff
*Vulgarian Rhapsody*
Micki Janae
*Of Blood and Lightning*
Aram Saroyan
*Still Night in L.A.*
Robert Silverberg
*The Face of the Waters*
Stephen Spotte
*Animal Wrongs*
Max Talley
*Peace, Love and Haight*
Richard Vetere
*The Writers Afterlife*
*Champagne and Cocaine*
Jessamyn Violet
*Secret Rules to Being a Rockstar*
Julia Watts
*Quiver*
*Needlework*
*Lovesick Blossoms*
Gina Yates
*Narcissus Nobody*

ESSAYS
Richard Katrovas
*Raising Girls in Bohemia*
Vanessa Baden Kelly
*Far Away From Close to Home*
Erin Wildermuth
*Womentality*

MEMOIR & BIOGRAPHY
Nassrine Azimi and Michel Wasserman
*Last Boat to Yokohama: The Life and Legacy of Beate Sirota Gordon*
William S. Burroughs & Allen Ginsberg
*Don't Hide the Madness*
edited by Steven Taylor
James Carr
*BAD: The Autobiography of James Carr*
Judy Gumbo
*Yippie Girl: Exploits in Protest and Defeating the FBI*
Nancy Kurshan
*Levitating the Pentagon and Other Uplifting Stories*
Hédi A. Jaouad
*The Immortal Journeys of Isabelle Eberhardt*
Judith Malina
*Full Moon Stages: Personal Notes from 50 Years of The Living Theatre*
Phil Marcade
*Punk Avenue: Inside the New York City Underground, 1972–1982*
Jillian Marshall
*Japanthem: Counter-Cultural Experiences; Cross-Cultural Remixes*
Alvin Orloff
*Disasterama! Adventures in the Queer Underground 1977–1997*
Angelica Page
*Bountiful: Growing Up with Geraldine Page*
Nicca Ray
*Ray by Ray: A Daughter's Take on the Legend of Nicholas Ray*
Aram Saroyan
*Before I Forget: A Memoir*
Stephen Spotte
*My Watery Self: Memoirs of a Marine Scientist*
Christina Vo & Nghia M. Vo
*My Vietnam, Your Vietnam*
(Vietnamese translation also available: *Việt Nam Của Con, Việt Nam Của Cha*)

DADA
*Maintenant: A Journal of Contemporary Dada Writing & Art (annual, since 2008)*

MIXED MEDIA
John S. Paul
*Sign Language: A Painter's Notebook (photography, poetry and prose)*

HUMOR
Peter Carlaftes
*A Year on Facebook*

FILM & PLAYS
Israel Horovitz
*My Old Lady: Complete Stage Play and Screenplay with an Essay on Adaptation*
Peter Carlaftes
*Triumph For Rent (3 Plays)*
*Teatrophy (3 More Plays)*
Kat Georges
*Three Somebodies: Plays About Notorious Rebels*

TRANSLATIONS
Thomas Bernhard
*On Earth and in Hell*
(poems; German and English)
Patrizia Gattaceca
*Isula d'Anima* (Corsican & English)
César Vallejo | Gerard Malanga
*Malanga Chasing Vallejo*
George Wallace
*EOS: Abductor of Men* (Greek & English)

PHOTOGRAPHY-MEMOIR
Mike Watt
*On & Off Bass*

SHORT STORY ANTHOLOGIES
SINGLE AUTHOR
*Alien Archives: Stories*
by Robert Silverberg
*First-Person Singularities: Stories*
by Robert Silverberg
*Tales from the Eternal Café: Stories*
by Janet Hamill, intro by Patti Smith
*Time and Time Again: Sixteen Trips in Time*
by Robert Silverberg
*The Unvarnished Gary Phillips: A Mondo Pulp Collection*
by Gary Phillips
*Voyagers: Twelve Journeys in Space and Time*
by Robert Silverberg

MULTI-AUTHOR
*The Colors of April*
edited by Quan Manh Ha & Cab Tran
*Crime + Music: Nineteen Stories of Music-Themed Noir*
edited by Jim Fusilli
*Dark City Lights: New York Stories*
edited by Lawrence Block
*The Faking of the President: Twenty Stories of White House Noir*
edited by Peter Carlaftes
*Florida Happens:*
edited by Greg Herren
*Have a NYC I, II & III: New York Stories;*
edited by Peter Carlaftes & Kat Georges
*Songs of My Selfie*
edited by Constance Renfrow
*The Obama Inheritance: 15 Stories of Conspiracy Noir*
edited by Gary Phillips
*This Way to the End Times: Classic & New Stories of the Apocalypse*
edited by Robert Silverberg

POETRY COLLECTIONS
Hala Alyan
*Atrium*
Peter Carlaftes
*DrunkYard Dog*
*I Fold with the Hand I Was Dealt*
*Life in the Past Lane*
Thomas Fucaloro
*It Starts from the Belly and Blooms*
Kat Georges
*Our Lady of the Hunger*
*Awe and Other Words Like Wow*
Robert Gibbons
*Close to the Tree*
Israel Horovitz
*Heaven and Other Poems*
David Lawton
*Sharp Blue Stream*
Jane LeCroy
*Signature Play*
Philip Meersman
*This Is Belgian Chocolate*
Jane Ormerod
*Recreational Vehicles on Fire*
*Welcome to the Museum of Cattle*
Lisa Panepinto
*On This Borrowed Bike*
George Wallace
*Poppin' Johnny*

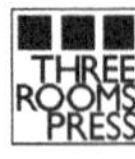


Three Rooms Press | New York, NY | Current Catalog: www.threeroomspress.com
Three Rooms Press books are distributed by Publishers Group West: www.pgw.com

www.ingramcontent.com/pod-product-compliance
Lightning Source LLC
Jackson TN
JSHW061915140626
103854JS00003B/4

*9781953103741*